ANCESTORS

ANCESTORS

The Prehistory of Britain in Seven Burials

ALICE ROBERTS

**SIMON &
SCHUSTER**

London · New York · Sydney · Toronto · New Delhi

First published in Great Britain by Simon & Schuster UK Ltd, 2021

1 3 5 7 9 10 8 6 4 2

Simon & Schuster UK Ltd
1st Floor
222 Gray's Inn Road
London WC1X 8HB

www.simonandschuster.co.uk
www.simonandschuster.com.au
www.simonandschuster.co.in

Simon & Schuster Australia, Sydney
Simon & Schuster India, New Delhi

A CIP catalogue record for this book is
available from the British Library

Hardback ISBN: 978-1-4711-8801-5
eBook ISBN: 978-1-4711-8803-9

Typeset in Perpetua by M Rules
Printed in the UK by CPI Group (UK) Ltd, Croydon, CR0 4YY

MIX
Paper from
responsible sources
FSC® C020471

For Linda

CONTENTS

'Into the underland we have long placed that which we fear and wish to lose, and that which we love and wish to save.'

Robert Macfarlane, *Underland: A Deep Time Journey*, 2019

PROLOGUE

Some of the clues to our past, our ancestry, lie buried deep underground. They may never be discovered. They may already have disintegrated, merging with the soil, dissolving into groundwater, rendered into fragments of molecules, before anyone ever had the chance to catch them.

Others have been prised out of the earth, though. The bones of ordinary and extraordinary people from long ago, whose antiquity and miracle of preservation guarantees them sacred status. They are kept in boxes in museums – new acid-free cardboard coffins to contain the relics that have been lifted from their original resting places. Strange codes are scrawled onto the outside of the boxes, identifying the contents by place and date of discovery. Sometimes, someone will come and check the boxes, opening them to look at the contents, making a note, then replacing the lid. Occasionally, someone will take a box down, and remove the bones for more careful inspection. They might take a piece of bone or a tooth away with them.

Or – some bones are laid out with reverence, in glass display cases, in the public spaces. And devout pilgrims make journeys to see them, to contemplate the vastness of time past, the strangeness of old ways, the inevitable fact of human mortality.

Our visits to museums, to gaze on such human remains, are a form of ancestor worship.

But the contemplation goes beyond mere looking. We can extract information from those ancient bones. We can scan them for clues to the identity of the dead – carefully recording the shape and texture of the bones, measuring them, comparing them. And they contain another sort of information too – the sort written in chains of nucleotides at a molecular level. Another strange code, in fragments that we have learned to assemble and decrypt until we have in our hands the genome of a person who died many centuries ago, redolent with meaning and mystery.

Rather too often, perhaps, we think of Britain 'beginning' with the arrival of the Romans. But that is a historical artefact – it's with the Romans that we start to have written records. That's when British history – in the sense of that documentary evidence of the past – begins. But archaeology allows us to push back into the unwritten past, into prehistory. And there, we uncover stories written in stone, pottery, metal and bone.

This book is about exploring changing prehistoric funerary rites through time – uncovering a prehistory of Britain through burials, but also exploring what those burials *mean*. It's about how people came and went from this island. I'll also explore the history of ideas about the human past, and find out how ideas are transformed by archaeological discoveries and new ways of interrogating the evidence. I'll look at how advances in genetics are transforming archaeology, and I'll let you in on the inception of an exciting and ambitious ancient DNA project.

This book is also about belonging; about walking in ancient places, in the footsteps of the ancestors. It's about reaching back in time, to find ourselves, and our place in the world.

1.

A THOUSAND ANCIENT GENOMES,
22 MAY 2019

Almost a year since we first met, I am meeting Pontus Skoglund again.

The first time was at Cheltenham, at the science festival, along with a gathering of people who'd been intrigued enough by the title of our event in the programme to buy a ticket and turn up. Our subject was 'Mapping the Human Journey'. We were joined by geneticist and writer Adam Rutherford and archaeologist Brenna Hassett, and for an hour we all talked about how archaeology and genetics were colliding and creating sparks. We were seeing more depth and complexity than ever before in the story of human origins, the colonisation of the globe by our forebears, the endless movement and migrations – the restlessness – of the past.

These once-disparate spheres of enquiry were fusing to create something new; something that went beyond the sum of its parts; a magnificent new alloy.

Archaeology – in all its grimy earthiness. With a slightly musty aura. Dirt under the fingernails. Objects and ancient bones prised from the ground. Dusty boxes tucked away under desks, secreted away in museum stores, full of ancient remains waiting to be discovered again. Heavy with history and tradition.

Genetics – in all its clinical brightness. Born out of white-walled labs where robots labour inside glass-walled chambers to polymerise, synthesise and decrypt. The molecules that make us – stretched out, broken up, translated – from chemical into digital archives. The cold white heat of technology, dazzling us with its intensity. Brave and brash in its newness.

Fusion is difficult to achieve. But it creates astonishing energy when it happens.

We're in the Crick Institute.

It's like a cathedral, this place. Or a monastery. Hushed conversations murmur at the fringes of audibility. Sunlight glances down from the high glass roof. A few high bridges cross the vast space of the central atrium, and I'm sitting in a booth on one of them. On each side of the atrium, glass-walled, cloistered offices and labs. That's where the work takes place – the careful drilling, detection, decoding. This is where the letters are assembled into words and sentences; where the scribes toil away assembling a vast library of life . . . and death.

Pontus could be a monk, I think, as he approaches. He exudes a certain calmness. He has a knowing quality to him, too, as though he has imbibed all the wisdom contained in the library; as though he knows the answers to questions I haven't even thought of yet. He sits down in the booth elegantly, folding up his long limbs. Two initiates join us, sitting on the other side of the table. Pontus introduces me to them: Pooja Swali and Tom Booth. Together, they are just about to start work on the most ambitious archaeological genetic project that has ever been carried out in Britain. They are hoping to sequence a *thousand* ancient genomes. And to *fully* sequence them – leaving no stone unturned, no stretch of DNA unread. It's only two decades since the first single human genome was sequenced. Sequencing is so much faster now, with the ability to compile DNA libraries drawn from the living – and the dead.

What do we hope will be revealed by all this effort, by these new genetic libraries? Connections. In Britain, outside Britain. Family ties. Comings and goings. All lost in the deepest past.

'We'll learn so much more about the history of people living in this island – really fascinating history,' says Pontus. 'If we use whole genome information, we'll be able to detect rare variants, shared between particular people – revealing recent common ancestry between people from different regions.'

Ancient DNA bears clues to forgotten journeys – memories of migrations long ago, written into genes. The rare variants Pontus hopes to unearth are crucial to unpicking that history. The sudden appearance of a rare variant – more common in another population – suggests the arrival of people from elsewhere. And with enough genomes, across enough depth of time, it should be possible to work out *when* that influx, that migration, occurred.

Previous projects have often focused on just a few individuals. Some have dealt in larger samples, but only decoding certain parts of the sequence – sometimes single letter changes – providing a sparse yet still illuminating scattering of information across each genome. But now Pontus is aiming to mine wide *and* deep – in pursuit of both scale and detail.

'You can imagine really fascinating, dramatic events affecting a population – but you won't see that in the DNA if you don't have high enough resolution – that's why we're going for the whole genome,' he explains.

5

It's not just human genomes that Pontus and the team are interested in. His lab, after all, is in the biggest biomedical research facility, not just in Britain, but in Europe.

'We're working here, in a biomedical institute that's dedicated to understanding patterns of human health and disease, where the British population is now becoming *the* model population for the genetic basis of human disease, through initiatives like the UK Biobank.'

The UK Biobank is a huge record of half a million people who are having their genomes sequenced, alongside blood tests and other measurements and lifestyle questionnaires – and they'll have their health tracked over time. The idea behind all this is that, with such large numbers involved, we'll learn much more about why some people go on to develop certain diseases, while others don't. The participants in the UK Biobank are all currently alive, in 21st-century Britain, but Pontus is now hoping to provide a historical counterpoint to that project with his ancient DNA project.

'There's an opportunity to add another dimension, and understand the evolution of human health and disease. That's where Pooja comes in.'

Pooja studied archaeology, anthropology and forensics at Bournemouth, then changed tack and went off to research infectious diseases at the London School of Hygiene and Tropical Medicine. Now she was setting out to combine her experience in these two areas in one project, as she embarked on her PhD with Pontus.

Pooja explains that in her part of the project, she'll be looking at the *metagenome*. Samples of ancient bone don't just contain the DNA of the human they once belonged to, but also genetic material from any pathogens that the human might have been carrying around with them. She would be looking for genetic traces of systematic infections, like TB, syphilis, plague; infections that travel around the whole body in the bloodstream, and settle into bones and teeth.

'What can you tell about those ancient diseases – beyond their presence – by looking at their DNA?' I ask her.

'I'll be looking for specific strains of the pathogens – seeing how they've changed in terms of their virulence and how that relates to what we see today. And how they've migrated across the world with us.'

'Any diseases in particular that you're going to focus on? Any burning questions?' I wonder.

'I just want all the pathogens! All of the pathogens, all of the time!' Pooja laughs. 'But seriously, I'm very interested to see how diseases change when agriculture emerges in the Neolithic – when people begin to live in larger, denser communities. And I think what will be fascinating is to see how virulence affects the way diseases spread. And what the history of diseases tells us about them today.'

A new genetic mutation can create a new strain of a disease – something that could end up either more or less virulent than its predecessor – which may also make a difference to how it gets passed from one victim to the next. Genetics has become fundamental to understanding how diseases erupted and spread through populations in the past. (And little did we know, of course, in May 2019, that just a year later, the Thousand Ancient Genomes project would be put on hold as the entire Crick Institute redirected its focus to understand and combat the spread of a brand new infection in humans. We were blissfully unaware at this point.)

In just the past few years, geneticists have turned up

astonishing revelations about one of the most notorious patho-gens in history – the plague itself. A team of researchers from Copenhagen and Cambridge Universities extracted DNA from the teeth of skeletons excavated from across Europe and Asia dating to the Bronze Age and early Iron Age. Among them, they found seven individuals whose metagenomes included the DNA of *Yersinia pestis*, the bacterium which causes the plague. And one of these individuals revealed that the plague had been infecting humans several millennia earlier than had been thought previously – right back in the early Bronze Age, nearly 6,000 years ago.

The study also shed light on how the plague had changed over time, becoming more virulent and spreading in different ways. The six oldest plague victims detected in the study had been infected with a version of the plague that differed in a very important way from later strains.

'There's a specific variant of the *ymt* gene,' Pooja explains. 'It's not there in early *Yersinia* samples, so the mode of trans-mission would have been very different.'

This gene and the protein it encodes – a toxic enzyme – was first investigated in mice, and names tend to stick around in genetics – *ymt* stands for '*Yersinia* murine toxin' – and it is indeed toxic to mice. But it's what this toxin does in fleas that is actually most important: it causes flea constipation. When a flea bites an infected rodent, it ingests *Yersinia* bacteria in that blood meal. But the bacteria are very likely to just pass through the gut of the flea and out the other end – unless they can clump together and form lumps too large for the flea to pass. This is exactly what *ymt* allows them to do – by protecting the bacteria from the flea's own gut enzymes. One to two weeks after that first meal of infected blood, *Yersinia* bacteria have multiplied and colonised the flea's gut so comprehensively that the flea can't digest its food and starts to starve to death. The hungry flea will bite and bite, getting very little sustenance, whilst puking up *Yersinia* bacteria from its guts into the blood of the next host.

For *Yersinia* itself, the *ymt* gene was a huge advantage – helping the bacteria to sweep through populations in a way it couldn't have done before. For fleas, mice and humans, the evolution of the *ymt* gene was bad news, on a biblical scale. This virulent variant was only present in the youngest individual in that sample of seven, dating to 951 BCE, from Armenia; in the next youngest, a skeleton from the Altai Mountains, dating to 1686 BCE, it was absent. As well as that *ymt* mutation, the youngest plague victim had also harboured a strain which contained another important mutation, in a gene called *pla* (meaning 'plasminogen activator'). This genetic variant is linked to the invasive, bubonic form of plague – as opposed to the less invasive, but still nasty, pneumonic plague – where the infection resides in the lungs, spreading like so many bugs, via coughs and sneezes. In bubonic plague, the bacteria enter the human lymphatic system and cause lymph nodes to swell into pus-filled buboes. So, highly virulent, bubonic plague was rife as early as the first millennium BCE. There seems to be a biblical record that fits the picture – in *1 Samuel* – describing a disease outbreak among the Philistines, after they capture the Ark of the Lord from the Israelites:

'Soon after receiving the Ark, rats appeared in the land and death and destruction spread throughout Ashdod. The Philistines, young and old, were struck by an outbreak of tumours in the groin and died.'

This is a passage that historians, archaeologists and doctors have enjoyed arguing about, over the years. While the 'tumours in the groin' have been interpreted as buboes by some, others have argued that the swellings described were more likely to have been haemorrhoids. And that, anyway, there were no black rats around in the Middle East in the first millennium BCE, to spread the plague. But then the discovery of characteristic plague fleas from Amarna in Egypt, dating to around 1350 BCE, suggested that the disease could well have been operating in the nearby Middle East early enough to make it into the Old Testament. And the existence of black rats in the Nile Valley was also pushed back to around this time. But the Copenhagen/Cambridge ancient DNA study surely provides the best corroborating evidence, with definitive proof that the pathogen itself – the bubonic form of the plague – was operating by the early first millennium BCE, in Western Asia.

Later on in *1 Samuel*, the Philistines decide that the Ark may have brought with it a curse in the form of this devastating disease. So they send it back to the Israelites – along with an offering of ten gold sculptures, five shaped as tumours and five as rats. Presumably the Philistines had made the connection between humans dying with swellings in their groins – and dead rats in the streets. Perhaps those gold sculptures were some form of votive offering – a plea to the Israelites and their god to take the curse back as well. Or perhaps they were a coded warning. Either way, the Israelites may have been very pleased to have their sacred Ark back – but now they suffered their own outbreak of the disease.

The Bible is an unreliable witness when it comes to ancient history, having been written by so many authors and revised so much over time. Many scholars believe the stories in the Old Testament to have been written down in the late Iron Age – drawing on earlier oral histories, of course, but with a healthy dose of legend mixed in. But the new dating of the emergence of bubonic plague makes it at least possible that this *is* the disease being described in that ancient text. At the very least, the author must have been familiar with the effects of the plague on its victims.

The Copenhagen/Cambridge study cleared up so many questions about the plague in prehistory. It showed that all the ancient – and indeed, more recent – *Yersinia pestis* strains descend from a common ancestor around 6,000 years ago; it showed that early plague must have been the pneumonic variety, spreading from human to human via coughing, while the more virulent, flea-spread bubonic plague – with its *ymt* and *pla* genes – came along later. And the geneticists had also shown that the bubonic plague went back early enough to have afflicted the Philistines, as described in the Bible.

There was so much more to discover about ancient diseases, by mining their DNA from the skeletons of people who had contracted the infections during their lives.

'And this is evolution in action,' Pooja enthuses. 'Those infectious diseases are adapting to different environments, different hosts, different vectors. We'll learn more about diseases that affect us today if we understand their past.'

Pontus breaks in to explain something about the sample of genomes he hopes to analyse. If we want to understand how *our* genomes today have been shaped by diseases in the past, anything before the British Bronze Age is largely irrelevant. This is because other studies have already suggested that there was a huge upheaval in Britain at this time, with a significant turnover of ancestry – a widespread population replacement.

'The people who lived in Britain before the Bronze Age didn't contribute much ancestry to later populations,' Pontus explains. 'But this isn't to say we're not interested in earlier time periods – Neolithic, Mesolithic as well.'

Those earlier periods wouldn't tell us much about our susceptibility or resistance to disease today, and how that's evolved – but the ancient DNA would still hold secrets about the pathogens around at the time, and about movement of people themselves, of course.

'And we're collaborating with a huge number of archaeologists on this project,' Pontus continues. 'They'll have their own questions – not just about whole populations, but also about the individuals they're interested in – and we'll be able to help them with those questions.'

Tom is already reaching out to archaeologists across the UK, and I'm helping to spread the word about this project too. Like Pooja, Tom also has a foot in two camps – archaeology and genetics. He studied archaeological science as an undergraduate, going on to do a PhD looking at bone preservation on a microscopic scale. Following that, he'd worked at the Natural History Museum, on a project where his role was meant to be advising on which bones would be most likely to contain DNA, based on preservation.

'But as soon as I started,' Tom tells me, 'it turned out that there was one obvious candidate – the petrous – that was usually good for DNA, whatever the preservation. So it didn't really matter – we just didn't need to look anywhere else.'

Sometimes science can be intensely frustrating, yet other times there are moments of pure serendipity like this. The petrous bone – or, more formally, the petrous temporal bone – is part of the base of the skull, and made of very dense bone indeed. It needs to be; it contains the workings of the inner ear, which demands particular acoustic properties.

'So how did that make you feel about your PhD?!' I joke.

'There's still some usefulness in it,' Tom smiles. 'And actually it turns out I can help Pooja, because a lot of what I'd been looking at was how bones get attacked by bacteria. Understanding the taphonomic histories of bones means you know where to find the DNA of all the little bugs that have lived inside the bone and have eaten it.'

Taphonomy is essentially the study of how things rot away – the stuff of Tom's PhD.

Tom grins again. 'So I'm still relevant. DNA hasn't destroyed the work of my early career. These new kids on the block aren't gonna stop me!'

But of course Tom *is* one of the new kids on the block – having immersed himself in ancient DNA research. So, does he think of himself as having joined the dark side, or was he finding a way to unite these two disciplines that had grown up largely independently of each other, with the older sibling more than a little wary of this brash newcomer?

'These huge advances in ancient DNA have only happened recently. And I'm one of probably very few people with an archaeological background who's been embedded within this ancient DNA revolution – so I understand both sides.'

Pontus nods. 'I think one important issue is that most archaeologists don't have an idea of the boundaries of what genetics can say. It's a very new field. A lot of the techniques we're using are new, not established. And it's really on us to communicate what sort of information it is, what its limitations are.'

When ancient DNA studies get into the press, which they often do, the headlines tend to evoke excitement, drama and intrigue. From 'Humans and Neanderthals were frequent lovers' to 'Archaic DNA rewrites human evolution' and

'Ireland's ancient kings married their sisters', the findings are reported in a way that leaves little room for nuance, doubt or probability. Perhaps it's not a surprise that the older generation of archaeologists can be suspicious of this powerful new tool, feeling their toes firmly trodden on, or feeling let down, perhaps, after expecting definitive answers to questions that ancient DNA simply can't resolve. But in the end, ancient genomics is set to transform archaeology in the way that modern genomics will transform medicine. And it's that power to *transform* that is also troubling. What we're seeing is a clash of cultures playing out, and Tom traced some of the opposition to ancient DNA to the enduring divide between science and the arts.

'I think it's been bubbling under the surface for quite some time,' he muses. 'We've seen an increase in the use of scientific techniques like stable isotope analysis, and ways of looking at big data, that go against some of the more traditional theoretical approaches in archaeology. They can be seen as a threat. Ancient DNA is the culmination of all this – it represents the pinnacle. A lot of the other revolutions – radiocarbon dating and stable isotopes – have been a bit more gradual and have taken the archaeological community with them. Ancient DNA has come out of the field of genetics, and for most archaeologists working in the field, this new science has just appeared on the scene; it's almost come out of nowhere, straight onto them.'

And the answers it's providing haven't always been welcome, either.

'They're being told that this is the result: that migrations *were* influential in prehistory. A lot of people who have spent their careers looking at this – suddenly being told that this is the definitive answer – feel like they've been shat on from a great height.'

But the evidence and answers from genetics don't mean archaeologists working in a more traditional way – interpreting patterns of culture – are obsolete. Far from it. The power of genetics to settle debates about population movement – migrations, replacements – changes the picture and the questions in an interesting way. Previously, when archaeologists studied changes in material culture over time, they would ask whether this represented a movement of people, or a movement of ideas. And in fact, studying the cultural artefacts alone would never resolve that question. Genetics, on the other hand, should tell us whether new ideas arrived with a significant influx of new people – or how much contact there was between populations across land masses and oceans. Then the question becomes not *why* a culture change has happened, but *how*. And while genetics provides a bigger picture of what was happening with human populations – from a biological perspective – we need archaeology to provide the local, fine-grained detail, focusing us back down on the human level, of individual lives. On those ancestors who were here before us. We reach back in time to touch those lives, to better understand ourselves.

Archaeology provides us with that tangible, physical connection to those past lives. We unearth objects that were last touched by human hands hundreds and thousands of years ago. We can walk through landscapes that have been inhabited through the ages. We are just the latest to walk in the ancient places, in the footsteps of the ancestors.

I leave the Crick Institute with my head full of thoughts, simmering with excitement about the start of this new project. I will help Pontus and his team reach out to archaeologists across the length and breadth of the country. And among those thousand ancient genomes in the genetic library that they will create, there will be a chapter on people who lived in a special place, on the border between Dorset and Wiltshire, over thousands of years – between the Neolithic and the time of the Saxons. The next time I see Tom and Pooja, it will be in the museum that holds the remains of these ancestors – in Salisbury.

2.

THE RED LADY

Have ye heard of the woman so long underground?
Have ye heard of the woman that Buckland has found,
With her bones of empyreal hue?
O fair ones of modern days, hang down your heads,
The antediluvians rouge'd when dead,
Only granted in lifetime to you.

Philip Duncan (1772–1863),
Fellow of New College, Oxford

*

The route down to the cave is steep and craggy.

A group of six people park their cars up on the farm track, then they follow a path to the cliff edge – and over it, descending in a narrow, V-shaped gully down to the sea. Some of them are carrying heavy equipment. They must proceed carefully. The path is rocky and uneven, testing balance. Lower down, the rock is bare, and carved into sharp-edged blades and Gaudi-esque pinnacles by the waves. Feet alone cannot be trusted; hands come into play to steady the body. It is low tide and the way to the cave is dry – down the rocks and across a short stretch of sand – then back up on the rocks again the other side. Now just a short ascent to the mouth of the cave: a black teardrop in the gull-grey, grassy cliff. This is Goat's Hole, sometimes simply known as Paviland Cave.

People are drawn to the Gower for its rocks and its waves. At the west-facing end of the peninsula, the golden sand of Llangennith Beach stretches out over 3 miles, backed by dunes and embracing the Atlantic swells that make it one of the most popular surfing destinations in the UK. Climbers make for the cliffs – including these ones at Paviland, just east of Port Eynon – pitting their wits and strength against the craggy limestone. There's a route that runs up close to Goat's Hole, with a sharp overhang near the top. And another, more demanding and difficult, just to the east – called 'Assassin'.

But we're not here to surf or to climb. We're just here for that cave. The cliffs are southwest facing, drenched in sunshine. The cave itself is about 10 metres above the high-water line – easy to scramble up to. As we enter the mouth of the cave, we pass into shadow. I'm here with Paul Pettitt. We taught together at Bristol University for a brief term, dividing up the course on *Human Origins* into stones and bones. Paul did the stones, but he knows a thing or two about bones too, especially when it comes to dating them.

Here at Paviland, we're following in the footsteps of a famous nineteenth-century antiquarian, who discovered the bones of a much more distant ancestor. Someone who died a very long time ago – though *exactly when* has been a subject of much speculation.

The reverend and the Lady

The antiquarian was a legendary character himself – a pioneer of early geology and archaeology – the Reverend William Buckland. He visited the cave in Paviland Cliffs in 1823, where a group of locals had started digging, and had turned up some curiously large bones.

Buckland was born in Devon in 1784, the son of a rector. He caught a brace of obsessions from his father – palaeontology and theology – and he would spend his life trying to reconcile the two. He studied at Corpus Christi College in Oxford, staying on to become a priest there. But he also pursued his academic interest in earth sciences, giving lectures on geology and palaeontology, and collecting rocks and fossils for the Ashmolean Museum. This was in no way unusual; at the time, most college Fellows were also clergy, funded by the church. And then, in 1818, he became Reader in Geology at Oxford – the first to hold this post. And when he gave his inaugural lecture, his subject was '*Vindiciæ Geologiæ*; or the Connexion of Geology with Religion explained'.

He opened his lecture by thanking the Prince Regent, the future George IV, for his regal munificence – Buckland having persuaded the Prince to fund his university post. It's strange for us to think of geology being essentially a new invention, but that's what it was, back in the early nineteenth century. And how resourceful of Buckland, to secure some royal backing for the new discipline – and of course, for himself.

'We may henceforward', Buckland told the assembled crowd, 'consider Geology as exalted to the rank of sciences.' He went on to argue that this emergent discipline should be grafted onto the classical humanities that formed the foundations of English education. In his defence of the 'new and curious sciences of Geology and Mineralogy', he made an argument for science for its own sake. The utility of science should not be measured in terms of 'mere pecuniary profit and tangible advantage', he insisted – the pursuit of truth was a far nobler aim. (Of course, by the mid-nineteenth century, geology would become, in its own right, a source of unimagined wealth – as the oil boom boomed; but Buckland wasn't to know that.)

The truth that Buckland believed to lie within the grasp of geology was the ancient history of the earth itself, and of earlier life forms, 'which by inhumation have passed over to the mineral world', becoming fossils. Zoology and botany were incomplete, he declared, without the fossil record. But then he moves on to the central argument of his lecture: that it should be possible to unite 'abstract science' with 'Religious Truth'. Indeed, in his view, any investigation of Natural Philosophy must ulti- mately lead back to the original, divine creator of it all – the 'Omnipotent Architect'. Buckland saw evidence of a benevolent God in the way that the earth appeared to be 'designed' with the support of humans specifically in mind. (There are plenty of cosmologists who make a similar argument today, extending it to the origin of the universe itself and the laws of physics, which seem to be so finely tuned – to have enabled *Homo sapiens* to evolve and flourish. I find it an odd argument. Just because we're lucky enough to be here, doesn't mean that it was *meant* to be. It could quite easily have turned out differently. And then we wouldn't be here to comment on it, would we?)

For Buckland, studying the earth meant studying the work of God: geology was a devoutly religious pursuit. But his theological approach went further than that: he wanted to be able to reconcile the origin myth in Genesis with the scientific evidence. He noted that 'geological investigations . . . may seem at first sight to be inconsistent with the literal interpretation of the Mosaic records.' But he went on to insist that the 'apparent nonconformity' of the science with the Bible was most likely to stem from problems with 'the yet imperfect science of Geology' – rather than with the biblical version of events. As an Anglican priest, how could he think otherwise? He thought he could explain how geology, in fact, fell neatly into line with the creation story in Genesis – and not only that, but the rocks also provided unequivocal evidence of the biblical Deluge. He quoted his friend, the French anatomist and zoologist, Georges Cuvier, on this subject:

> . . . if there is any circumstance thoroughly established in Geology, it is that the crust of our globe has been subjected to a great and sudden revolution, the epoch of which cannot be dated much farther back than five or six thousand years ago; and that this revolution had buried all the countries which were before inhabited by men and by the other animals that are not best known.

The biblical flood myth was 'in perfect harmony with the discoveries of modern science', Buckland proclaimed; the Bible describes just one episode of destruction since humans came into existence, and this is what geology affirms. Buckland bravely struggled to shoehorn the geological record into agreement with the biblical account. And if he could do this, it would help to reduce any theological opposition to his beloved geology. Buckland knew that geological strata contained evidence for a whole series of 'revolutions', between which 'new races of organised beings have successively arisen and become extinct'. But he believed the very last revolution – the one which he and Cuvier thought had happened just 5,000 or 6,000 years ago – to be the biblical Deluge. This was also the only one relevant to human history, and therefore the only one mentioned in the Bible. In the early nineteenth century, after all, the very concept of *human* prehistory – the idea that the story of humanity extended back before any written history – was only just starting to crystallise.

In Buckland's mind, that great Deluge had happened relatively recently, while the story of the earth itself extended back much further, through deep time, to the moment of creation. Geology could hope to illuminate those lost ages between creation and the flood that were passed over in the biblical account.

Buckland granted himself considerable room for interpretation in his approach to scripture. While some biblical literalists were concerned that the Bible didn't mention extinctions, and recorded instead that Noah had managed to rescue a pair of every kind, Buckland had a more pragmatic explanation. Accommodating both the fossil record of clearly extinct animals and the biblical story, he reasoned that, with limited space and fodder on board the ark, Noah would probably have focused on rescuing animals useful to humans. He also thought that, while some species had been wiped out in the great flood, others may have been created later. Creation, for Buckland, wasn't a one-time-only event.

Buckland seems to have been able to roll with the cognitive dissonance emerging from scientific challenges to the stories told in scripture. He was as firm in his religious faith as he was in his belief in science. And yet he apparently approached both with a lightness of spirit that helped to diffuse tensions. When Buckland presented his views on prehistoric England at the annual dinner of the Geological Society in 1822, Lyell commented, 'Buckland in his usual style, enlarged on the marvel with such a strange mixture of the humorous and the serious, that we could none of us discern how far he believed himself what he said.' He loved practical jokes, eliciting some raised eyebrows, and – to some eyes – undermining his gravitas. He may have been too thick-skinned to care; or too clever. After all, it's harder to feel outraged at a potentially heretical idea if you're smiling at the joke it's wrapped up in.

He knew that difficulties already existed in reconciling these two approaches to the world – the scientific and the religious. But he hoped that those stumbling blocks would be overcome with further investigation – with no serious damage to either mode of philosophy, saying 'neither will the ardour of science be discouraged, nor the full confidence of religious myth be shaken'.

And so, having stated his case, he settled into his double life, as progressive priest and geological inquisitor. He would pursue science – but he would start out with the very firm idea that any evidence he collected had to fit within a prescribed theological framework. Science could not be permitted to question or threaten religious tenets. The proper place for science was as 'the faithful auxiliary and handmaid of Religion'. Any evidence he collected would fit into a history of the earth that included a global deluge, just 5,000 or 6,000 years ago.

Five years after his inaugural address at Oxford, Buckland made his way to the coast of South Wales, just 16 miles west of Swansea. He was drawn there by news of the discovery of ancient animal bones – in Goat's Hole. This came hot on the heels of his exploration of another cave, up in Yorkshire.

In Kirkdale Cave, in the Vale of Pickering, Buckland had found bones from hyenas, as well as from many other mammals and birds. He'd made the startling claim that the cave had been a hyena den in deep antiquity, and the smashed-up bones of other animals represented the leftovers from these predators' meals. It seemed that the ancient denizens of Britain had been very different from those roaming around in modern times. Buckland's claims were startling, at a time when old bones found in caves had often been interpreted as being the remains of unicorns or giant humans. On the few occasions when mammoth bones had been recognised at least as some form of elephant, it had been suggested that the Romans must have imported these creatures to Britain. Another suggestion was that the bones of large, exotic animals could relate to the biblical Deluge moving things around – washing the remains of animals from faraway lands into caves in Britain.

Buckland, however, thought something else was also going on at Kirkdale Cave. While he still very much entertained the idea that some ancient bones represented victims of the flood, floating great distances from their lands of origin, he thought that at least some of the bones in the Yorkshire cave had belonged to local inhabitants. He was content with the concept that the sort of animals that roamed Britain before the biblical flood could have been quite different from modern fauna. His hyena den in Yorkshire supported this idea – hyena bones had not been merely washed into Kirkdale Cave; these animals had clearly *lived* there. The cave yielded the gnawed bones of large mammals – whose carcasses must have brought into the cave in pieces – as well as hyena bones. But the smoking gun was Buckland's discovery of balls of crushed, white bone – the remains of hyena faeces.

News of Kirkdale Cave reached the Talbot family of Glamorganshire – the landowners of the Gower. Buckland had previously corresponded with the Talbots and visited them at Penrice Castle. Lady Mary Cole – the widow of Thomas Mansel Talbot, before she married navy captain Sir Christopher Cole – was an avid botanist and apparently also keenly interested in the new science of geology, as were her daughters. Buckland had encouraged Lady Mary and the 'Misses Talbots' to undertake a survey of Glamorganshire for him. They created a geological map of the area and sent it to him for inclusion in Greenough's *Map of England and Wales*, published by the Geological Society in 1819. In return for all that work, he sent Lady Mary a sketch of fossil trees, and some seeds from the Alps.

It's a stark reminder of the deeply patriarchal nature of science – that Buckland's name is firmly connected with the nineteenth century archaeological investigations on the Gower, while Lady Mary and her daughters tend to drop out of history. And yet their role in this story of discovery was absolutely crucial.

When Lady Mary and her daughters heard about

Buckland's finds at Kirkdale Cave, they were reminded about a collection they had in their possession at Penrice Castle – an assemblage of bones that had been recovered by quarrymen from a fissure called Crawley Rocks, on the Gower, at the end of the eighteenth century. They packed up the bones and sent them to Buckland, who was intrigued. He wrote back in November 1821 to ask if they could look around for any more such caves:

> I shall be very much obliged if you will have the kindness to examine carefully the state of the Lime Stone Rocks there, to ascertain if there be any traces of Caverns or fissures still remaining, which may have been connected with that in which the Bones were discovered.

But then, in the summer of 1822, inspired by the stories about ancient bones from the Crawley fissure, two men from nearby Port Eynon set out to explore Goat's Hole at Paviland Cliffs. One was a doctor and the other a curate, and they both went by the name of Davies; they might well have been brothers – but history is unclear on that. But we know what they found in the cave. Daniel Davies and John Davies did some digging around and did indeed find bones – and the tusk of an 'elephant', which they left in the cave. They also found two Roman coins, which they took to Penrice Castle for the Talbot family's museum. Somehow, news of the cave reached Buckland. On Christmas Eve 1822, he wrote to Lady Mary Cole:

> Pray oblige me with a line to say whether there really has or has not been a Discovery of a New Cave full of Bones in your neighbourhood . . . be so kind . . . as to oblige me with

a line to clear up the obscurity which at present hangs over this matter.

The letter seems to have spurred Lady Mary Cole's oldest daughter into action. In late December, Mary Theresa Talbot headed to Paviland Cave, in the company of another local landowner and amateur geologist – the Swansea pottery magnate Lewis Dillwyn. Together, they dug up the tusk that the Davieses had left, and carted off several baskets of bones and teeth, back to Penrice Castle. Mary Theresa Talbot sent Buckland a tooth from the cave, which he identified, writing back swiftly on 31 December:

> Many thanks to you for sending me up the Tooth which I will return to you as soon as I have compared it with my fossil teeth from the German Caves. I have no Doubt it is one of the Molar teeth of the Lower Jaw of a Bear . . .

And then he went on to ask a whole string of questions about the nature of the cave and its deposits: was the floor of it flat or inclined? How big was it? Was it on the coast or inland? Was there a crust of stalagmite above the mud?

'I am impatient for further accounts,' he ended, 'and the moment I can stir will if possible run down to get a peep at what remains in the Cave, for as yet I do not understand its history nor how the animals got there – meantime pray have the mouth closed up again to prevent total destruction.'

Buckland didn't waste too much time – he was down on the Gower on 18 January 1823 to get his peep at the cave. Despite the prior removal of basketfuls of bones and teeth, there were plenty of intact sediments for Buckland to get his trowel into, towards the back of the cave. By modern standards, the excavation was very rushed – Buckland himself cannot have spent more than one or two days there. Digging through a layer of reddish-yellow loam, he came down upon a deeper stratum, which contained seashells and bones. Among the bones, he found parts of the skull of an 'elephant', but there was a surprise in store – when human bones started to turn up.

Buckland described the discovery in great detail:

In another part . . . I discovered beneath a shallow covering of six inches of earth nearly the entire left side of a human female skeleton. The skull and vertebrae, and extremities of the right side were wanting; the remaining parts lay extended in the usual position of burial, and in their natural order of contact, and consisted of the humerus, radius, and ulna of the left arm, the hand being wanting; the left leg and foot entire to the extremity of the toes, part of the right foot, the pelvis, and many ribs . . . All these bones appeared not to have been disturbed by the previous operations (whatever they were) that had removed the other parts of the skeleton.

The bones, he wrote, 'were all of them stained superficially with a dark brick-red colour, and enveloped by a coating of a kind of ruddle, composed of red micaceous oxyde of iron, which stained the earth, and in some parts extended itself to the distance of about half an inch around the surface of the bones. The body must have been entirely surrounded or covered over at the time of its interment with this red substance.'

The cave was limestone, with a floor of yellowish sediment. Why were the bones stained red and coated in 'ruddle'? Perhaps red ochre had been sprinkled into the grave when the body was interred, or the body had been wrapped in red-stained blankets or clothes. Or perhaps the ochre had been painted onto the skin. And, as Buckland reported, there were also objects that had been carefully, deliberately, placed in the grave.

> Close to that part of the thigh bone where the pocket is usually worn, I found laid together, and surrounded also by ruddle, about two handsfull [sic] of small shells of the *nerita littoralis* [periwinkle] in a state of complete decay, and falling to dust on the slightest pressure . . .
> In contact with the ribs, I found forty or fifty fragments of small ivory rods nearly cylindrical, and varying in diameter from a quarter to three quarters of an inch, and from one to four inches in length . . . most of them were also split transversely by recent fracture in digging them out, so that there are no means of knowing what was their original length . . . some small fragments of rings made of the same ivory, and found with the rods, being nearly of the size and shape of segments of a small teacup handle; the rings when complete were probably four or five inches in diameter. Both rods and rings, as well as the nerite shells, were stained superficially with red, and lay in the same red substance that enveloped the bones; they had evidently been buried at the same time.

Although, in his report, he described finding a female skeleton, Buckland's initial interpretation had been that the bones were those of a man — perhaps, he even suggested, a murdered excise-man. There were plenty of stories of violent clashes between smugglers and excisemen around the coast at that time. But just a few weeks later, he seems to have changed his mind.

In February, having returned to Oxford, he wrote to Lady Mary Cole:

> the Man whom we voted an Exciseman turns out to have been a Woman, whose history wd. afford ample Matter for a Romance to be entitled the Red Woman or the Witch of Paviland for some such Personage must she have been; but for what purpose she used her ivory Rods and Rings & the shells in her Pocket I have yet to learn . . . but how she came to be buried in ruddle or what was her motive for living in such a place I cannot tell.

The reason for his change of mind seems not to have been anything to do with the physical characteristics of the human bones themselves, but the fact that this individual had been buried with ivory rods and rings. Buckland wasn't sure what these objects were for, but nonetheless thought them much more likely to be female accoutrements. In a later letter to the British Archaeological Association, he wrote: 'There never was, nor ever will be a period, when, even among uncivilized races, the female part of our species were not, and will not be, anxious to decorate themselves with beads.'

His idea that this woman could have been a witch was based on another find from the cave (though not with the burial): the scapula of a sheep. He wrote: 'The Blade Bone of Mutton gives grounds for a conjecture, wh[ich] favors the Theory that she was a Dealer in Witchcraft'. His theory drew on the work of two historians. One of them, living in the twelfth century, was Gerald of Wales, who had recorded a curious occult practice in Pembrokeshire where people cleaned up the shoulder blades of rams to use in divination. An apparent persistence of the custom in Cardiganshire (now Ceredigion) had been noted by Buckland's contemporary, the nineteenth-century historian Samuel Rush Meyrick. Strange as it sounds to modern ears and sensibilities, this particular form of fortune-telling – known as scapulomancy or omoplatoscopy – was widespread in antiquity, popping up in records from ancient Greece to China, Japan and North America.

Buckland elaborated on his far-fetched theory about the identity of the Red Woman in his letter, suggesting to Lady Mary Cole that this could be good material for a novel:

> I think you may easily get up amongst you a good romance on the old lady, who was very tall and very thin, as a Witch ought to be, and then the Rods and rings & tooth pick made of Wolf Toe & Pocket full of yellow Nerites & the tongue-shaped Bits of Ivory, & Giants Bones in the Shape of an Elephant, wd. have been her conjuring tools, not forgetting the shoulder Bone of Mutton, for whose virtues see Meyrick and [Gerald of Wales].

As for the date of the 'Red Woman', Buckland was absolutely convinced that she could not possibly have lived at the same time as an ancient elephant – a mammoth. He thought that 'antediluvian' humans existed in Asia, the cradle of humankind, but not in Europe. Wrestling to reconcile his scientific and religious ideas, Buckland was a creationist – but not a young-earth creationist. He accepted the contemporary geological understanding of the deep antiquity of the earth, but rejected any ideas about evolution which were just starting to take hold in biology. He accepted evidence for change, and accepted that species could go extinct. But he thought that species appeared through creation, not evolution, and that humans had been a relatively late divine creation, only introduced to the earth once it had been adequately prepared by God – which included wiping out potentially dangerous animals in Europe. Antediluvian humans lived in Asia, and were mainly wiped out by the Deluge. Then, after the flood, the descendants of Noah would have repopulated the world; a Bronze Age, Middle Eastern origin myth was being worked hard to explain human history from a global perspective.

Buckland had found some fragments of Roman pottery in the cave as well – though not in the grave itself. So, to him, the remains in the cave seemed best explained as a jumble of time periods – with ancient remains of antediluvian creatures mixed up with a *much* later human burial. The Witch's ivory objects, if indeed contemporary with her bones, must have been made from a more ancient tusk that she had happened upon in her cave.

He was firm in his letter: 'we cannot . . . admit our Red Woman to have been Antediluvian'. Instead, he connected the burial with an ancient British camp on the clifftop, deciding that 'there is reason to conclude that the date of these human bones is coeval with that of the military occupation of the adjacent summits, and anterior to, or coeval with, the Roman invasion of this country'.

Lady Mary Cole had boxed up the bones and, towards the end of March 1823, dispatched them to Buckland in Oxford, for closer inspection. Buckland was late writing back to acknowledge receipt of the bones, and to thank her. He excused himself; he was busy finalising the text – with 'the extreme Pressure of the Printers on me' – of his magnus opus on the great flood: *Reliquiae Diluvianae* – 'Relics of the Flood'. Or, to give it its snappy subtitle: *'Observations on the organic remains cont-ained in caves, fissures, and diluvial gravel, and on other geological phenomena, attesting the action of an universal deluge'.*

The Red Woman of Paviland appears in the *Reliquiae*. This time Buckland didn't mention witchcraft, but instead focuses on her relationship to that nearby British camp:

> The circumstance of the remains of a British camp ... seems to throw much light on the character and date of the woman under consideration; and whatever may have been her occupation, the vicinity of a camp would afford a motive for residence, as well as the means of subsistence.

Treading lightly around a delicate subject for his Georgian readers, Buckland hints another possibility: that the human remains at Paviland were those of a prostitute, a 'painted lady' – a scarlet woman – buried with her ivory armlets. He seemed to enjoy this story and elaborated on it in later talks. On a visit to Plymouth in 1841, he was reported as giving an 'amusing account of a cave in Wales, in which he had found the skeleton of a female who had been buried among fossil remains, and who had evidently kept a sort of sutler's shop as appeared from the remains of Celtic implements of gam-bling, and other amusements of a camp.' The mysterious ivory objects in the cave had morphed into gaming counters, and the cave itself into some sort of ancient casino. In the nine-teenth century, sutler's stores would supply military posts with provisions, as well as being dens for gambling, drinking and prostitution. These were opinions that Buckland seemed happy to pontificate about in front of all-male audiences at scientific meetings – and he was very clear that women should be excluded from such gatherings. That didn't stop him, of course, using contributions from women towards his own work, often without credit. Indeed, the *Reliquiae Diluvianae* would have been much impoverished were it not for discoveries made by the Talbot sisters – and by a certain Mary Anning in Dorset. Another woman provided the illustrations for *Reliquiae* – the keen fossil collector Mary Morland, who had already illustrated one of Cuvier's books. In 1825, Mary Morland would become Mary Buckland, and she continued to help her husband with his work throughout his life, illustrating as well as editing his later writing.

Buckland's hefty tome on the 'Relics of the Flood' proved to be an instant success, with the first edition selling out within the year – but there were dissenting voices. Although Buckland was looking to provide scientific evidence that could be marshalled into line to support the Genesis flood myth, for some his science went too far. A particular criticism flowed from the pen of Granville Penn (the grandson of William Penn, who founded Pennsylvania). Granville Penn was an evangelical Anglican and an ardent armchair geologist, who was also a steadfast young-earth creationist.

Buckland wrote to Lady Mary on 3 December 1823, telling her all about the success of his new book, but also grumbling about Penn's criticism:

I am not however without opposition from Mr. Granville Penn who has published a Kind of Reply, but so very weak that it would deserve no kind of answer but for the sake of that Part of his readers who are totally ignorant of Natural History, and ready to believe with him that nothing can be true in Physical Science that is not revealed in the Bible.

This was the kernel of Penn's criticism — he took the Bible literally and, not only that, viewed it as exhaustively comprehensive. If an event was not described in the Bible — it had not happened. Any scientific claim had to be corroborated with scripture. Penn had criticised Buckland before — taking him to task over that ancient hyena den at Kirkdale Cave. He attacked Buckland's claims with an ingenuity and imaginative resourcefulness that is familiar in the arguments of conspiracy theorists today. Buckland had argued that the presence of rhinoceros and elephant (mammoth) bones in the cave was explained by the action of hyenas, dragging chunks of carcasses back to their den. Many of the bones bore the tooth-marks of hyenas, after all, and there were also those tell-tale white lumps. Buckland convincingly reasoned that these were ancient hyena faeces, packed with splintered bone — modern hyenas produced similarly bone-rich excrement. Penn, though, offered an alternative explanation for how elephant and rhino bones had ended up in the cave. He accepted the cave entrance was too small for such large animals to squeeze in on their own — but instead suggested the cave had formed *around the bones*. Penn argued that the bones of large (as he thought, tropical) mammals that had ended up in Kirkdale Cave had been washed from south to north and accumulated on the seabed of the flooded globe. When the waters retreated, the 'soft and yielding' sediment had *then* hardened around the bones to form a cave. He drew an analogy with seashells trapped in limestone, but then ties himself up in knots as the bones were *loose* inside Kirkdale Cave. He goes on to suggest that the festering, fermenting bodies of the drowned animals would have produced bubbles of gas inside the fluid rock — cavities which persisted when the sediment hardened. Penn's extraordinary flight of fancy transformed the hyena and elephant bones at

Kirkland Cave from evidence for the existence of a very different fauna in northern Europe in the distant past – as Buckland recognised – to evidence for a global flood.

Penn laces his criticism with disingenuous praise for Buckland, 'the eloquent Professor of Mineralogy'. Buckland, he writes – channelling Uriah Heep – has left him no choice . . .

> The equity of this highly respected writer must here, therefore perceive, and will, I am well convinced, as candidly acknowledge, that he has himself imposed upon me the ungrateful task to which I very reluctantly submit, – of [deciding] . . . whether there remains *no other alternative* than to *'admit'* that the animals, whose remains are found in the cave, *'MUST once have inhabited it.'* [Italics the ever-so-'umble author's own.]

Penn perfects that Dickensian combination of obsequiousness and sticking-the-knife-in, but he flails around for a convincing alternative explanation, his preferred ones being just as amorphous and lacking in substance as the 'soft limestone' of his hypothesis.

Ultimately, though, Penn's objection to Buckland's ideas comes down to the fact that Buckland's interpretations stand separate from the revealed truth laid out in the Bible.

'But that which constitutes the most weighty and really important objection to this ingeniously inventive *hypothesis,*' he writes, 'is its direct contradiction of . . . Mosaical [scriptural] Geology'.

Penn admits being somewhat torn, however, because of course Buckland has set out in *Reliquiae Diluvianae* to establish 'the truth of the *sacred history of a deluge*', as Penn puts it.

I've read Penn's take-down of Buckland's ideas so you

don't have to. It goes *on and on* (my italics). He rambles and repeats himself; he vacillates between obsequiousness and sneering; he returns again and again to his absolute certainty that different fauna could never have inhabited northerly latitudes — because the Bible would definitely have mentioned this important fact. As it's not mentioned in the Bible, therefore, it never happened.

It's curious, especially from a 21st-century perspective, with all we now know about the antiquity of the earth and the geological processes that have formed its rocks and preserved its fossils. Here are two men — arguing over how far the Bible could take us in understanding Earth's history. Both believed in the literal truth of Noah's flood — a global inundation that had wiped out some animals and left its mark on the landscape. For Penn, though, geology could and should only illustrate what is already attested in scripture. For Buckland, the Bible was not so perfectly comprehensive and exhaustive — he clearly thought it completely in keeping with his faith to be open to geology and palaeontology providing him with unforeseen surprises. It makes me wonder how he'd make sense of all we know now, if we were to drag him into the present. Would Buckland still be able to reconcile his science and his faith? The distance between people like him and people like Penn has grown into a very wide gulf. Science has provided such comprehensive answers to questions about the origin of the earth, and the universe itself, and to the emergence of these strangely brainy apes that can make some sense of it all, that there is really no room for divine revelation to compete. There are gaps to be filled, but the Bible doesn't come near to filling them. This isn't surprising, of course, as the Old Testament is a compilation of Bronze Age and Iron Age myths, written by people who were trying to make sense of how things were, before science spilled the beans. Many Christians today accept that way of interpreting the Bible – especially the Old Testament – as a collection of stories written by *people*, and containing some grains of truth, perhaps, but open to interpretation. In this way, they manage to accommodate both faith and science inside their heads. Would Buckland be one of those open-minded Christians today, or would he find very little left to believe in, and become – as so many people brought up as Anglicans have recently become – a humanist? There are some evangelical Christians around, of course, who still maintain an extreme position – a Penn-like adherence to biblical revelation, taking it literally. To do that requires overlooking the internal inconsistencies in the Bible, of which there are many, as well as turning away completely from science – which has revealed so much more about the real fabric of the world since Penn's and Buckland's time. Buckland occupied a sort of halfway house in the early nineteenth century, between the extreme views of those like Penn – whose biblical literalism could admit no scientific addition, much less a challenge, to the events and processes laid out in the good book – and more scientifically inclined geologists, for whom the explanatory power of the biblical flood was receding. Penn thought the bones of exotic animals in northerly caves, as well as other features of the landscape, were explained by the Deluge. In contrast, Buckland thought that the bones were those of indigenous fauna, different from the animals inhabiting those environments today – but did still think that flood had been the major factor in carving out valleys and depositing gravels in the landscape.

Buckland seems to have been slightly needled by Penn's criticisms – though, as indicated in his letter to Lady Mary, he was most concerned to help disabuse Penn's readers of the idea that science could never produce any answers that were not already 'revealed in the Bible'. If Buckland could have described Penn in modern terms, he would surely have considered him a purveyor of fake news. Buckland consoled himself with the fact that other eminent scientists had been similarly denigrated by Granville Penn: 'It is satisfactory that he finds the same faults with Cuvier and Wollaston and Sir I. Newton that he does with Mr. Buckland, so that I am in good company'.

And yet Buckland's geological and archaeological interpretations were seriously constrained by his adherence to biblical chronology and his belief in the factual reality of the Deluge. In *Reliquiae*, Buckland had described ways in which the biblical flood had left its mark on the landscape, in 'immense deposits of gravel that occur occasionally on the summits of hills, and almost universally in valleys over the whole world; in situations to which no torrents or rivers such as now are in action could ever have drifted them.' He was absolutely sure he could see the signs of the biblical flood written upon the earth – in the shape of hills and valleys, in those great beds of gravel. All the signs pointed, for him, to that very recent deluge. In fact he couldn't even conceive of any other explanation that could account for these phenomena he and others had observed. His mind was so entrammelled by the religious story that he'd been brought up with, that he'd pursued through university – he simply couldn't see it any other way.

But Buckland was out of step with many geologists of the day. A school of geology called uniformitarianism was gaining ground – which was essentially the idea that rocks and landscapes had been formed over vast stretches of time by processes which still operated today, such as the gradual formation of valleys by the persistent erosive force of rivers. These processes were uniform through time – so the present provided a key to the past.

The pioneering geologist James Hutton had laid out this theory in two volumes published in 1785 – *Theory of the Earth* – describing how rocks were eroded, formed shifting sediments, became buried and compressed, then pushed back up, in a cycle which must have lasted much, much longer than the 6,000-odd years granted to the planet's existence by most natural philosophers – who were essentially young-earth creationists. The rocks showed signs of change – and yet any change must be immeasurably slow, Hutton argued, as rocky features around the Mediterranean were – nearly 2,000 years later – imperceptibly different from descriptions made by classical writers such as Polybius or Pliny. For Hutton, fossils, as well as the rocks themselves, provided important clues to the deep antiquity of the earth: 'We find, in natural history,' he wrote, 'monuments which prove that those [primitive] animals had long existed; and we thus procure a measure for the computation of a period of time extremely remote . . .'. Hutton's ideas were enthusiastically embraced by Charles Lyell, who was born in 1797 – the year that Hutton died. Lyell wrote his own book, *Principles of Geology*, published in 1830, which helped to popularise the concept of the extreme antiquity of the earth. Lyell would himself become a close and influential friend of Charles Darwin, whose insights into the evolution of life on Earth depended on this relatively new appreciation of deep time in geology.

Buckland was just behind the wave. He was still trying to fit environmental evidence to a biblical version of events. Writing to Lady Mary in 1828, he told her that he was working on a second volume of the *Reliquiae*. But by then he and his fellow Diluvialists were losing ground to the uniformitarians, or 'Fluvialists', as Buckland called them. Buckland had already expanded his reconstruction of the past to include several catastrophic global floods – the idea of a single Deluge as described in the Bible was crumbling in the light of the physical evidence. One of Buckland's students – Charles Lyell – would call out his former mentor, saying that the arguments against the flood myth were now 'enough to sink the *Reliquiae Diluvianae* for ever'.

Buckland's epic had been greeted enthusiastically upon its publication, especially by those already troubled by the potential of science to challenge accepted religious world views; *Reliquiae* provided them with what looked like a reconciliation between scripture and science. But the promise would soon fall through. Buckland may have clung on to the flood myth much longer than others, but even he would eventually reject it. In his later years, he was persuaded that the landscape features he once believed to prove 'the truth of the Mosaic records', the biblical flood myth, were in fact laid down not by a global deluge, but by the action of great ice sheets. Glaciation, not inundation. The Swiss geologist Louis Agassiz had carried out painstaking geographical work that demonstrated that many features of glacial landscapes were found preserved in regions that were currently ice-free. I remember a personal Damascene moment when I saw this evidence for myself – in a trip to Greenland to explore the movement of glaciers, quickly followed by a visit to the Scottish Highlands. I had the powerful impression of the ice sheets *just* having melted in Scotland – leaving traces that are so obvious once you know what you're looking at. That curious trick of cognition leaves us wondering why it took so long to see what seems like clear evidence to us today – knowing what we know, and not being able to 'un-know' it. Once Darwin pointed out the evidence (and the mechanism), everyone could see that evolution had happened (if they dared to look). Similarly, once Agassiz had articulated it, everyone could see the evidence for glaciation. A modified uniformitarianism – where processes similar to those at work today had operated in the past, although sometimes in the context of a much colder climate and much more extensive glaciation – took hold. The Deluge was dead. Glacial Theory won the day.

It's rather easy for us to look back, 200 years and marvel at how incredibly short-sighted Buckland was in his adherence to the flood myth. Yes, there are signs of ancient floods in the landscapes of the northern hemisphere. Vast lakes breaking through dams and scouring landscapes. Sea levels rising and flooding the land. But these are events that have happened time and again, not just once – and their causes lie not in a flood sent as divine retribution – but in global changes, as the earth cycled in and out of Ice Ages, over hundreds of thousands of years.

For those of us who have rejected religious dogma today, or indeed are able to separate religion from science in our minds – as two separate systems of explanation – Buckland's attempts to reconcile the legends in the Bible with the actual history of the earth seem risible, at best foolhardy. But we shouldn't be too smug. We're looking back with the benefit of hindsight, with the advantage of all the scientific knowledge that has accumulated over two centuries. And there will certainly be things we're wrong about even now.

We humans are cultural creatures; we live and breathe the stuff. Our own cultures will have shaped our minds too. Even as we strive to be objective, there will be patterns of thought that seem so natural to us, we're not even aware that they're influencing our interpretations in ways that drag us further from the truth. This, perhaps, is the most important lesson for the sciences from the humanities. We can never entirely escape our subjectivity: it is part and parcel of the human condition. And archaeology and anthropology have a long history of grappling with this challenge, leaving us with insights that may be applicable to sciences more widely. Science can never happen in a political, social, moral vacuum. Because it is done by political, social, moral creatures. By humans.

Nevertheless – science advances. And it does so through human effort, and because humans can be wise enough to admit being mistaken. Buckland proved himself to be a scientist in the end.

He'd been wrong about Noah's flood – and eventually he accepted the evidence adduced by Louis Agassiz, admitted he'd been wrong and recanted the whole diluvial thing.

He was right, though, about his hyaenas living in their den in Yorkshire.

One thing he never did quite get to the bottom of, however, was the mystery of the Red Lady of Paviland. That would prove to be a conundrum that would take almost two centuries to unravel, with a story that takes us right back into the Ice Age, when glaciation was scouring and gouging the British landscape, leaving behind its telltale valleys, erratic boulders, clay and gravel.

After Buckland's work on the human remains from Paviland Cave, the bones of the Red Lady herself remained at Oxford. But many of the other finds from the cave stayed in the collections at Penrice Castle. There's a record from the Swansea Scientific Society, from 1893, when some of its members visited the castle and saw a collection of ivory rods, pierced shells and some 'bone and ivory eardrops' from Paviland Cave. Some of this collection was donated to the National Museum of Wales in 1915, but the rest of it seems to have gone missing. A few other finds, including three flint blades and a chert flake, had apparently been kept by Buckland. His grandson would eventually deposit them in the British Museum, in 1946. At the time of discovery, these stone tools had been thought to be 'Celtic' – a catch-all term that was used to describe anything thought to be pre-Roman in date. The whole of human prehistory, then, was effectively squashed into that category.

Buckland's *Reliquiae* meant that Paviland Cave became a magnet for other collectors, with numerous antiquarians – and in the 1890s, even a whole posse of schoolboys from Clifton College in Bristol – making pilgrimages to the Gower and digging up more remains from inside the cave. Various finds were reported over the nineteenth and into the early twentieth centuries, ranging from human bones and a tooth, Roman coins and pottery, more fragments of ivory rods, other fragments of mammoth ivory and of reindeer bone, to hundreds of flint and chert flakes and tools. A few artefacts made their way into museums, but many went missing. Apart from a couple of bones, including a humerus dated to a mere 7,000 years ago in the Natural History Museum, no one has been able to track down any of the additional human remains that were discovered after Buckland's original excavations in the cave and his discovery of the Red Lady.

Meanwhile, archaeologists were attempting to understand the chronology of the deep past – how human culture and technology had changed over time – and this would be essential to unravelling the real story of the Red Lady.

In the early nineteenth century, the Danish antiquarian Christian Jurgensen Thomsen, organising an exhibition of prehistoric artefacts in the National Museum of Denmark in Copenhagen, had decided to arrange the artefacts in a chronological fashion – Stone Age, Bronze Age, then Iron Age. We're so used to talking about the past in this way, it's difficult to imagine it being a new thing, along with the concept that humans might have discovered how to extract and work with certain metals at different times. So it wasn't just that people used different materials in the past; they used different materials at different times. Thomsen described his 'three-age' system in a paper published in 1836, and it was widely adopted. Then the Stone Age was divided up – into 'Old' and 'New' – with politician and polymath John Lubbock (now perhaps more famous for 'inventing' bank holidays) coining the terms 'Palaeolithic' and 'Neolithic' in 1865. And it went on; people started to carve up the Palaeolithic into different sections. Charles Lyell had alluded to 'different degrees of civilisation, and in the art of fabricating stone tools' in the Palaeolithic. But he was less clear about whether that reflected a chronological sequence, or whether there had just been varying degrees of sophistication among contemporary groups of stone-tool makers in Europe.

In the latter half of the nineteenth century, a much better understanding of how Stone Age cultures had developed over time was unfurling, driven largely by discoveries in France – and by a curiously niche debate between philosophical materialists and Catholics.

In 1861, the French geologist and palaeontologist Edouard Lartet wrote about his discoveries at Aurignac Cave in southwest France, where he had found clear evidence that humans had coexisted with extinct fauna. He divided up the bone caves of the Palaeolithic not by types of technology, but according to the animals that were around: the Cave Bear period, the Elephant and Rhinoceros period, and the Reindeer period. It was an unusual approach – where others were focused on ideas of human progress and technological evolution, Lartet was attempting to bring together human and natural history. Another Frenchman, Gabriel de Mortillet, proposed an alternative classification for the Stone Age based on stone tools in museum collections. He diagnosed characteristic styles, which he named after the sites where they were first discovered: Acheulian (St Acheul), Mousterian (Le Moustier), Solutrean (Solutre) and Magdalenian (La Madeleine). Such a chronology was infused with a concept not just of change or adaptation to certain environments, but of inherent progress through human history. It was as though there were an intrinsic programme of development, a march of progress, that humans were working their way through. What was emerging was the philosophical idea of culture-history – that would permeate archaeological research for so many years to come. De Mortillet's periods didn't just represent self-contained, characteristic cultures – each was a rung on a ladder of progress. In this model, there was little room for migration to play a role: human cultures everywhere were progressing through predictable stages of development.

At the end of the nineteenth century, a Catholic seminary student in the suburbs of Paris, Henri Breuil, was developing a passionate interest in prehistory. His interest in archaeology was more than a passing fad, and would divert him entirely away from a career in the church (though he always retained the title of Abbé – being a sort of minister without portfolio, as Paul Pettitt puts it – an abbot without an abbey!). When apparently ancient cave paintings were discovered in Spain and France, Breuil was among the first to consider them seriously – as genuine works of art from the early Stone Age – when many had thought them to be fakes. He was one of the first to see the astonishing cave art in Altamira in Spain and Lascaux in France, soon after those iconic sites were discovered.

Henri Breuil also became obsessed with trying to understand the sequence of stone tool types and artistic styles in the early Stone Age. He became embroiled in what became known as the 'Battle of the Aurignacian' – not a prehistoric conflict but an early-twentieth-century battle of ideas. The finds from Aurignac Cave had lent their name to stone tools of a similar type all over the place – the 'Aurignacian'. It was thought that this style related to a particular time-period, but there was debate over how old this stone tool-kit really was. De Mortillet had categorised the Aurignacian period as part of the last Palaeolithic culture he recognised, the Magdalenian. But Breuil thought it dated to much earlier – to before the Solutrean. The battle was on – and it was curiously heated for what seems like a very esoteric debate among scholars (although admittedly these can be some of the most vitriolic arguments ever). And it's particularly pertinent that Breuil was a churchman and that the Catholic Church permitted – perhaps even sponsored – his diversion into archaeology. The emerging scientific consensus on deep time, evolution and the antiquity of humans represented a threat to traditional Christian doctrine. A group of priest-scientists – including Breuil – set about trying to rein in the science. It's not clear how much their efforts were encouraged, sponsored or directed by the Church. But there was more at stake than just refining a chronology for the Palaeolithic.

Breuil made room for migration in his Stone Age chronology — for ideas arriving from the east, flowing into western Europe. Archaeologists could not yet pin precise dates on sites and objects — as they can today, using a variety of radiometric dating techniques, from radiocarbon to uranium series dating, as well as more exotic-sounding methods such as electron spin resonance and optically-stimulated luminescence. Before those techniques were developed, archaeologists relied on relative dating — piecing together chronologies by looking at the style of objects — and the depth of layers in which they were found.

Although Breuil accepted that, generally speaking, older technologies tended to be simpler than later ones — he didn't think that was a hard-and-fast rule. He thought that the position of artefacts in their layers, in their strata, was much more revealing and dependable when it came to reconstructing the chronology of the deep past.

Nevertheless, he recognised an important watershed at the end of the Mousterian — a clear divide that he thought was a sign, not of a sudden advance in culture within indigenous Europeans, but rather of a population replacement. He wrote, in 1912, 'it appears established that the arrival of the upper paleolithics [sic] brought about, at the end of the Mousterian, a social and industrial change and a racial substitution so profound . . . [to consider it to be] a division of equal greatness to that which separates this period from the Neolithic epoch.' (Chazan, 1995)

We know now that he was right about this watershed moment; it did indeed represent the replacement of a preceding people, with their own particular way of making stone tools, with another group, with another distinctive lithic culture. The earlier people, that *race première*, are none other than the Neanderthals — *Homo neanderthalensis* — the makers of the Mousterian. The incomers, the *race deuxième*, were modern humans — *Homo sapiens.* They appeared to arrive making Aurignacian tools — which was, as Breuil had worked out, winning that particular battle, a pre-Solutrean technology.

What's particularly curious, from a modern perspective, is that Breuil's interpretation is more genuinely evolutionary than de Mortillet's ladder of progress. Breuil saw cultures evolving across time and geographic space in a branching pattern, but also allowed for populations to move and replace others. Somehow, that seems to have fitted better with Catholic sensibilities. But maybe that's just because a priest had formulated it. Science was starting to tackle big questions — Who are we? Where do we come from? — that had previously been the exclusive preserve of religion. Perhaps the tension between science and religion would have been even greater if clerics like Buckland and Breuil hadn't engaged with this sphere of enquiry.

Paviland Cave was in the mix when it came to understanding the Palaeolithic cultures of Europe. In 1863, Edouard Lartet visited the museum at Oxford University with his friend, the banker and collector Henry Christy, to see the bones of the Red Lady. They were bemused by Buckland's interpretation of the bones as female. When they later wrote up their findings, they remarked that the skeleton 'was regarded by [Buckland], we know not why, as that of a woman'. Having measured the bones, Lartet and Christy concluded that 'they belonged to an individual of very great stature'.

A few years ago, I laid out the bones of this skeleton in the Oxford University Museum of Natural History, in the office of the curator, with its wonderful mural. There were a few ribs; a coccyx was the only part of the spine to have survived; and then there were bones belonging to a left arm and left leg, and a few bones from the right leg and foot. The bones are chunky: 'robust' as we anthropologists would say. The joints are large. They're not the bones of a slight woman; they looked very clearly male. And the left pelvic bone – the pelvis being the best clue to the sex of an archaeological skeleton – bore male features: the angle beneath the pubic bone was steep; the greater sciatic notch behind the hip was narrow; and the whole bone was robust and well-developed where muscles would have been attached to it. The bones were adult – the ends of the bones had fused to the shaft, and there were few signs of the line of fusion on the surface of the bones; just a trace on his hip bone, where the hamstring muscles attach. That suggests not only that the male was an adult, but that he was old enough for his bones to have remodelled and mostly mask those signs of growth during adolescence. The joints of the hip bone – at the front, the pubic symphysis, and at the back, where it meets the spine at the sacroiliac joint – had an adult but not aged appearance. He must have been at least in his mid-twenties. From the length of his bones, his stature can be calculated: around 5ft 6. There were no signs of disease in the bones. He was healthy – if dead.

I felt very privileged to be able to lay out these bones and look at them up close. And it seemed strange to me that Buckland had apparently been so swayed by the inclusion of what he thought were ivory beads in the grave that he couldn't imagine the Red Lady to be anything other than female. Neither could he imagine just how ancient the burial really was. He found a mammoth skull, complete with tusks, at the head end of the grave. But he still thought the two were quite separate – the mammoth being much older.

Lartet and Christy, though, saw similarities between the burial practices in Paviland – and at Crô-Magnon rock shelter, where human remains had also been found associated with seashells, red ochre and ivory objects. Whereas Buckland had been sure that the human remains at Paviland were quite recent – Roman or Celtic – Lartet saw no reason to doubt that the human and mammoth bones came from the same time, and that this burial in Paviland Cave in fact dated all the way back to the Palaeolithic. But others still argued, doubting that Palaeolithic humans would even have been capable of carrying out burials of the dead.

In 1911, Buckland's successor, Professor William Sollas, reviewed the finds from Paviland in the collections at Oxford, and decided that the time was right to revisit the cave itself, and do a little more digging. He was accompanied by colleagues from Oxford and Cardiff – and by Henri Breuil. Together, they dug down through the remaining sediments in the cave, noting them as 'much disturbed' and sieving them to retrieve even the tiniest fragments. They retrieved over 4,000 pieces of flint and chert, and also plenty of fragments of bone and ivory.

The task of classifying all the finds fell to Henri Breuil. He would sit at a table littered with stone flakes and tools, or 'cailloux' – pebbles – as he called them. His hands would dart over the table, selecting and sorting, occasionally throwing rejects over his shoulder. Some 'pebbles' he classified as Mousterian, but most as Aurignacian: Lower, Middle and Upper. Most of the finds, each piece inscribed with what is thought to be Sollas' handwriting, ended up in Oxford University Museum, with some later donated to the National Museum of Wales in

Cardiff. Sollas and Breuil were also sure that the mammoth skull had been deliberately placed in the grave – that it was contemporary with the human bones.

In 1926, the palaeolithic archaeologist Dorothy Garrod – whose accolades included being the very first female professor at Cambridge, and who was a friend of Breuil – wrote of the skeleton of the Red Lady: 'its Palaeolithic age cannot be doubted'.

The story that Buckland had dreamed up about those ochre-stained bones was receding. Nearly a century after their discovery, the consensus had changed – these were not the bones of woman who had lived a few thousand years ago, but those of a man who had been buried in the cave way back during the Great Ice Age, the Pleistocene epoch, when bands of hunter-gatherers making Aurignacian stone tools inhabited Europe, when mammoths still roamed the landscape.

But the last piece of the puzzle – the precise date of the burial – would only fall into place after the latest campaign of investigation, when the secrets contained in the ochre-stained bones could be unlocked by the latest advanced methods in radiocarbon dating.

Land of ice and snow

To even begin to understand where the Red Lady fits into the Ice Age story of Britain, we need first to zoom out to look at the repeating cycles of glaciation that characterise the geological epoch known as the Pleistocene. The name literally means 'most recent' – coming from the Greek πλεῖστος (pleîstos, 'most') and καινός (kainós, 'new') – and was coined by Charles Lyell himself, though the meaning he was trying to encapsulate was something more like 'almost modern'. He based his definition on the fact that rocks from this period, and where he'd studied them, in Sicily, bore fossil molluscs that were largely similar to today's species. In contrast, the preceding era was the Pliocene – 'more recent' or perhaps 'nearly modern'. The epoch we're living in now is the 'completely recent' or 'wholly modern' Holocene – from ὅλος (holos, whole) and καινός – though some scientists have begun to refer to this latest phase in Earth's history as the Anthropocene – the epoch defined by humans' impact on global climate.

The Pleistocene epoch began a fairly eye-watering 2.6 million years ago and ended a mere 12,000 years ago. It is also known as the 'Great Ice Age', but the world wasn't solidly gripped by ice for this entire period. Glaciations – which are referred to simply as 'Ice Ages' – came and went, interspersed with short warm periods. Each glaciation would leave marks on the landscape – as Agassiz realised and Buckland finally accepted. But working out just how *many* glaciations had taken place over these millions of years, how long each lasted, and how quickly the world moved in and out of Ice Ages, would take some serious sleuthing – with clues emerging from ancient beetles, the deepest seas and layers of 'fossil' ice still frozen today.

In the early 1950s, Russell Coope – who would become Professor of Quaternary Science at the University of Birmingham – was studying gravel pits near Bromsgrove in Worcestershire. Or, to be more specific, he was scrutinising the animal remains in the gravel. He'd first become interested in this site because of the large bones – and tusks – emerging from it; rather like Buckland being drawn to Paviland by those reports of elephant bones. There were bits of mammoth, woolly rhino and bison at Upton Warren. But when Coope started to look at the sediment around the larger bones, he found it packed with minute fossils – even pieces of tiny insects. And it appeared that no one had studied this before. It very quickly became clear to him that these silty deposits – sandwiched between layers of gravel – had built up in the bottom of three ponds, at different times.

Coope started by shovelling the black mud into a biscuit tin, before sticking it in his rucksack and catching a bus home. Then he had to separate the minute fossils out. He removed the pebbles from it by hand, then sieved it. The final, fine mesh with holes about 0.6mm wide would collect sand grains, tiny scraps of plants, pieces of shell, rodent bones – and parts of insects. Before each sample dried out, Coope looked carefully for the iridescent colours of beetle wing-cases – which he knew would fade to black as the sample dried out. Some of them were stunningly beautiful – and their colours were important for identifying which species the beetles belonged to: crucial to Coope's investigation. Some species were familiar – but others, intriguingly, were very unfamiliar. In a later interview, he shed light on what drove him as a scientist – and it wasn't just answering questions; it was about responding to beauty in the world. He said, 'At no time did I ever think, in those early days, "This might come in handy one day to unravel climatic and environmental change" – it was all because it was so exciting, because it was something beautiful.'

(Coope sounds like a real character. Paul Pettitt recalls attending a lecture by him, when he was an undergraduate at Birmingham in 1988. Coope, he told me, 'was famous for swallowing beetles to establish taphonomic changes as they went through the gut'!)

Russell Coope used radiocarbon dating to determine when

the silty layers from Upton Warren, with their microfossils, were laid down. He came up with a date of around 42,000 years ago, which has since been pushed back to between 43,000 and to 48,000 years. This was a period of climatic amelioration – though still colder than today – during a longer glacial phase. The great glacier that covered the Irish Sea was retreating and the forerunner of the River Salwarpe, a tributary of the Severn, was laying down gravel and sand on its floodplain.

The bones of cold-loving mammoths and woolly rhinos from the Upton Warren gravel pits certainly suggest that the climate was much colder back then than it is now. The scarcity of tree pollen – even of robust species like pine, birch and willow – lent weight to the idea that, around 45,000 years ago, now-leafy Worcestershire was a virtually treeless tundra. But then – alongside those clues indicating a relatively harsh, cold climate – Coope found something odd, something apparently inconsistent: signs of a warmer climate. There was pollen from small plants now more familiar from *southern* Sweden – implying a warmer temperature.

But it was the beetle fossils that revealed the real detail of ancient climate. Some beetles like it cold, others like it warmer. While some of the beetle species that Coope identified are extinct today, others are still around – but many of them are no longer found in Britain. Quite a few of these species are resident in northern Scandinavia and Siberia – suggesting a 'rigorous Arctic climate'. Other beetle species were similar to those present in Britain today – but now only in live in the far north, or up mountains in the south.

But then there was a twist – there were some species of beetle in the sample which were clearly much more warm-loving, as they now live in southern climes. Coope was sure the mud that had settled in those layers was undisturbed – it didn't look at all as though it had become mixed up over centuries or millennia. So those cold-loving and warm-loving beetles must have been living at Upton Warren around the same time. Coope concluded that there was only way that would have been possible: his ancient beetles had lived through a period of extremely rapid climate change. The rapidity of change was such that some cold-loving species of beetle were still clinging on as the temperature quickly rose, while other, warm-loving beetles arrived to join the party. The remains of those muddy pools bore the hallmarks of a profound change in climate happening over just a few decades, at most.

It was a controversial theory. The old concept of sudden, global catastrophes – tied in with the biblical flood myth – had been overthrown and the prevailing model at the time was one of very gradual change, in and out of cycling Ice Ages. There were no historical records of any radical changes in climate happening over short timescales. In Sweden, pollen records from lakebeds – with sudden peaks of the cold-loving alpine, the eightpetal mountain-avens or *Dryas octopetala* – had indicated some short, sharp shifts in climate, but these were just thought to be local blips rather than global changes. But Coope knew his beetles couldn't lie – and he was eventually proved right.

More evidence emerged through the 1960s and 70s, when researchers were using deep-sea cores – samples drilled out from the seabed – to pin down Ice Ages, and fluctuations of temperature and climate, with increasing levels of accuracy. Once again, the clues would come from the remains of fossilised creatures – but these ones were much, much smaller than beetles. They were minute, single-celled microorganisms called foraminifera – between half a millimetre and a millimetre across. Foraminifera, or forams for short, are amoeboid – the single cell has long, filamentous protrusions used for movement and for catching food particles. Another key characteristic of forams is that they make shells around themselves; and it's for this reason they're sometimes called 'armoured amoeba'. The shells may be made of tectin, a flexible material, or out of sand grains stuck together with calcite, or purely from calcite. The shells possess tiny holes, allowing those tendril-like filaments to protrude through them. And the Latin word for aperture, *foramen*, gives these little amoeboids their name: foraminifera – the 'hole-bearers'.

The calcite in those tiny shells, from thousands of years ago, and buried deep in the seabed, provides an astonishing record of past climate – through its influence on the water cycle, as that cycle is partially interrupted during an Ice Age. Calcite is a type of carbonate – a crystal-forming molecule containing atoms of the elements calcium, carbon and oxygen. Each element can exist in a few different forms, called isotopes. Some isotopes are unstable, and decay into alternative forms over time, emitting ionising radiation when they change. These are referred to as radioactive isotopes, or radionuclides. Others – which never seem to change – are called 'stable isotopes'. Oxygen exists in three different stable forms: oxygen-16 (^{16}O), 17 (^{17}O) and 18 (^{18}O), but oxygen-16 is by far the most abundant. In Earth's atmosphere, out of every 10,000 atoms of oxygen, 9,976 are oxygen-16, twenty are oxygen-18 and just four are the rare beast that is oxygen-17, which we'll respectfully set aside for now. In the oceans, the ratios of the light oxygen-16 to the heavier oxygen-18 are affected by evaporation and condensation. Water molecules evaporating from the surface of the sea contain relatively more of the light type of oxygen, oxygen-16, than the sea itself. As air rises, or moves towards the poles, that evaporated water will start to condense. Now it's the other way round – it's the water containing heavy oxygen that condenses most quickly. Rain falling near the equator contains more oxygen-18 than rain or snow at higher latitudes. But eventually, of course, a lot of that water – wherever it falls – finds its way back to the oceans. During a glaciation, though, the water cycle is literally frozen. Snow falling closer to the poles, full of light oxygen, becomes frozen into ice sheets – while the oceans are enriched with heavy oxygen-18. And floating around in the sea, those minute forams capture a record of the oxygen isotopes in their immediate environment when they build their tiny, delicate calcite shells. When they die, their shells fall to the sea floor, buried ever more deeply as millennia pass – then are eventually wrested from their cold, deep tomb by the coring drills of palaeoclimatologists. Layers in the cores can be dated using the very unstable, radioactive isotopes of another element – uranium. And so the palaeoclimatologists can unlock a record of changing oxygen isotopes – and fluctuating climate – through time. By 1960, research on deep-sea cores was suggesting that major temperature shifts of 5 to 10°C had taken place on timescales of less than a thousand years.

Another incredible record of climate comes from ice itself – from layers of 'fossil' ice that are preserved very deep in the ice sheets that persist over Greenland and Antarctica. Once again, those deep layers can be sampled by coring. And in those ice cores, a high level of heavy oxygen-16 indicates a cooler period, when ice sheets were forming: a glaciation. Tiny bubbles trapped deep in the ice provide more detail; they're effectively pockets of ancient atmosphere, allowing palaeoclimatologists to assess concentrations of carbon dioxide in the atmosphere in the past. By the end of the '60s the resolution had improved, and researchers were talking about rapid changes happening within a century.

The deep-sea cores and ice cores have revealed that climate change could indeed be incredibly rapid – just as Russell Coope had predicted – with big swings happening in just decades. As we look deep into the past, over vast stretches of time, the apparent stability of geography and climate that we perceive as individuals melts away, and we see instead a picture of changing climate, with sea levels rising and falling, and whole ecosystems in flux. But in fact the apparent stability that we perceive turns out to be something of an illusion – or, at least, not the whole picture. There have clearly been times in the past when major climate shifts have happened over short timescales – over just decades – certainly within the span of a human lifetime. And these climate shifts were global. The oxygen isotope records in the ice cores showed that the rapidly changing climate indicated by pollen in Sweden – and indeed by beetles in Worcestershire – were not just local aberrations, but rather windows onto local ecosystem disruption during global climate change.

These short, sharp changes in climate are superimposed on much longer cycles that last about 100,000 years. Rather than a simple, smooth wave form, the detailed record of past climate is more jagged, sawtooth in nature, with rapid switches between cold glacials – or Ice Ages – and warm interglacials.

The long cycle underneath all those rapid changes is governed by celestial rhythms. The earth's orbit is not a perfect circle, and so there are times when the earth is nearer the sun, and warmer, and other times when it is further away, and colder. These orbital cycles last around 100,000 years. Superimposed on those are other rhythms: the tilt of the earth's axis varies, on a 41,000-year-long cycle, affecting the degree of difference between the seasons. And then the earth also wobbles a little around its axis, on a 23,000-year cycle. At times, orbit and tilt conspire to create exceptional chilliness – a glacial period or Ice Age. At other times, the factors come together to produce a very warm period, called an interglacial. This theory of super-imposed oscillations affecting climate was developed by the Serbian mathematician Milutin Milankovitch in the early twentieth century – we refer to them now as Milankovitch cycles.

The Great Ice Age, the Pleistocene epoch, more than 2.5 million years long, embraced more than twenty of those long cycles, where long cold glacial periods (with those shorter-scale climate oscillations superimposed on them) were interspersed with relatively short warm, or interglacial, periods. Pleistocene ice sheets grew down from the north pole and reached as far as Gower peninsula in South Wales at least three times. We know this because of glacial erratics – great boulders carried by the glaciers – entombed in silt deposited by later glaciers. The first glaciation to reach down to South Wales was about 650,000 years ago. The second was around 450,000 years ago. And the last was around 23,000 years ago. The ice reached down almost as far as the Red Lady's grave. The edge of the ice sheet ran right across the Gower, from northwest to southeast, lying just 4 miles north of Paviland Cave itself.

The first attempt at directly determining the age of the Red Lady's bones came in the late 1960s, resulting in a radiocarbon date of about 18,000 years before the present. It was a difficult date to stomach – the stone tools at the cave looked similar to types in France dating to 10,000 years earlier. The author of the study argued that British hunter-gatherers had continued to make these types of stone tools long after their French counterparts had moved on to making new tool-kits. But other scientists were deeply sceptical. The stone tools weren't the only problem. The date placed the burial extremely close to the peak of the last Ice Age – the Last Glacial Maximum – when the ice sheets had reached almost as far as the cave itself. Perhaps it would still have been possible to visit the cave in summer, it was suggested. But as more research and more dates poured in from the European Palaeolithic, it became clear that there was no evidence for any human presence in South Wales around the Last Glacial Maximum. In fact, there was no human presence in Britain; indeed, no humans north of the Loire. The radiocarbon date *had* to be wrong.

In the late 1990s, another attempt was made to radiocarbon date the Red Lady (whose name has stuck fast) – using improved techniques. The researchers were able to use bone powder left over from the previous test, and this time the date came out considerably earlier: 31,000 years ago. This made much more sense from an environmental perspective; it meant that the burial dated to well before the peak of the last Ice Age, before the ice sheets reached their maximum extent, when human hunters could still survive in Britain. It also made sense looking at the style of the burial: all that ochre in the grave, the mammoth bones, the ivory artefacts and shell beads – this is a practice seen at many other sites across Europe, before the last Ice Age reached its icy maximum.

But in 2006, archaeologists decided that improvements in radiocarbon techniques meant that it was worth having yet another go at dating the material from Paviland. This time, the researchers were also being very careful to avoid taking any samples contaminated with old museum glues – which had been used to consolidate some of the bones, and which could potentially skew the result. In many cases, the new dates were very similar to the previous set. But some of the animal bones were turning out to be a few thousand years older. So the team decided to re-test the human bones as well, taking one sample from a piece of rib and another from a shoulder blade, or scapula. The samples were washed in acetone to remove any possible traces of contaminants, then the bone mineral was dissolved away, leaving the protein component of bone – collagen. This was then reduced to soluble gelatin and filtered to remove small, potentially contaminating molecules. When this cleaned-up sample was assessed using mass spectrometry, the ratio of radioactive carbon in the bone protein indicated that the Red Lady had died an astonishing 34,000 years ago.

Links across the landscape

This is, by far, the earliest burial found anywhere in Britain. Modern humans had probably only reached the fringes of western Europe a few millennia before this. The style of the burial in Paviland Cave is echoed across other sites in Europe and into Russia – which also include ochre and shell beads, as well as the bones of large, dangerous herbivores such as mammoths. But this very ancient date places the Red Lady much earlier than most of the other, similar-looking burials (assuming the dates of those are correct). Perhaps the Red Lady is still culturally connected with those burials, though, and simply represents a very early example of this very particular approach to death and burial. Some of the stone tools from Paviland also echo this connection to a wider culture of hunter-gatherers, who used similar hunting technology as well as having that common approach to burial. The culture has been named the Gravettian, after the site where it was first recognised – La Gravette in the Dordogne. Gravettian burials give us a precious insight into the rich culture of the 'Hunters of the Golden Age', which flourished before the global cooling at the peak of the Last Ice Age. There are plenty of examples of these burials right across Europe, with particularly rich archaeology from this period found around the Danube.

Gravettian burials in central and eastern Europe tend to be in open-air sites, whereas those in the south and west are found in caves. At Sunghir in Russia, the graves of a man and two boys, dating to around 34,000 years ago, were accompanied with ochre, spear tips and thousands of small mammoth ivory beads (though no stone tools that are strictly Gravettian in style). At Buran-Kaya in Ukraine – a 36,000-year-old site – there was no formal burial, but archaeologists found fragments of human skull associated with Gravettian-style stone tools, ivory ornaments, shell beads and ochre. At another Russian site, Kostenki, a child burial with two mammoth scapulae over the body, and other mammoth bones placed above them, was dated at 28,000 years old. At Krems-Wachtberg in Austria, two newborn babies were found buried together in a pit, with a third infant in another pit, dating to 27,000 years ago. One of the infants in the double burial was accompanied by more than thirty drop-shaped ivory beads. There was ochre in this grave too – its distribution suggesting that at least one of the infants was wrapped in a red shroud, pinned at the head with a mammoth ivory pin. A mammoth scapula was placed over both of them in the grave. Near Brno in the Czech Republic, archaeologists discovered the burial of a man, accompanied by ochre, animal bones and pieces of shell; stone, bone and ivory discs; an ivory figurine; and, nearby, a mammoth tusk and scapula dating to around 25,000 years ago. (Intriguingly, this is a secondary burial – it looks as though this man had been first buried elsewhere, then moved to a new grave, after his soft tissues had decayed away.) In the Grotte de Cussac in south-western France, several skeletons were found, deep inside the cave, laid into ready-made depressions in the floor – old bear nests. The bones were covered by silt from floods in the cave – but the bodies had clearly just been laid in the hollows, not actually buried. Some bones were covered with red pigment, but this time there were no beads. Cussac is unique as a site containing Gravettian human remains together with cave art.

Apart from those quite extraordinary burials, archaeology provides us with other insights into this Palaeolithic culture. Those hunters were well adapted, even comfortable, in those bitterly cold and bleak landscapes of Ice Age Europe. They would have been nomadic, on the move throughout the year. And yet they seem more settled than earlier hunter-gatherers, staying in one place for longer. They often set up large camps in valleys where they would have been able to intercept the migrating herds of horse, bison and reindeer that they depended on. In some places, they made semi-subterranean houses, with sunken floors dug into hard ground or ice. They had animal-fat lamps made of stone to supplement the flickering firelight. They made tanged stone points that probably formed the tips of small spears or javelins, possibly to be thrown with a spear-thrower. They also made tools out of bone and mammoth ivory – and presumably out of all manner of organic materials that have not stood the test of time. At Oblazowa Cave in southern Poland, archaeologists excavated an extraordinary collection of artefacts that may possibly have been grave goods, including pierced fox teeth, bone beads and a shell – and a thrown hunting stick, the world's oldest boomerang, made out of mammoth tusk. From impressions in clay, we know at least that they were capable of making and knotting cord. Butchered bones from Gravettian sites show they were successfully hunting large herbivores, primarily reindeer, probably with bow and arrow – but also smaller animals such as hare, presumably using nets or snares. Mammoth remains account for half of the volume of animal skeletal material from central European Gravettian sites – but the hunters may have been scavenging useful bones and tusks from carcasses, or even from mammoth 'graveyards', where already-ancient bones are found washed into the bends of rivers. Near the coast, they also dined on river fish, shell-fish and marine mammals such as seals. Plant material tends to rot away very quickly, but archaeologists recovered a range of charred plant remains from the Czech site of Dolni Vestonice, including bulbs and roots from the arti-choke family. (Some sites even show evidence of wild cereal grains being ground down into flour – even if modern 'Paleo' diets eschew bread!) Nevertheless, the variety of plants found at Gravettian sites is less than in the Aurignacian, or at sites after the peak of the Ice Age. The Gravettian toolmakers must have eaten some plants, but in the depths of the Ice Age winter, they would have relied mainly on meat, just as the reindeer herders of the high Arctic do today. As one research paper puts it, 'when the cold-dry conditions meant less plant biomass, [this] favored a hunting-dominated economy concentrated on large ungulate herds', or, if I can paraphrase – 'If you can't get vegetables, eat reindeer instead.' And it's highly likely that the Gravettian hunt-ers were not just using fire to keep themselves warm, but also to cook their food.

They didn't make pots, but they knew that clay could be moulded and fired – as we see with the famous 'Venus' figurine from Dolni Vestonice. And in fact this is the era of many of those famous female mini-statues – from Monpazier in France and Willendorf in Austria, to Savignano in Italy. Art found its way onto the walls of caves as well – from the spotted horses of Pech Merle Cave and hand stencils at Cosquer Cave in France, to some of paintings in Altamira Cave in Spain.

But who invented the Gravettian? Where did it start? The preceding Aurignacian is accepted to be a type of stone-tool technology brought into Europe in the hands of some of the very first modern human hunter-gatherers to live in the continent, moving into the territory of the indigenous people there, the Neanderthals. The later Gravettian, on the other hand, is more complex. Does its appearance and spread represent a particular group of people – the 'Gravettians' – whose population expanded across Europe, perhaps replacing, perhaps mixing with, others? Or was it more of a movement of ideas than people themselves? It's that crucial, knotty question that has vexed archaeologists for so long – wondering about the origin and spread of any prehistoric culture. It is a question that ancient DNA should be able to cast some light on. So far, there are some genetic links to the Near East, revealed in the DNA extracted from human remains at the Ukrainian site of Buran-Kaya – a very early, potentially Gravettian site. That DNA bore similarities to people from the Eastern European plain, as well as to later Gravettian toolmakers in central Europe – supporting the idea of an east-to-west spread of people at this time. As more ancient DNA studies are carried out, we'll get a clearer idea of just how much population movement underpinned the spread and evolution of this Palaeolithic culture.

The stone-tool technology itself offers some clues, though. Although some researchers have expected to find a local origin for the Gravettian, and have looked hard for traces of the earlier Aurignacian stone-tool industry *evolving* in a Gravettian direction – they've failed to find a convincing sequence. But there are types of stone tool from the Eastern Mediterranean that could conceivably have evolved into the Gravettian, implying that a second wave of people may have entered Europe from the east, after the initial incursion represented by the arrival of Aurignacian culture. If so, then these incomers didn't start off with the 'full Gravettian package' – the large camps, art and symbolism, and richly ritualised burials – that later developed and blossomed around the Danube. Still, the date of the Red Lady places his burial somewhat earlier than the earliest Gravettian sites in eastern and central Europe, which go back to about 30,000 years ago. Another, northern Gravettian site, however – Maisières-Canal in Belgium – has recently been dated to around the same time as the Red Lady. This lends some weight to another idea: that the earliest Gravettian culture in western Europe developed in the north, during a slightly milder episode within the Ice Age, then the population spread southwards as the climate grew more frosty.

At the moment, there are three 'big ideas' about how the Gravettian emerged and took root. One hypothesis sees it emerging somewhere around the Danube, then spreading east and west. This has the advantage that a lot of Gravettian archaeology has been found around the Danube – but this could just be because – that's where people have been looking for it for a long time. Another idea is that the Gravettian forms by lots of ideas coming together from different places – from the Near East, from Russia and Ukraine, and possibly from western

Europe too. The third hypothesis is about hunter-gatherers virtually independently responding to environmental changes in similar ways across a wide landscape. Now, I can see how that might explain changes in stone tools, and a switch from a fairly constantly on-the-move lifestyle to more settled, seasonal camps. But a common burial culture?

There are, of course, those sites that seem at first sight to be rather annoying but are probably, in reality, the most important to understanding the flow of ideas and sequence of events; sites where the evidence doesn't seem to quite fit the expected pattern. Like those early burials at Sungir in Russia, which look like 'classic Gravettian' graves, but without any 'classic Gravettian' stone tools – so that some researchers say we shouldn't even admit Sungir to the Gravettian club. But arguments over labels aside, perhaps that site is telling us something important – that the ideas about stone-tool technology are spreading in different ways from the ideas about how to bury your dead.

Anyway, if archaeologists settle on the Danube origin for the Gravettian, that means we'll have to invent another name for what was happening on the Gower 34,000 years ago – as the earliest Gravettian in the Danube basin emerges 4,000–5,000 years later. Palaeolithic archaeologist Stephen Aldhouse-Green reached for an alternative explanation for the elaborate, ancient burial to which he'd dedicated so many years of his own life. Was Paviland the origin? The 'naissance of a ritual tradition in the isolated tundra of southern Britain', as he so poetically put it, positioning Paviland Cave as the birthplace of the Gravettian? We all like a good origin myth, especially if it's *ours*.

As every research paper used to end, before it became a cliche best avoided: more work needs to be done. But it's also a reminder to be thoughtful about the labels we attach to past cultures and past people – they're useful tags, but they're constructs. At low resolution, we can see patterns across vast stretches of space and time – patterns the hunters of the Palaeolithic would not have been aware of. Their concept of humanity was bound in different ways from ours. Palaeolithic hunters may have travelled hundreds of miles over the course of a year, building complex mental maps of their own migration routes; they may have had connections with other tribes who told them stories of distant lands. They would undoubtedly have had a better appreciation of their place in the ecosystem than we do – in our urbanised, industrial societies where food is usually so far divorced from its source. But they wouldn't have known just how far ideas could travel.

The latest interpretation of the finds from Paviland Cave, incorporating the new radiocarbon dates, is that the cave was visited during the Aurignacian – around two dozen stone artefacts belong to this phase. These tools were based on flakes of stone, struck off a core. Then the flakes were chipped to make them into scrapers (for preparing animal hides) and burins (used like chisels). Charring on some bones suggests that fires were lit in the cave, for warmth and perhaps to cook food. But human inhabitants are likely to have alternated with other occupants, including spotted hyenas and, later, brown bears.

A single, indisputably early Gravettian-type stone tool was found in the cave – a broken, tanged point – which may have been attached to a handle as a knife, or a longer shaft as a spearhead. And then there's the burial, with all the other typically Gravettian material associated with it: the ochre, the ivory objects, the mammoth bone. It seems reasonable, for the time being, to call it Gravettian. There were more than sixty items made of ivory, bone or shell among the collections recovered over the decades at Paviland Cave, including the most recent excavations there. Buckland recorded pierced shells, fragments of ivory bracelets and around forty broken pieces of somewhat mysterious ivory rods. The shell beads, found near the hip, may have been sewn onto the bottom of a coat, or the top of trousers, perhaps – or contained in a bag. They're common periwinkles, still common on our shores. The sea was much lower back then – and the coast 70 miles away from Paviland, but that's not a huge distance for a hunter who might have travelled a round trip of a few hundred miles over the course of a year. Periwinkle shells are common ornaments, from the Aurignacian, through time. I still pick them up on visits to the beach today – small jewel-like treasures along the tide line – as though driven by some ancestral urge. The carved ivory rods are much stranger – they demand more imagination as we try to interpret them. Buckland found forty to fifty cylindrical fragments of mammoth tusk, 6–18mm in diameter, ranging from 2 to 10 centimetres long. Sollas found even more. Similar rods have been found at Aurignacian sites in Belgium, and also at the Gravettian site of Maisières-Canal and at Brillenhöhle in Germany. But what are they? Twenty-three of the pieces of ivory rod have survived in the collections now held at the Oxford University Museum of Natural History. Some of them can be fitted back together to make longer rods. Stephen Aldhouse-Green, leading the most recent excavations and re-analysis of the previous finds at Paviland Cave, thought the ivory rods could have been fragments of magical wands. They could, alternatively, be a stage in the production of ivory beads – bead 'blanks', perhaps. If so, a collection like this could conceivably represent some sort of Palaeolithic concept of wealth (like being buried with a load of gold ingots, once metalworking developed). Whatever they were, they can be safely assumed to represent something of value, placed in the grave of this man.

Fragments of ivory rings, wide enough to have been bracelets, were also found next to the man's bones – but not at his wrists or ankles. They seem decorative, but are probably not bracelets or armlets as Buckland supposed – unless they were childhood adornments that he'd kept hold of – as the diameter is too small. Some have suggested they may have been shamanic symbols, or even castanets. Who knows? The Red Lady, and he took that secret to the grave.

There's another – deeply strange – ivory object from Paviland Cave, but not necessarily from the grave, that defies explanation. It looks like a large egg made of ivory, around 8cm long. It's known as the 'Sollas egg', and it seems that it is not a beautifully hand-carved sculpturette, but actually an odd pathological growth inside a mammoth tusk. Sollas discovered it, but Buckland had excavated a mammoth tusk which had a cavity into which the egg fitted! It had been noticed in antiquity – removed from the tusk and modified, with holes drilled into it – clearly to suspend it. It looks like a fishing weight. Perhaps it is something both aesthetically pleasing and utilitarian like that. But how strange that the tusk it came from should have ended up in the grave as well. The two objects must have been kept together, perhaps remembering that special mammoth who made a pearl within her tusk.

Then there's a small collection of pierced fox and possible deer teeth, pointed pieces of bone and ivory that may have been parts of needles. And three bone 'spatulae' – each with a thickened waist and notches at the side. Stephen Aldhouse-Green thought they represented the female form. I think they look like toggles for a coat. Perhaps I downplay the symbolic potential of these things, but they just look more functional to me. Paul Pettitt has another functional explanation: that they could be shuttles for weaving. He points to similar ethnographic examples from Polynesia, and we know – from impressions in clay – that woven cloth existed in Gravettian Europe. (I like to imagine the Red Lady in a fur overcoat, fur boots and calfskin trousers, perhaps, and concealed beneath – bright red linen underwear.)

The other animal bones reported from the cave may or may not be associated directly with the burial. Buckland said he found a mammoth cranium – in fragments but with six-inch-wide tusk sockets, which would have meant hunters carrying a very heavy, adult mammoth skull into the cave. Dorothy Garrod thought it was part of the burial. More recently, Roger Jacobi thought it was related to ivory-working at the site. But why bring in a whole skull – weighing in at 300–400 kilograms – when you could just carry the tusks back to your workshop? Others have suggested that the cave was perfectly big enough back in the Ice Age for a mammoth to have wandered in and died there – its remains to have been later plundered by opportunistic hunters.

As for the red ochre staining the bones of the Red Lady and the objects buried with him – was that really part of the burial ritual, or just iron-oxide-rich clay in the cave? A few lumps of ochre from earlier excavations were analysed as part of Stephen Aldhouse-Green's re-examination of the site. They turn out to be not native to the cave, but not from a million miles away either. Veins of matching haematite run through the rocks of the eastern Gower, on the beaches around the Mumbles headland, just west of Swansea. It seems the ochre was brought in then, and chemistry shows how iron oxide can permeate and dye bones – but we're left guessing at the reasons for the ochre coming into the cave and ending up in the burial. But there are some conclusions we may usefully draw. The ends of the bones, where they meet at joints, are not stained red. This suggests that the body was still articulated – not divided into disjointed bones – at the time of burial. Ochre powder or paste could have been applied to the burial – or it could have been used to colour the clothes the corpse was dressed in. It is likely that we will never know precisely how the Red Lady became so red.

Although many interpretations of hunter-gatherer societies involve conceptions of egalitarian societies, where resources are shared, where a form of communism exists, the extraordinary burials of the Gravettian – or whatever we wish to call this funerary practice of the Ice Age – hint at the special treatment of a few, chosen individuals. Are they leaders, chieftains, priests or shamans? And if they did have some kind of high social standing, were those roles – whatever they were – hereditary, explaining the honour afforded to the Krems-Wachtberg infants and the Kostenki child? If these burials do indeed reflect high status in society – that status must have been inherited or ascribed rather than earned.

This doesn't mean the Red Lady hadn't earned an honourable burial. He could have been a hero, a well-loved or much-feared leader, a prestigious hunter, a revered shaman. His last rites, buried in his clothes, with red ochre staining those garments or added to the grave, with all those mysterious ivory objects must – the archaeologists have emphasised – have been a piece of impressive theatre, perhaps even presided over by shamans, sending him off to wherever they believed he was headed, or simply giving him back to the earth.

It's easy to be drawn into romantic reconstructions of the past. We have to remind ourselves what we do know, what we don't know – and, in fact, what we can never know – about this burial. The circumstances of this man's death, his position in his society, the reason for his unusual burial in that cave – these are all facts that are lost, and now we can only look at what the physical remains *suggest* to us. So this involves an act of imagination on our part too. While we engage our imaginative faculties, though, we should also try to think of as many explanations as possible – construct as many hypotheses as we can – before testing those out again, going back to the facts of the physical remains, looking at archaeological and ethnographic comparisons. We need to be hard on ourselves. We might *like* a particular explanation – but could there be an alternative?

As an alternative to the idea that the Red Lady could have been a leader, shaman or hero, Paul Pettitt has suggested an alternative hypothesis to explain his elaborate burial – based on the manner of his death. He proposes the possibility that what we're looking at is a 'deviant' funerary practice. We see such practices in many different time periods and locations – and they represent a break from the norm. Something about the individual or the way they died somehow requires a special, unusual treatment. For instance, in Ireland, unbaptised or stillborn children were historically buried in unconsecrated cemeteries; Roman burials with corpses laid face-down, or decapitated, are thought to be the bodies of people who were criminals – still feared in death. In historical times, people

74

who died suddenly or were murdered could be buried in strange ways – prone, or with rocks on their chests, or mutilated – to prevent them 'coming back'. Whatever the standard mortuary practice in the Gravettian – it doesn't leave a trace. So the Red Lady could be seen as a deviant burial, making us wonder if he was either a 'bad man' or died a 'bad death'. Hero or villain – we'll never know now. But he was buried in a special way, in what could already have been seen as a special place.

Here is what looks like a Gravettian burial in a cave once used by Aurignacian stone toolmakers. There's a similar pattern at the famous site of Crô-Magnon, where early layers with charcoal from ancient hearths also contain Aurignacian stone tools, with dead bodies later placed at the back of the shelter, in Gravettian times. A shelter for the living becoming a sanctuary for the dead? That's how we see it now, perhaps, but we'll never know if those Gravettian people chose to lay their dead in Paviland Cave and Crô-Magnon rock shelter *because* of any association with earlier ancestors. The selection of those caves for burials, as Roger Jacobi and Tom Higham noted when they published the new radiocarbon dates for Paviland Cave, may have been nothing more than serendipity. And as Paul Pettitt points out, the evidence for occupation at Paviland Cave is very ephemeral anyway.

So perhaps Paviland wasn't all that special before the Red Lady was buried there. But when he was – when this man was given his 'grave with a view' – he could lie there in his scarlet and ivory luxury and keep watch over the hunting grounds of his surviving relatives and friends. Whether they feared or revered him, he would stay in that place, guarding a Gravettian time capsule.

The cave – now and then

Collectors continued to visit Paviland Cave in the twentieth century, though there was precious little left to find, after Sollas and Breuil had so carefully sieved through the sediments. In 1997, Professor Stephen Aldhouse-Green, then Head of Archaeology at Newport University, planned a comprehensive reinvestigation, intent on fully mapping out the interior of the cave for the first time. But he and his team also did some digging, to see if any intact, undisturbed sediments remained, after nearly two centuries of investigations there – and whether any protection was needed. Although the cave is high on the cliffs, storm surges can occasionally push up into it, potentially threatening any remaining archaeology. The archaeologists found new beaches of sandy shingle inside the cave, washed into two hollows on the bedrock floor, up against the northern wall of the cave, on the left as you enter. The Red Lady himself was probably buried within the first hollow, nearest to the entrance.

When I visited the cave with archaeologist Paul Pettitt, in 2005, it was a warm, sunny day. We scrambled down among the jagged rocks, an hour or so before the lowest tide. Then we trekked back up to the cave mouth. It's a wide, high entrance today – about 10 metres high and 5 metres wide, a teardrop-shaped gash in the cliffs. But towards the end of the Palaeolithic, so much sediment had built up in the cave that the entrance would only have been 2 metres high. I filmed an interview with Paul inside the cave – talking about the radio-carbon date he and his team at Oxford had obtained from the bones in the late 1990s, as part of Stephen Aldhouse-Green's reassessment of Paviland. Paul's team had pushed the date back to about 29,000 years ago – not quite as ancient as we now know it to be, after the most recent analysis.

Paul and I wondered about what the cave would have been like, back in the grip of the Ice Age. Very different from today. At the moment we're enjoying a nice, warm phase (admittedly getting even warmer now, which could leave us facing other climatic challenges this century). We're living in an interglacial (literally 'between the ice') that officially started 13,000 years ago. Before this current interglacial, the last time the earth was nicely warm was ages ago, between 130,000 to 74,000 years ago: the 'Eemian' or 'Ipswichian' interglacial. From 74,000 to 13,000 years ago, the world was much cooler, but with a slightly milder – or, at least, not as horrendously icy – period sandwiched between two bitterly cold Ice Ages. That milder period lasted from 59,000 to 24,000 years ago – embracing the time of the Red Lady. But, most of the time, it was still much cooler than today, and so much water was already locked up in the ice sheets that the sea level was around 80 metres lower than today, and the coast 70 miles away. The Severn Estuary would have been a wide, grassy plain, with a much smaller river snaking west across it to the sea. At times, herds of red deer, reindeer and bison, as well as woolly rhinoceroses and mammoths, would have roamed that landscape – rich pickings for predators like wolves and hyenas, and human hunters.

Between his time and ours, then, the ice sheets of the last Ice Age grew and deepened, eventually reaching down almost as far as Paviland Cave itself. South of the ice, Britain – as merely part of a peninsula off northwest Europe – was treeless tundra, abandoned by humans. It's hard to imagine this transition – or to know the details of just how rapid the descent into ice and tundra was. Perhaps it did happen within a human lifetime, or at least quickly enough for those hunters to be aware of the change:

spring coming later and later each year; the herds of reindeer shifting further south; the winters longer and more difficult to bear than ever. Human numbers in northern Europe dwindled. The north was eventually abandoned – not by people migrating away, but by populations disappearing – local extinction. That peak in iciness, the epic-sounding Last Glacial Maximum, drew a veil over Britain for thousands of years, during which time no humans could survive here. The Red Lady represents some of the last Palaeolithic hunter-gatherers to live in this corner of Europe before the world got too cold. And while their culture was so different from our own, the burial itself speaks of a need to mark a death in a way that we still understand today.

We can imagine the day of his burial. He could have been a murderer, or murdered. But let's allow ourselves to envisage him as a fallen hero.

A small group of people are scrambling up from the plain to the foot of the cliffs, their backs to the afternoon sun. Some of them are carrying something heavy – a body. They lay it down for a moment and recover, before picking it back up and trudging up the talus slope to the dark triangle of a cave entrance in this rocky outcrop that's such a familiar landmark in this wide valley that they always move through at this time of year, autumn, following the herds of reindeer on their migration.

The hunters are all clad in furry reindeer hide and Arctic-fox fur – bulky, hooded coats, leggings and boots. They have hunting weapons – light javelins – tied to their backs. The body is fully clothed, too, with three bone toggles closing his hooded reindeer-fur coat. Inside the cave, the hunters gently lie the body down on the sandy floor. They push their hoods back and we can see their faces. Men, women, children. They start digging a hole to the left of the cave, right up against the wall. Some pick up bones from the back of the cave to use as picks; others seem to have brought bone and antler tools with them. Loosening the sediment, they use their hands, too, to scoop the loam aside.

A woman with streaks of grey in her matted locks kneels down beside him. She uses her reindeer-hide cape to wipe some of the dried blood from his face. He was killed in a hunt just the day before – running beside a herd of reindeer, losing his footing – and kicked in the head by the panicking animals. She's lost other children, but none of those had grown to adulthood. She didn't expect to lose him. Now, his body lying stretched out on the sandy floor of the cave they have carried him into, he somehow looks taller than he was in life. His hide leggings have seashells sewn onto them. He has bags slung around his waist, made of animal skin attached to ivory rings. The woman opens a bag of her own and begins to rub powdered, red ochre on his hands, face and clothes. She doesn't really know why – it's just how they've always honoured someone killed in a hunt.

After some time, they've dug out a long pit. They place stone slabs at each end, then lift the body and place it into this grave. One of the children found a mammoth skull half-buried at the back of the cave – with the help of some adults, they've dug it out and now they drag it towards the grave, to lie near the dead man's head. It seems the right thing to do.

Everyone gathers round the grave. Each of them places a rod of mammoth ivory – the precious raw material they tend to carry round, in this form, for making beads and toggles – in the pit with the body. Another honour for a dead hunter. One of them places a dart with a broken stone point in the grave; a broken spear for a broken hunter. Then they all help to scrape the loam over the reddened body, entombing it.

And they exit the cave, scrambling down the cliff and then making their way home south to their camp by the river that loops across the plain. His mother and sister are the last to leave the cave. They hold each other, shaking with grief, as they turn their backs on the grave of the hunter-hero, son and brother.

Four of the other five people with us on that pilgrimage to Paviland Cave in 2005 were television-makers. The story of that ancient burial was one I was desperate to include in a series for BBC Two about the prehistory, history and wildlife of the British coast. The fifth person was my husband, Dave, who knew the cave and the tides there very well. He'd been part of the team that reassessed the cave, led by Professor Stephen Aldhouse-Green, more than twenty years ago. Dave had surveyed the cave – by hand, using tapes, a clinometer and trigonometry. He knows its crevices, secret places – and its spiders – in perhaps more detail than anyone alive. The monograph on the cave contains his precise plans and section drawings. Sitting down to write this chapter, I pull this book down off the shelf at home – a large, black, cloth-bound hardback. On its spine, there's an image of one of those bone toggles, picked out in gold, along with the lettering:

PAVILAND
CAVE
AND THE
'RED LADY'

———

Aldhouse-Green

When I open the book, I find three black-and-white photographs tucked inside the flyleaf: a trowelled section through a mound of dirt and stones, with a ranging rod propped up for scale; a view of the inside of the cave, with two archaeologists in hard hats crouched down near the wall on the left and, in the distance, a floodlit section of the cave where another archaeologist bends over a trench. The third photograph is a wide, slit-like crevice, which can only be perhaps 30cm high – I can infer this because the soles of two boots are providing the scale here. The archaeologist himself is disappearing into the bowels of the earth.

I show the photographs to Dave. Are they Paviland? They don't look quite right. No. They are from another cave he knows well, at the other end of Wales. Another Ice Age story, but one that takes us even further back in time: Pontnewydd.

3.

THE FLOWER PEOPLE

Another cave – this one in the Elwy Valley in North Wales, where the river is full of fat, wild brown trout. Close to the small village of Bontnewydd, 'New Bridge', the cave itself is known by the unmutated Welsh version of the name: Pontnewydd. This was another cave, like Paviland, that Stephen Aldhouse-Green set out to re-examine in the last decades of the twentieth century, once again treading in the footsteps of early, nineteenth-century pioneers of archaeology.

William Boyd Dawkins wrote about his own discoveries in Pontnewydd in his book, *Cave Hunting*, published in 1874. He opened with a tug of the forelock to Buckland:

'The exploration of caves is rapidly becoming an important field of enquiry,' he wrote. 'Since the year 1823, when Dr. Buckland published his famous work, the "Reliquiae Diluvianae" . . . the momentous discovery of the human relics along with extinct animals in caves and river deposits has revolutionised the current ideas as to the antiquity and condition of man'.

The book introduces the history of cave exploration

in Europe, then focuses on how caves are formed, before embarking on a tour of 'historic caves' – where archaeological discoveries had been made. Boyd Dawkins rambles around Britain, with no particular chronology in mind, mentioning 'Romano-Celtic' caves in the same chapter as Picts and Scots, the 'Neolithic Stratum' and Pleistocene hyenas. He has a whole chapter dedicated to Neolithic skulls from western Europe, classifying them by shape into dolicho-cephali and brachy-cephali. Then a chapter on 'Caves Containing Human Remains of Doubtful Age', starting with Paviland.

Boyd Dawkins seems to have been unaware of Edouard Lartet's assessment of the Red Lady, as a Palaeolithic burial contemporary with the mammoth bones in the cave, as he writes that, 'The Cave of Goat's Hole at Paviland . . . offers an instance of an interment having been made in a pre-existent deposit of the Pleistocene age,' and that 'Dr Buckland's con-clusion, that the interment is relatively more modern than the accumulation with remains of the extinct mammalia, must be accepted as the true interpretation of the facts.'

Pontnewydd Cave, though, was included in Boyd Dawkins' gazetteer as firmly Pleistocene. A range of 'ossiferous caves and fissures' in the North Welsh valleys of the Clwyd and Elwy, had been described in 1833 by yet another reverend with a penchant for antiquarian pursuits: the Rev. Edward Stanley – later to become Bishop of Norwich. William Boyd Dawkins explored one of these caves, near 'Pont Newydd', in the company of a Mrs Williams Wynn – and of course, an obligatory reverend – this time the Rev. D. R. Thomas. In this horizontal cave, they discovered water-worn bones embedded in claggy boulder clay. Among them, Boyd Dawkins identified the remains of brown, grizzly and cave bear. But there were signs of a human presence as well: stone tools, which he described as 'rude implements of felstone' – and intriguingly, 'a human molar of unusual size'.

The bone caves quickly became famous and attracted many visitors – including a 22-year-old Charles Darwin, fresh out of university. A few, smaller excavations took place into the early twentieth century. And then, during the Second World War, the cave was converted into a store for explosives, with a gateway built into the entrance.

But in 1978, a certain Stephen Green (not yet Aldhouse-Green) from the National Museum of Wales decided it was time to re-examine the cave. He and his team wanted to look at evidence for the formation of the cave, as well as searching for traces of the advance of the ice sheet during the last glaciation – and they were on the look-out for animal bones, human bones and archaeological artefacts as well. The original tooth from Boyd Dawkins' dig had sadly been lost in the intervening years, but Stephen Green hoped that there might be more human remains to be found.

The archaeologists dug through the cave floor, going down about 4 metres. Limestone caves are born of water – sculpted out by subterranean rivers and streams, but constantly being augmented as well. Water percolating through the limestone of the cave dissolves the calcium carbonate and redeposits it as flowstone, stalactites and stalagmites. The topmost layer of the cave floor was a crust of stalagmitic limestone, crystallising out of the water still dripping and flowing through the cave. Under that was a thick wedge of clays and sands laid down by an earlier stream in the cave, and beneath that, a layer of fine, red cave-earth. Then there were hard layers of breccia – where silt, sand and chunks of limestone had become cemented into hard rock – by calcium carbonate crystallising out of water. The deepest layers were mixed-up silt, sand and gravel; the lowest of these full of small pebbles. Some of the deposits looked like they'd been washed in, pushed in as mud, or had settled out of ponds. Others looked like the sort of silts left behind when ice sheets and glaciers thaw. Using uranium series dating, they could determine the age of the layers: the stalagmitic crust at the top was around 20,000 years old. The lower layer of breccia was at least 200,000 years old.

Like Boyd Dawkins, Stephen Green and his team found plenty of bear bones distributed among the layers of deposits in the cave. Although the bones had been bashed around before ending up in the breccias, they could identify species – as well as bear: beaver, lemmings and voles, fox, lion, horse, rhinoceros, red deer and reindeer, and ancient cattle and sheep. And they also found human remains. This time: a tooth, a piece of jaw, and a fragment of a vertebra. The tooth was a large upper molar. The cusps of the tooth were only slightly worn down – suggesting that it had belonged to someone who had been a young adult when they died. Upper molars usually have three separate roots. Even though this tooth's roots were partly broken, it was possible to see that they were fused together for much of their length, with a very large pulp cavity inside. This pattern is known as 'taurodontism', which literally means 'bull-tooth'; the tooth looks a bit like cattle teeth, which are long and rectangular in shape, with fused roots. It's an unusual condition, and doesn't cause any problems itself – though it can make dental work tricky today. It's sometimes associated with other genetic anomalies, but there's also a possibility it may have been advantageous in people with tough diets in the past. The fused roots can become hardened and continue functioning as a decent grinding tooth after the crown has worn down. Taurodontism is quite rare today, affecting 1–5 per cent of the population. But it was more common in the past – among another group of humans: Neanderthals. And this tooth was found in the mixed, gravelly layer under the lower breccia, making it more than 200,000 years old. The animal bones found near it helped to refine the date to around 230,000 years ago. This was a period of relative warmth during the Pleistocene – in a gap between glacial cycles. But it was still cold compared with North Wales today. The animal bones tell us what the landscape would have been like: a mixture of open steppe grassland, judging by the presence of lemming bones, with some patchy woodland, given the presence of wood mice and roe deer as well.

The piece of human jaw was from the back of a mandible, with a back tooth *in situ*. It's a molar with five, simple cusps – and still held in the embrace of the bone of the mandible: it hadn't yet erupted through the gums. As it has such a simple shape, it's hard to pin down *which* molar it is. Without a firm identification, it makes it difficult to know how old this individual was when they died. It's unlikely to be a first molar, though, as this would make its owner around three years of age – and the jaw itself is too large to be that of a three-year-old. If it's a second molar, that would imply an age of eight to nine years old; if it's a third molar, its owner is likely to to have been an older child – more than eleven years old when they died.

The fragment of vertebra is frustratingly difficult to interpret as well. It's a piece of the back of a vertebral body, with facets for ribs – so it must be a thoracic vertebra. Beyond that, it's impossible to say anything else about it.

There were other signs of humans too: the archaeologists

found around 300 stone tools and flakes made of hard rock –
some of flint. But it didn't look like these artefacts had been
brought into the cave by humans. Instead, they'd ended up deep
inside the cave in the same way that the sand and gravels, pebbles and bone fragments had been deposited in there – by the
action of thawing ice, water and slumping mud. They probably
haven't travelled far, though; the entrance of the cave may have
been used as a site for butchering animal carcasses. Among
the artefacts were Acheulian hand-axes, scrapers, cores from
which blades had been struck, and lots of waste flakes.

In their early paper on the site, Stephen Green and his
colleagues are very wary of saying which people made those
tools, and even what species the fragments of teeth and bones
represent. It turns out they were right to be cautious about
those human remains. The piece of jaw and the vertebra
fragment came from disturbed layers left behind by previous
excavations – and are now thought to date to well after the Ice
Age. Taurodont molars may have been more common among
Neanderthals – but some modern humans have that pattern
too. The taurodont tooth came from under the hard breccia,
however, which was dated to 200,000 years ago. The earliest
modern humans – *Homo sapiens* – reached Europe between
40,000 and 50,000 years ago.

Pontnewydd clearly held more secrets, and Stephen Green
kept returning to the cave throughout the 1980s and into the
mid-'90s, finding more and more evidence of Ice Age animals –
and humans. Over the years, the archaeologists would recover
more than 1,500 stone tools and flakes from the cave, and more
teeth – all coming from that lower layer of breccia.

Sometime later, two palaeoanthropologists working in
the Natural History Museum – Tim Compton and Chris

Stringer – took a closer look at the teeth from Pontnewydd Cave, carefully comparing them with other ancient teeth from Europe, Africa and Asia in order to try to work out which species they belonged to – because Neanderthals weren't the only possibility.

Before modern humans reached Europe, the continent was home to Neanderthals – *Homo neanderthalensis* – and before that, to another population – one that may have eventually evolved into Neanderthals, the species known as *Homo heidelbergensis*. The transition between these species would have played out as a long, drawn-out process over thousands of years, with different features changing in a mosaic fashion. The Pontnewydd teeth may lie towards the end of that transition.

The teeth do look odd. Five of them have that taurodont shape, with roots fused together. Modern human upper molars usually have three roots and look a bit like a three-legged bar stool – an upside-down three-legged bar stool, if you orient them the right way round, as they sit in the upper jaw or maxilla. The taurodont molars, on the other hand, look like chunky hourglasses – wide at the crown, slightly cinched in at the start of the thick root, then broadening out towards the end of the root. Tim and Chris examined seventeen teeth from Pontnewydd Cave – two still embedded in a fragment of maxilla, and the rest found loose. All were permanent except for one milk tooth. There's a variety of different types of teeth represented in the sample, and they must have come from at least five different individuals – but possibly as many as sixteen. The crown of a tooth is like a small mountain range, with cusps rising in peaks, and grooves and fissures dividing them like passes. Mapping the topography of each crown, Tim and Chris found striking similarities between the shape of the Pontnewydd teeth and teeth from a site called Sima de los Huesos (the 'sink of the bones') in Atapuerca, in northern Spain. The hominins from Sima de los Huesos date to around 430,000 years ago, and are thought to represent a transitional stage between an earlier species known as *Homo heidelbergensis* and 'classic' Neanderthals, which date to later than 200,000 years ago. Like the Spanish material, the Pontnewydd teeth seem to represent a human population 'on its way' to becoming full-blown Neanderthals.

But the hominin teeth are stray finds in that Welsh cave: they're on their own, not anchored in a skull and associated with the rest of the skeletons they were once part of. How did they get there? The stone tools and flakes suggest that early humans were using the cave as a base, perhaps camping in its entrance. Some of the animal bones from the cave bore cut-marks – evidence of having been butchered. But – we don't know if the human teeth were brought to the cave by other humans, or by scavengers like wolves or hyenas. They represent what's left of between five and fifteen individuals, and Stephen Aldhouse-Green thought the most likely explanation for their presence was 'a conscious deposition of the dead in the dark recesses of the cave'. Others have disagreed, pointing out that the human remains seem to have been washed deeper into the cave in the same way that the rest of the sediment, pebbles and bones have been – by meltwater from the retreating glaciers as the Ice Age came to an end. If they were originally buried in the cave – no traces of those graves remain.

Despite the fact that we can't say much about what those pre-Neanderthals were doing in North Wales, the teeth and stone tools at least show that they were *there*. And these remains represent the most northerly evidence of hominins at this time – these early pre-Neanderthals – showing just how widespread these populations were, right across Europe.

But we're still not any closer – at least based on the evidence from Pontnewydd – to knowing if these early humans buried their dead, or practised any sort of funerary ritual at all.

The bone sink and the rising star

There are a couple of even more ancient sites where archaeologists have argued that human remains have been deliberately brought into caves. One of those sites is that Sima de los Huesos shaft in Spain, where the remains of at least twenty-eight individuals have been recovered, along with a stone hand-axe. The identity of these Sima hominins was hotly debated from the moment of discovery, but it was the ancient DNA revolution that offered an answer. The DNA from these 430,000-year-old fossils is – at the time of writing – the earliest human genetic material to have been sequenced, and it reveals the Sima hominins to have been 'pre-Neanderthals'. The other heated discussion around these fossils is about how those bodies ended up at the bottom of a 13-metre-deep shaft inside a cave. The original excavators argued that the bodies had been deliberately thrown into the shaft – making this the earliest example of mortuary practice anywhere in the world. Other anthropologists have countered this claim, suggesting that the accumulation of human remains could represent unfortunate accidents occurring over time, bodies washed in by water flooding through the cave or carnivores bringing their prey into the cave. The last suggestion can be fairly easily dismissed – very few bones show any evidence of having been bitten and gnawed by carnivores. Analysis of the breakage patterns on the bones – particularly the skulls – suggests that these individuals could have been victims of violent deaths, their skulls smashed in. It's gruesome, but still doesn't explain why all those bodies ended up in the pit of bones. The case is far from closed.

Another very ancient site which has been suggested to provide evidence of mortuary practice is the Rising Star cave system in South Africa. In excavations starting in 2013, hundreds of fossils were found deep inside these caves, dating to between 240,000 and 340,000 years ago, and representing a species never seen before: *Homo naledi*.

Those old bones belonged to at least fifteen individuals, and this species combined a weird mix of modern-looking with more archaic features. While the hands and feet look quite similar to those of modern humans and Neanderthals, their ribcages seem more like those of much earlier hominins, from millions of years ago. The bones were found inside chambers deep within the cave system, and could only be reached by crawling through two very narrow squeezes – at one point, only 20cm wide. The archaeologists that excavated them thought it highly unlikely that the bones had ended up in the cave by being washed in or taken in by scavengers – they argued that other *Homo naledi* individuals must have deliberately pulled the bodies through to the chamber.

Other experts – including Chris Stringer – were sceptical of this explanation. *Homo naledi* had a tiny brain, about half a litre in volume, around the same size as a modern gorilla's. Rather than these hominins practising a strange funerary ritual, it seems more likely that the skeletal remains represent accidental deaths in the cave. Perhaps, individuals fleeing attack or predation sought refuge in its deep recesses and never managed to make it out – dying, terrified and alone, in the depths and the darkness. The pile of bones in the cave could represent many such isolated incidents, over hundreds or even thousands of years. The discoverers of the site contest that, if those hominins represent accidental deaths, you might expect to see evidence of other ill-fated primates, such as baboons, down there – and there are none (while Paul Pettitt still thinks the bones could represent a carnivore cache, as some of the remains are partially articulated limbs, but there are no whole skeletons).

It seems like an esoteric debate – whether those ancient bones ended up in the cave through carnivore agency, personal accident or intentional 'burial' by others. But it's crucial if we're to trace the earliest manifestations of a behaviour that carries with it connotations of human ways of thinking. Moving dead bodies around seems to be about something other than just survival. Even if we don't know what past people were thinking when they performed funerary rites, the practices themselves speak of *some sort* of symbolic thinking – some sort of appreciation of the difference between being alive and being dead, the meaning of loss, the importance of ritual.

Symbolic thinking goes to the heart (or brain) of what we believe is unique about us humans. We can hold abstract ideas in our heads in a way we think other animals cannot – at least, not to the same degree. Abstract ideas and symbolic thinking also underpin our language – which is far more complex than that of any other animal. Language and ideas don't fossilise. It's not until people invent writing, around 5,000 years ago, that we can read the thoughts of our ancestors. (Even then, we can only read the thoughts they cared to submit to clay, papyrus or stone. And most of those are – somewhat tediously – records of who owes what to whom. Yes, you can blame accountants for the invention of the most transformative technology in human history.) Before the invention of writing, what can we reasonably look for among the physical traces left by our ancestors that could help us know if they thought 'like a human'? The empty spaces inside their fossilised skulls are just that – empty spaces. We can measure the size of brains and even the relative shape of parts of the brain, but that doesn't get us very close to knowing what they were thinking about. The traces of what they made and did are far more informative. Archaeologists look for evidence of sophisticated tool-making – creating tools which require several steps and forward-planning in their manufacture. The earliest stone tools of any sort go back over 3 million years ago and are very crude – pebbles are bashed together and useful flakes with sharp edges fly off. Around 1.8 million years ago, a new style of stone tool appears in the archaeological record – the Acheulian hand-axe. These are hefty teardrop- or oval-shaped implements, some of which may indeed have been hand-tools, while others may have been hafted – stuck onto handles of some kind. Archaeologists argue about what they were used for, and how. But that's almost beside the point when it comes to what they can tell us about the mind of the maker. In order to create such an artefact, the stone knapper must choose a suitable rock, then set to work chipping away at it – with, all the time, an idea of the finished shape in their mind. An abstract idea – 'teardrop' – is made real. A capacity for symbolic thinking is demonstrated by the ability to make that symbol into a physical object. A virtual concept wrought in Real Life.

The appearance of Acheulian hand-axes seems like a watershed moment: the first glimmer of a modern mind in the making. And yet that same shape continues to be churned out by generation after generation within some hominin populations, from *Homo erectus* to *Homo heidelbergensis* . . . there's very little going on in the way of innovation. Around half a million years ago, things do start to change, with a shift in stone-tool technology that sees the one-size-fits-all hand-axe replaced by tool-kits with a range of different forms and functions. Around the time modern humans are appearing on the scene, more diverse tool-kits, some including carefully formed blades, are becoming more common. Those features – diversity and blade manufacture – have long been thought to represent hallmarks of a modern mind in action.

Other indications of 'modernity' – products of something you could interpret as a modern human mind – have been proposed: the use of bone to manufacture tools; traces of artistic expression and communication – with pierced shells and animal teeth, hinting at personal adornment; ancient lumps of ochre ground down to release the red powder, presumably as pigment; and then – spectacularly – the profusion of painted caves in Spain and France, where the wild, extinct megafauna of Europe are frozen in time, running across limestone landscapes.

And then there is burial. A ritual which seems to encapsulate a familiar concept of life and death, the need to mark an ending, to achieve closure by folding the dead into the bosom of the earth. Other funerary rituals speak similarly of that acknowledgement and marking of a life that has ended. Fire sends the cremated body up in smoke, becoming part of the air and wind, with calcined bones left to be scattered in the landscape, naturally or by human hand; or buried in an urn. Excarnation reduces a body to its most enduring elements – flesh is cut or rots or is torn away by scavengers – leaving the bones, hard as stone. Is the skeleton somehow seen as the essence of a person? Left after knives, teeth and decay have stripped away the mortal vestment? However we do it, marking death with ritual that transforms the body takes us beyond just mourning. Elephants and chimpanzees mourn. Humans seem to translate mourning into a physical demonstration of loss and transformation, with mortuary rituals: burial, cremation, excarnation.

Archaeologists used to speak of the 'five Bs' of modern human behaviour: blades, bone (tool-making), beads, beauty and burial. And the greatest of these – it could perhaps be argued – is ritualised burial. Funerary rituals seem to represent something about the way we think about the world, and our place in it – that we believe is uniquely human.

We know that, once, we were not in the world – and then we were born. We know that one day, we will leave this world – that we will die. We understand that each of us, as individuals, had a beginning, and that we will not endure for ever. It's unavoidable. And I suspect that all of religion is, at its roots, concerned with providing us with solace in the face of this frankly unimaginable – but at the same time, incontestable and unavoidable – fact. The idea of an afterlife is so appealing that many people believe in it even today, when there is of course no reliable evidence for any meaningful existence after death. Even when that goes against everything we understand about physics, biology and consciousness.

We don't know what any of our prehistoric ancestors believed about what happened to people when they died, but we can see that those ancient mortuary rituals – at least, the physical traces that we are left with, after the elegies, songs and dances have echoed away – are rich with symbolism, even if we can't get at the precise meaning of the symbols.

Aside from thinking about the possibility of an afterlife,

rituals associated with the dead suggest that the people car-rying them out had, at least, an appreciation of the passage of time; that they could remember the past, when the dead were living – and imagine a future, when those still alive would also die.

We can't really be sure about how either the skeletons in the Rising Star cave system, or in the Sima de los Huesos, got into those deep chambers. The evidence isn't conclusive – as shown by the weight of eminent experts arguing both for and against intentional mortuary practice, in both cases. And even if it *is* mortuary practice, such caching of dead bodies seems to fall into a different conceptual category from funerary practice, which implies a more thoughtful, symbolic approach to death and the dead.

This leaves us wondering whether the capacity to understand death and the need to mark the passing of a life is something that only came along with the evolution of our own species – modern humans: *Homo sapiens.* The earliest fossil evidence of our own kind comes from Africa – from Moroccan finds dating to around 315,000 years ago, and Ethiopian discoveries dating to between 160,000 and 200,000 years ago.

What appear to be genuine graves containing the skeletons of modern humans come along later. Multiple burials at the caves of Skhul in Israel date to between 100,000 to 130,000 years ago. Another Israeli cave, Qafzeh, contains burials from 90,000 to 110,000 years ago. And a child's body deposited in a pit at Taramsa, in Egypt, dates to 75,000 years ago. These sites are considered transitional – some 'burials' use natural fissures into which bodies are placed; others involve the digging-out of shallow pits.

And yet, burial may not be an exclusively modern human

activity, after all. While the evidence from Sima de los Huesos and Rising Star – and indeed from Pontnewydd Cave – is inconclusive, there are other sites that suggest at least one other human species did practise burial. The debate – you won't be surprised to learn – is far from settled, but there are a handful of discoveries, dating to later than those early modern human burials at Skhul, Qafzeh and Taramsa, that suggest that Neanderthals themselves may have buried their dead.

The Chapel of the Saints

In 1908, a Neanderthal skeleton was discovered during excavations of a cave in the Bouffia Bonneval, in La Chapelle-aux-Saints in southern France. The skeleton was fairly complete – the skull, most of the spine, some ribs, the long bones of the arms and legs, and some of the hand and foot bones, were there. The skull is 'classic' Neanderthal, with arched brow ridges jutting out above the eye sockets, a sloping forehead and bulging cheekbones. He was an old man when he died – at least forty, if not quite a bit older than that; he'd lost most of his teeth, and was wracked with osteoarthritis. But it's how this 50,000-year-old skeleton got into that cave that is most pertinent here.

The original archaeologists claimed that the body had been deliberately buried – in a crouched position, in a pit that had been purposefully dug. But others were more sceptical, and doubt persisted. Sites like this – discovered and dug more than 100 years ago – are always problematic. Archaeological techniques were not as advanced as they are today – recording could be somewhat sloppy – and so it's hard to draw reliable conclusions. More than a century later, archaeologists returned to La Chapelle to re-excavate, re-analyse and test the conclusions of the original excavators. After careful consideration, the new team thought it most likely that the Neanderthal skeleton represented a deliberate burial. In particular, they argued that the skeleton would not have survived in such an intact, articulated state if it had been left exposed – vulnerable to weathering and scavengers.

But questions remained. Why was the pit in the cave, originally described as rectangular and steep-sided, now a very rounded-off rectangle and shallow? And is the depression in the bedrock that is visible now simply where the first excavators dug the skeleton out of the clay and sandstone cave floor – or was there really an ancient pit that the remains had been placed in? This is really difficult to know from the surviving records of the first excavation and the way it was carried out. Today, archaeologists would dig a small, straight-sided trench across a possible pit or grave – to provide them with a cross-section that should show up the edge of any hole that had been dug – the 'grave cut'. A section like this would also usually show a clear difference between the rock or sediment that the pit had been dug down into, and the mixed-up material that had been put into the grave to cover the body – the 'grave fill'. In 1908, no such section was cut – so the illustrations of a box-like grave, cut down into the cave floor, must be considered to be schematic rather than an accurate representation.

The early-twentieth-century archaeologists had found another depression, near the mouth of the cave, which was found to contain parts of a bison skeleton. Other modern archaeologists suggested that the depressions – based on comparison with other caves – could have been dug out by cave bears, as nests. The depression shown in the original drawing was also very large – at least twice as big as would have been necessary just to accommodate the skeleton. Why would anyone dig a grave so much bigger than it needed to be? Having said that, the depression is also large for a bear nest. In the exchange of views over the modern interpretation of the site, the shape of the pit is much discussed. Is it too round to be a grave, or too rectangular to be a bear's nest? I end up shrugging my shoulders. It's a sort of rounded-off rectangle. Either possibility seems . . . possible.

The position of the skeleton, lying up against one side of the pit, suggests a certain scenario perhaps – that this old Neanderthal man crawled into the hollow, rested his head on the side of it, and fell asleep there – never to wake up. The final – perhaps – nail in the coffin is that the sediment that covered the 'burial' doesn't look as though someone deliberately covered up the body, filling in a grave; it appears to be a natural deposit, which is spread right across the cave floor.

As for the intact nature of the buried bones, it's true that many parts of the skeleton were present, and in natural, articulated positions. But then more than 100 bones were still missing. And reindeer and bison remains in the cave were also found in anatomically joined-up patterns – and no one is arguing that those were deliberately buried. It seems instead that any body parts ending up in hollows in the cave, for whatever reason, had a good chance of becoming naturally covered up by sediment, and so protected from trampling, scavengers or weathering. Only a small number of all the bones from the cave show any signs of having been gnawed, and there were very few carnivore bones – less than 2 per cent. Modern ecological studies also show that the assumption that any unburied carcass will always be scavenged is just not right. It depends on the number of scavengers around, of course – and what else they have available.

The Neanderthal bones seemed to be in better condition than reindeer bones found in the cave, but without knowing precisely when and where those bones were deposited, it's difficult to draw any conclusions. Preservation can vary a lot, even within one cave.

Finally, there's nothing associated with the Neanderthal skeleton which could be interpreted as grave goods. The original diggers found some ancient aurochs, or bison, foot bones near the human remains – but it's clear that bones like these are just scattered through the sediments in the cave. There's nothing special or obviously symbolic about the bovid bones close to the Neanderthal.

Where does all this leave us? The recent re-excavators of La Chapelle say the best approach is a 'parsimonious' one – asking which is the simplest, most obvious explanation for the skeleton in the pit. They argue that the most parsimonious conclusion is that the skeleton in the Bouffia Bonneval got there by being deliberately buried, by other Neanderthals. But others say that the implications are so important here – Neanderthals carrying out funerary rituals, and thinking in symbolic ways about death – that the burden of proof rests with those arguing for burial. And that the evidence from La Chapelle is circumstantial and far from conclusive.

Both arguments seem persuasive. The evidence for Neanderthals – those much-maligned close cousins of ours – acting in 'modern' ways has mounted up impressively in recent years. Pigment use, drilling small holes in shells and animal teeth to make them into pendants, making stone tools that were just as useful as those made by contemporaneous modern humans, and perhaps even using feathers as decoration – all these things that we used to think were exclusive to our own kind, modern humans, have turned up in Neanderthal archaeological sites. In that context, it seems easier to imagine that they might have had ways of thinking about death and ritualising the loss of a loved one that seem familiar. But of course, just because we can now imagine this more easily, with this other evidence of rich and complex culture having come to light, doesn't mean we should accept it without question, without careful interrogation of the facts.

In some ways, it's a shame that La Chapelle was discovered when it was. If that burial (whether natural or carried out by humans) had been excavated closer to the present day, we would have had better answers. Instead, we're left with a lot of questions, and will probably never know for sure if that old man crawled into the cave, finding his own spot to die in, or whether he was laid to rest in there by his kind.

But there are other potential Neanderthal burials. They're all contentious – and anthropologists have argued that it's important to distinguish between mortuary practices – focused solely on the disposal of dead bodies – and funerary rituals – imbued with symbolic meaning. That's easier said than done, of course. If a burial contains no obvious grave goods, or any other potential markers of symbolic thinking – how do we know what the thought processes of the grave-makers involved?

Some have argued that there are no convincing examples of Neanderthal burials. Others say modern human burial practices are immensely varied, even among contemporary populations – perhaps we are being too stereotyped in our assessment of past possibilities.

My old friend and colleague Paul Pettitt has spent a lot of

time pondering Neanderthal burials – did they or didn't they? He thinks there's enough evidence – at least thirty examples accepted by many as true burials, including finds from Amud and Kebara caves in Israel – to come down firmly on the side of 'they did'. (Although he caveats this: some of the Neanderthals did bury their dead, some of the time!)

Those burials aren't there right from the beginning – from the earliest appearance of classical Neanderthals, around 200,000 years ago. They seem to appear from around 60,000 years ago onwards – coming along later than the earliest modern human burials. Paul believes that the archaeological record shows that at least some Neanderthal groups practised funerary rituals – burying infants and adults in shallow pits, sometimes after cutting into the corpse, for reasons which must remain obscure. He has written:

> It may have been on occasion too that certain enclosed sites served as mortuary centres, and that their function as such was perpetuated in the memory of Neanderthal groups either through physical grave markers or social tradition. In all it would seem that at least in some Neanderthal groups the dead body was explored and treated in socially meaningful ways.

But this is still a hotly contested issue, because underneath that question of 'Did the Neanderthals bury their dead?' is the deeper question: 'Just how similar to *us* were the Neanderthals?'

And there's a famous Neanderthal site – a long way from North Wales – that may be about to finally lay that question to rest.

Shanidar Cave

In the 1950s, Neanderthal remains were discovered in a cave in the Baradost Mountains of northeast Iraqi Kurdistan. The remains of ten individuals were found in Shanidar Cave – men, women and children – and some appeared to have been intentionally buried. On the basis of radiocarbon dates on fragments of charcoal associated with the burials, three were thought to date to around 50,000 years ago – right at the limit of radiocarbon dating – and seven, in deeper layers, from even earlier.

Among the burials was one which suggested that Neanderthals were doing much more than simply disposing of the dead, covering them up to protect them from scavengers. Burial 4 at Shanidar was full of flower pollen.

Soil samples from elsewhere in the cave contained little pollen. But Burial 4 was replete with it – in clumps that suggested whole flowers had originally been present. It looked like this Neanderthal man had been laid to rest one summer – some 70,000 years ago, the archaeologists estimated – on a bed of grape hyacinth, yarrow and groundsels. Some scholars suggested the plants had been specially chosen for their medicinal properties; that this individual, buried in such a special way, could have been a Neanderthal shaman or medicine man.

When the lead archaeologist, Ralph Solecki, published a book about the site in 1971, he gave it the title *Shanidar, The First Flower People*. In it, he wrote,

> With the finding of flowers in association with Neanderthals, we are brought suddenly to the realisation that the universality of mankind and the love of beauty go beyond the boundary of our own species. No longer can we deny the early men the full range of human feelings and experience.

But in the same book, Solecki had made several mentions of rodent burrows close to the burials:

> leading me to suspect that these animals must have been looking for the flesh of the dead. I remembered that rodent burrows were associated with most of the human skeletal remains we found. Indeed, one way of determining the possibility of a human skeleton was to plot the number and angle of the rodent holes, because they seemed to me most numerous around human bones, and seemed to zero in on them from different directions.

Gerbils, such as the Persian jird, which still lives in the area, habitually store plant material and seeds in their burrows. But they're not exclusively vegetarian – local Kurds used to catch them using pieces of raw meat as bait. There were plenty of gerbil bones found in Shanidar Cave, as well as their burrows. And another excavation, in the Zagros Mountains in the 1970s – this time focusing on gerbil burrows, not ancient humans – revealed side tunnels stuffed full of flower heads.

The most parsimonious explanation here, then – but certainly not the most romantic – may be that all the pollen around Burial 4 was not from garlands placed in the grave by mourners, but from gerbils who liked a side of flowery veg with their dinner of dead Neanderthal flesh.

Other research suggested that the wide cave mouth meant that, even without the agency of gerbils and their burrows, pollen was likely to have simply blown in from the surrounding landscape, just as it still does today. Pollen could also have travelled into the cave on the backs and legs of bees; bees' nests are always crammed full of the stuff. There's yet another possibility – and this one does involve humans, but in very recent times. The cave is a popular picnic spot, and the pollen may even have come from very modern flowers plucked by picnickers! All this environmental evidence brings us back down to earth with a hard, objective bump. Hungry gerbils, hardworking bees and whispering winds blow away that vision of the first Flower People, petals and wishful thinking scattering on the breeze.

A fierce enough interrogation of the facts at Shanidar Cave present us with another, somewhat disappointing, possibility: perhaps the 'burials' are not burials at all. Ralph Solecki thought the completeness of some of the skeletons made interment likely but, as with all that discussion around the Neanderthal skeleton at La Chapelle, there are other ways in which a largely intact dead body may become naturally buried underground.

Starting in 2015, a series of new excavations were carried

out at Shanidar, by a joint UK–Kurdish team led by Professor Graeme Barker, of Cambridge University. There was a theory that the Neanderthals had died out because of an inability to adjust to changing climate; Graeme and his colleagues were keen to gather more information about ancient climate and environment, to test that theory, but they also wanted to tackle some of that uncertainty about what exactly those Neanderthals had been up to in the cave.

It was a challenging site to excavate. In fact, one of the highly experienced leaders of the investigation, environmental scientist Chris Hunt, said that it was *the* most difficult site he'd ever worked on. At one point the previous year, when they'd been recceing the site, armed forces belonging to the Islamic State group ISIS had drawn 'uncomfortably close', and the archaeologists had been forced to evacuate. Not to be deterred, they returned in 2015, digging in spring, then again in the heat of summer, when the temperature in the open hit 50°C.

They cleaned up the trenches that Solecki had dug, while taking new samples for dating and further pollen analysis. And in the next couple of seasons at Shanidar Cave, they uncovered more Neanderthal remains – in what they knew, from Solecki's records, was the area where the sixth partial skeleton had been excavated from the cave during his investigations. The details of this new skeletal material were published in the *Journal of Human Evolution* in 2017. Like the bones in the original discovery, these ones were partially crushed, very fragile – some articulated, some more jumbled. Among those new bones were pieces of vertebrae, pelvis, femur, tibia and fibula, two foot-bones and a single wrist bone. All of those elements had been missing from the previously excavated remains designated as Shanidar 5. Emma Pomeroy was the biologist anthropologist on the team, and it was her job to carefully excavate the remains – and then, later, to pore over them and work out how they fitted into the existing jigsaw puzzle. These new bones turned out to match the earlier set of bones, known as Shanidar 5, in size, shape and signs of ageing. They had belonged to a man who was about 5ft 6 and who had been some forty to fifty years old when he died. He had the beginnings of bony growths around the edges of joints, characteristic of early stages of osteoarthritis – to be expected in someone who has lived an active lifestyle, like these ancient hunter-gatherers. Shanidar 5 was one of the later burials in the cave, with radiocarbon dating – albeit of bits of charcoal found near the skeleton, not the bones themselves – confirming an age of 46,000 to 50,000 years.

The original Shanidar 5 skeleton was found right at the end of the very last of Solecki's excavations at the site in 1960 – and at the time the archaeologists suspected that more bones might well be found, if ever anyone returned to the cave to dig.

That particular individual looked as though he might have come to a sticky end. In the original excavation, the skull was found on top of a large rock, but his pelvis had ended up underneath the same rock – the sort of arrangement you might expect if a rockfall collapsed on someone's head. The other bones of the skeleton were fragmentary, and many looked as though they'd been moved around afterwards, perhaps by rodents. In the recent excavations, the archaeologists once again noted evidence of burrowing close to the bones.

Rather than a deliberate burial, Solecki had thought that Shanidar 5 could be evidence of a personal disaster – a fatal rockfall, the bones preserved where the Neanderthal man lost his life, rather than a body being brought into the cave to be intentionally laid to rest. This jumbled skeleton was several metres away from the original 'flower burial' and a cluster of others.

The new excavations uncovered plenty of cultural artefacts, suggesting that various Neanderthals – over millennia – spent time in the cave. And there was also charcoal from ancient hearths entombed in the sediments. But what exactly was going on here? Were all these skeletons in fact the remains of Neanderthals who had met with unhappy accidents in a cave that they were living, and perhaps sleeping in – victims of sporadic rockfalls; or were at least some of them intentionally buried? Was Shanidar Cave a burial site at all, or just a stone-walled home that occasionally caved in and squashed its unlucky inhabitants?

Reading the published material from the recent excavations left me with too many questions. I needed to talk to the archaeologists themselves, to find out if they had further insights up their sleeves. I told Professor Graeme Barker about the book I was writing, and I asked him about his recent investigations at Shanidar Cave. Why did he want to revisit the site?

'We'd gone back to Shanidar mainly to address questions around Neanderthal extinction,' he explained. 'Changing climate may have had an impact, so we wanted to get a strong palaeoclimatic sequence from the cave. As far as burials were concerned, I assumed we wouldn't find anything. We hoped simply to identify *where* in the cave they'd been found, and date the sediments around them. So it was a real surprise to find more remains.

'We've been going back now every year since 2014, and we've opened up and exposed the part of the Solecki trench where he found most of the Neanderthals. But we never expected to find any more articulated remains.'

But then they did – and what's more, as I already knew from the 2017 paper in the *Journal of Human Evolution*, Emma Pomeroy had been able to match those bones up with Solecki's Shanidar 5 individual.

They kept digging, and further down, around 7 metres below the cave floor, they reached the level where Solecki had found the famous 'flower burial' – Shanidar 4. The story of the original excavation was quite extraordinary, as Graeme described.

'Solecki cut out a whole block of sediment, protecting it with wood and plaster of Paris, and took it to Baghdad Museum to excavate. They had to get it on the roof of a taxi which was going off down the mountain, and it was then driven to Baghdad. By the time anthropologist Thomas Dale Stewart got to look at it in the museum, the whole specimen had been bounced around and it was difficult to work out what was what.'

The anthropologist on the team in the 1950s painstakingly combed through the remains, assigning most of them to Shanidar 4. There were also remains from at least three other individuals, from lower in the block, including an infant burial – Shanidar 6, 8 and 9.

'It's an extraordinary cluster,' said Graeme, who knew he had reached the precise level of that block lifted in Solecki's excavations when they started to find flecks of the white plaster from 1960 in the sediment.

'And we can add to it now,' he went on, 'because in 2016, we found the articulated remains of an upper body – sex as yet unknown, but it is adult.'

I tried not to sound too excited on the phone. This was new news. Not even hot off the press – it hadn't made it to press yet.

'Emma exposed and lifted the skull,' Graeme continued. 'It was very crushed – flat as a pizza. And underneath that were parts of the arms. And underneath that, in 2019, she went on to find the backbone and ribcage.'

I was very glad I'd contacted Graeme. That excitement of discovery is contagious, and I was catching it. The new find was due to be published in the journal *Antiquity* very soon, and Graeme said he'd send me the draft – as long as I promised not to reveal anything before publication.

A few days later, he did, and I was able to read the details of the new half-skeleton. The teeth of the flattened skull were well worn, suggesting that this adult had been at least mid-thirties by the time they died. The left hand bones lay directly underneath the skull. The right humerus had been chopped off in the earlier excavation. The clavicles and upper ribs were in place, below the skull, where you'd expect them to be. Preliminary dating results suggested that the new skeletal remains, together with the original cluster – Shanidar 4, 6, 8 and 9 – were 60,000 to 70,000 years old. Solecki couldn't establish those dates with any certainty as this is earlier than the limit for radiocarbon dating. Graeme and his colleagues were able to use other techniques, like OSL (optically stimulated luminescence), which dates the age of quartz and fluorspar grains, to pin down these earlier dates.

Finding part of a new burial – with the opportunity it represented to do a painstaking, modern excavation, with all the archaeological scientific techniques now available – was a prize the archaeologists had not anticipated.

'It's the first articulated Neanderthal found for something like twenty years,' said Graeme, over the phone. 'It's the upper half of a body that was lying on its back. We don't have the lower half, but we suspect it belongs to that block of sediment that contained Shanidar 4 and the other remains.'

He was hoping that further careful work might reveal, once again, whether they had found missing bones from other incomplete individuals that Solecki had excavated. It was possible that the new bones were part of either Shanidar 6 or 8 – and Emma Pomeroy was already on the case, planning further work to reassess the previously excavated remains and work out exactly where their new finds fitted into the puzzle.

But with the opportunity to freshly excavate this individual in the cave, as well as the extra bits of Shanidar 5, did Graeme think these remains represented deliberate burials – or merely the unfortunate victims of rockfalls?

'Our sense is in fact that none of them were killed by rock-fall. Some are *amongst* rockfall. With Shanidar 5, there's a whole succession of rockfalls above and below – but not actually part of the same layer as the body. The indications are that these *are* burials. Or, at least, *most* of them are. The bodies really were deliberately placed there. And the bones we've most recently excavated were placed in a shallow scoop that's partly a water channel, but partly definitely cut – by someone.'

That had been an important new discovery from these recent excavations. It suggested that the grave itself had been delib-erately dug out and prepared (even if this was a shallow scoop rather than a straight-sided shaft that the word 'grave' tends to invoke in our minds) – the body wasn't just placed in an exist-ing trough or depression in the cave floor. The sediments they'd found lying below and above the bones were different in colour and texture. Work had begun on sifting through the material on top of the bones, to identify plant fragments. 'There was a curious lithic near the neck,' Graeme went on. 'We can't tell if it was placed there deliberately. But it also looks like there are some big stones on top of the burial that don't seem to be part of the rockfalls from the roof.'

Such tantalising suggestions of grave goods and perhaps even stones placed as grave markers. But it's so important not to let the imagination run wild. There was clearly a lot more work to do, but Graeme now clearly thought it unlikely that few, if any, of the Neanderthals in Shanidar Cave had been victims of rockfalls, and that they were much more likely to have been burials, covered by later rockfalls.

'So there's *no doubt* in your mind, then, having carried out these new excavations, that this *is* intentional burial?' I pushed him. Graeme laughed.

'Well, we're always trying to prove to ourselves it's not natural. Chris Hunt would always say the starting point has always got to be, "Show me it's not natural." But the accumulating evidence is that the body is in a scoop which is partially dug out, and the sediments around the bones haven't been washed there; they've arrived there by other means.'

So this was definitive evidence for Neanderthal burial, then. With careful excavation, modern archaeological techniques, and the discovery of new bones *in situ* in what looked convincingly like a deliberately dug-out grave, there seemed to be little room for alternative explanations here. And of course it wasn't just one burial.

'The assemblage of closely placed bodies in this lower, Shanidar 4 group is completely unique in Neanderthal archaeology,' said Graeme. 'Now, the cave is enormous. A great aircraft-hangar of a cave. Where the excavations were is in a small area – right under an enormous crack in the roof, which is the source of rockfalls over time. This cluster of burials is up against the rocks – in a sort of protected area.'

If it was a near-contemporary cluster, then is it reasonable to call this a Neanderthal cemetery? Neanderthals had clearly lived in the cave, but did it become, at some point, a place dedicated to the dead? Graeme was very cautious, and wary of circular reasoning. Especially when he was still waiting for results of a whole panoply of analyses to come in.

'Our major task now is to try to unravel whether those bodies could have been buried around the same time, within one person's lifetime and memory, or whether these are in fact separate burial events, centuries or even thousands of years apart.'

Did he have a hunch about which scenario had played out at Shanidar Cave, I wondered? Graeme was very cautious – so many investigations were still in progress. If the burials were close in time – a cemetery – then that would imply some kind of concept of a special place, persisting through time, that was dedicated to the dead. Paul Pettitt had suggested as much. Again, that's a concept that has been associated with modern humans and our ways of thinking. Could Neanderthals have entertained similar ideas? The answer to this question would have to wait.

But by now, I had plucked up the courage to ask the question I was dying to know the answer to. What was all that pollen doing around Shanidar 4, did Graeme think? Could it have been an ancient 'flower burial'?

'We've been trying to find the original sediment samples that were taken from around the bones of Shanidar 4,' said Graeme. 'And Chris Hunt and his PhD student have been looking at how pollen gets into the cave now. The main way that pollen enters today is on the feet of tourists! But those rodent burrows are also clearly important to look into. Chris is looking at what kind of pollen is in the burrows, and what kind of pollen is in the sediments – and not in the burrows. All of that research is going on right now.'

Even if this ongoing research ended up suggesting that flowers *had* been deliberately brought in and placed on a grave, there were other interpretations to consider – Graeme stressed – alongside the flowers being a gift, a floral tribute of some kind. Neanderthals may have simply covered up the bodies with vegetation, for instance. Graeme was also careful to stress the distinction between mortuary behaviour – referring to a more prosaic treatment of a dead body, perhaps just removing it from sight – and funerary behaviour, involving an element of symbolism and ritual.

Funerary behaviour is thought to be unique to modern humans today, and that's why it's so interesting and important to consider whether it existed among other types of humans, like Neanderthals. But mortuary behaviour – doing things to the dead bodies of individuals from your own species – is certainly seen in other animals. Chimpanzee mothers sometimes carry around the body of a dead baby for weeks. Cetaceans do the same. Elephants return again and again to a corpse. Crows make alarm calls when they see humans holding dead crows (although, to be fair, that's probably a good survival instinct rather than mourning). Even termites have been seen to clear up or cover the dead bodies of other termites in their nests. The underlying drive for these behaviours may be quite different. In social insects, the need to remove a corpse from a nest or hive seems to be a powerful instinct – presumably because the dead colleague represents a potential source of disease in a densely populated colony. In clever vertebrates, such as mammals and birds, it is thought that a corpse represents a real cognitive challenge: the dead body looks like a member of your species, even an individual you know well, but it does not react. It should be alive and moving, and yet it is still, inert. The conflicting stimuli provoke strong emotional responses, and those can translate into dramatic behaviour – attacking the corpse, even attempting to copulate with it, or to eat it. Removing the corpse from sight may be hygienic, but may also remove the clashing stimuli that create emotional turmoil.

This happens every time we try to draw a hard, fast line between us and other animals, or between *Homo sapiens* and other, now extinct human species. Layers of culture have built up over the years, centuries, millennia – until we feel ourselves quite separate from the rest of nature. But we are natural beings, and even the most ritualised behaviour has its roots in much simpler acts that are better understood when we cast around and look at what other animals do. The act of burial itself may be a human manifestation of a much more general tendency among social animals to clear the dead away from living spaces. But then we start to ascribe more meaning to it. You could argue it is that extra layer of meaning, rather than the act itself, that makes us human. Even if flowering vegetation was placed over the body in that Neanderthal grave – and we still don't know for sure that it was – we can't rush to conclusions about what that *meant*. On the other hand, the fact that mortuary behaviours are seen in other social animals tells us something very interesting about ourselves, I think.

'Although we can't be sure about the flowers – yet,' Graeme said, 'what is absolutely clear is that the particular body we've found was put there. It *is* a burial.'

In some ways, the flowers in the grave with the body (if there were flowers), and the determination that Shanidar really does represent evidence for Neanderthal burial, are not as important as if there were multiple burials in a relatively short space of time – because the flowers could just be about covering a dead body with vegetation, to hide it, and a single, simple burial could also just be about removing the body from sight (and smell). In other words, these could represent mortuary – rather than funerary – behaviour. Things that, after all, termites do. Without any obvious grave goods, it's hard to argue for a ritual aspect to the behaviour. But it was the possibility of Shanidar being a place for the dead, a Neanderthal cemetery, that surely moves us towards the rich world of symbols and complex culture. The latest excavations and the ongoing analysis may yet provide an answer.

If the cave was, at some point, a place for the dead, it was clear that there were moments when it was very much a place for the living, too. Graeme and his colleagues had also found plenty more evidence of Neanderthals spending time in the cave – alongside the burials, which always attract the most attention. There were clearly times when people were living in the cave: below the level of Shanidar 5 was a layer containing pieces of knapped stone, bits of butchered animal bone and burnt plant remains. Thin layers of charcoal in the sediment layers at different levels persisted as subtle traces of ancient hearths. This evidence of occupation – or at least, of people spending time in the cave – raises the question of whether those ancient people were both living in the cave and burying their dead in it, at the same time. Was it place of life *and* death, simultaneously?

Studying microscopic blocks of sediment taken from each hearth, Graeme had concluded that each fire – whether from Neanderthal times, or later, modern human use of the cave – represented a single, brief event; as he put it, 'People coming in, lighting a fire, being around for a bit, retooling, sharpening tools – chasing a few ibex then going away again.'

This is the world of classic Palaeolithic archaeology: ephemeral traces of people who moved around a lot, living hunter-gatherer lifestyles. Perhaps they thought of the whole landscape as their home, instead of just one small part of it, as we do. And yet, as successful hunter-gatherers, they must have had a 'mental map' of their landscape-home in their heads, perhaps dotted with prominent places – places that could help them navigate, and to which they might have returned again and again within a lifetime. Shanidar Cave – on the edge of a steep gorge and flanked by cliffs – could well have been such a prominent, important place. As well as that, it just sounds like it would have been a great place to hang out – with a spring in the valley nearby, plenty of animals around to hunt, and stunning views out to the Greater Zab valley, and the mountains in the distance.

There was a chance the burials might shed some light on what those Neanderthals thought about themselves, as well.

'We have males, females, young and old in Shanidar,' said Graeme. 'Emma wants to reanalyse all the bones to see if there are any clues as to whether they are placing themselves in any sort of categories. The Shanidar material can tell us about whether Neanderthals did bury their dead – but should also tell us something about Neanderthal identity. Thinking about how they represent themselves in death has all sorts of implications for how they thought of themselves in life as well, and their society.'

There was also the question of overlap with modern humans. The burials – as I think we can now reliably call them – at

Shanidar Cave date to an interesting period of time, when Neanderthals and modern humans were both around in western Asia. Neanderthals may have spread south into the area during periods of warmer climate. Modern humans – emerging as a species in Africa – started to venture eastwards out of their homeland after 100,000 years ago, and we find intermittent traces of them in the Eastern Mediterranean and the Arabian peninsula. Although the two groups could potentially have passed 'like ships in the night', never actually occupying precisely the same geographic area, the last ten years have seen a succession of discoveries based on ancient DNA, showing that Neanderthals and modern humans certainly *did* make contact. They made enough contact to swap genes with each other, to put it delicately.

'In principle, modern humans could have been around in the Shanidar area at the time of the Neanderthal burials,' Graeme said. 'Neanderthals could have been around for the first part of the time when modern humans are meant to be there, making a certain type of stone tool-kit that we find in higher, later layers in the cave. Ancient DNA from sediments in the cave might help shed light on that.'

It felt like Shanidar Cave – though just one site – could hold answers to lots of questions – and not just 'Did Neanderthals ever bury their dead?' (Yes, they did.)

'It's an iconic site,' said Graeme. 'There's a richness of data to be plumbed – about Neanderthals, and their concepts of death, their relationships with modern humans, their disappearance . . . a lot of answers lie in that cave.

'We're going to have to go through everything so carefully before we can say any more, though. These are such big questions. There's the whole debate about whether Neanderthals buried their dead or not – and if they did, what on earth that *meant*. You're dealing with a species which stretched from Portugal to the Urals, across some 300,000 years – it's highly likely they dealt with bodies in many different ways. But this Shanidar assemblage gives us a unique opportunity to investigate burial practice in that place, at that time, with all the benefits of modern science – to help us understand their culture.'

Variability seemed an important concept here. Perhaps more than burial itself being a marker of a 'modern mind', of 'modern behaviour' – it was that Shanidar Cave gave us a glimpse of just one of the ways Neanderthals treated the dead. From what we already know about Neanderthal culture, across huge landscapes and through time – we should expect variability: not one way of doing things, but many.

'Now we have clear instances of Neanderthal burial, the interesting question is about variability. You've got burials here, cannibalism there, something different elsewhere . . . and they could have been doing things that seem completely alien to us today. Given that vast canvas, you expect a great deal of variability.'

Pontnewydd fits into that varied picture, somehow – although with just a few fragments of bone and teeth, it's difficult to know whether there were ever any burials in that cave.

What we also need to be clear about is that, whenever we do find evidence of early burials – like the Neanderthals at Shanidar Cave, or the Red Lady at Paviland – that certainly wasn't the *norm*. Very ancient burials are few and far between – sporadic. Only a small number of people were ever treated in this way when they died. Remains of both Neanderthals and modern humans from the Palaeolithic are rare, and are mostly just fragments of bones, sometimes associated with carnivore activity, collected by the likes of hyenas.

The rare, early burials are not part of a sweeping cognitive and cultural change. Instead, they indicate a capacity for a certain type of ritual which seems very human to us – but it was incipient, occasional, and certainly not embedded in those Ice Age cultures.

What seems to be important, then, in this period of time – and, in fact, whether we're talking about modern humans or Neanderthals – is not just the appearance of burials for the first time, but the fact that this represents variability in behaviour. Across large geographic expanses, and through time, these Palaeolithic people were doing things in many different ways – from the types of stone tools they made to the way they treated the bodies of the dead. And it's that variability – which surely represents the ability to create culture, to innovate, to think and behave in ways which seem *human* – that tells us that these people, tens of thousands of years ago, had minds like us.

Perhaps even more than their predilection for mark-making – using pigments and painting caves – and their beads and their bone tools, it's burial that brings Neanderthals out of the shadows, closer to us. For so long, they've been seen as inferior, an unsuccessful experiment in being human. Or at least: an experiment in being human that survives only in pieces of DNA tucked away in our own genomes. But the idea that – in some places, at some times – they may have mourned like us, felt the need to mark the passing of a friend or loved one with *something* – to create a physical expression, to memorialise – that makes them feel less like unfeeling brutes. More like cousins.

And yet Emma Pomeroy and her colleagues, writing about Shanidar Cave, argue against looking for stereotypical signs of 'modern human behaviour' in the archaeological record – at all. We should be wary of trying to identify progress from mortuary behaviour to funerary behaviour as a marker of some sort of Palaeolithic enlightenment. We need to look at each site with 'the utmost rigour and with as few preconceptions as possible', making comparisons. Thinking, in each case, about *why*.

It's the *why* that is meaningful, that is human. Because that is surely the real hallmark of modernity, the 'modern human' mind – the ability to answer that question, to create meaning in our lives, through our actions, through our rituals.

'Are you going back to Shanidar?' I asked Graeme. It was early 2020, and things were heating up between Iran, bordering Iraq to the east, and Western states. British citizens had already been advised to avoid travelling to Iran.

'We're scheduled to go back in September 2020,' he said. 'It's over 40 degrees then, but a bit cooler in the cave. Emma likes it, though – better than the spring – because the consolidants she uses for the bone go off quicker!'

Graeme, though, preferred Shanidar in springtime.

'When the Kurdistan government first invited me to contemplate Shanidar, it came as a bolt out of the blue. I emailed Ralph Solecki and he was incredibly enthusiastic.'

Ralph Solecki died in March 2019, aged 101, knowing that a new generation of archaeologists was continuing his legacy at Shanidar.

'The first email from Ralph said, "The flowers at Shanidar in spring are very beautiful." And it's perfectly true,' said Graeme. 'We've been out in spring, and in late April, just for a few weeks, there's an absolutely fantastic bloom of flowers – most of which are the flowers that are there in the "flower burial". They're in the landscape now, still – for that brief period.

'It's lovely to see that flush of green. And it's a great time to be there at Shanidar – whether you're a Neanderthal or a modern human.'

4.

THE CANNIBALS OF CHEDDAR
AND THE BLUE-EYED BOY

We're back in Britain – and moving on through time. Right through the Great Ice Age, the Pleistocene, and out the other side – when the whole globe experienced a springtime. We find ourselves in yet another cave, this time deep in the Mendip Hills of Somerset. But before we descend into that cave, coming across human remains and grisly tales of cannibalism, no less, we should think about how different the landscape of Britain was during the fluctuating grip of the Ice Ages. For much of the time, it was simply uninhabitable. And when humans *were* here, they existed in a very different landscape to the one we're familiar with today – in a wild Britain.

More Ice Age tales

The meagre remains from Pontnewydd Cave reveal the presence of early Neanderthal populations in Britain, during the Pleistocene, around 230,000 years ago – even if they don't shed much light on what those people thought about death, or how they treated the dead. What those remains do tell us, though, is that the people of Pontnewydd must have been very much at home in what we can fairly describe as a bitterly cold environment.

Earlier types of humans had spread to live in what is now Britain during warmer periods in the Pleistocene. But the early Neanderthals at Pontnewydd must have been hardy – cold-climate survival experts. We can presume that they had basic clothing, and we know they had fire, as we find their hearths – lenses of smudged black charcoal revealed by the archaeologist's trowel. It seems that they particularly thrived in the cold conditions that prevailed during transitional periods – between full-on glaciations and balmy interglacials. When ice sheets descended over Britain, Neanderthals disappeared – not surprisingly: most other life was forced out, too. But they were also absent from Britain during the last interglacial – between 130,000 and 74,000 years ago – when the ice was gone, and the landscape transformed into dense woodland. Neanderthal happy hunting grounds were, it seems, the more open, grass-land environments which would have prevailed in the millennia bridging between glaciations and interglacials. We can imagine those grasslands teeming with herds of reindeer, horse and aurochsen – ancient cattle. A land of plenty for predators such as wolves, cave lions – and Neanderthals.

The story of the Pleistocene is one of ice advancing and retreating, populations of plants and animals shifting accord-ing to those climatic cycles. And of course, whenever we see human populations arriving in Britain after a period of absence – they've come from *somewhere*, and that somewhere was continental Europe. When glaciations bound the north of the continent in ice, undoubtedly forcing local extinctions across higher latitudes, the south was still habitable. Neanderthals could survive in refugia around the Mediterranean – and when the climate ameliorated, there was the potential for populations to bounce back, and to expand northwards once again.

As we're imagining these movements of people – and other animals – in and out of the islands of Britain as the Ice Ages of the Pleistocene cycled though, it's important to remember that these islands were high and dry for much of the time – and not islands at all. During glaciations the sea level was much lower – more than 100 metres lower than today – and Britain would have been part of the continental landmass of northwest Europe. Unfortunately, at the same time, most of the area that corresponds with Britain today would have lain under a thick ice sheet. So – although humans could have walked here, keeping their feet dry (if cold) – it wasn't exactly an inviting place. During interglacials, when the ice had melted away, the sea level rose, cutting off Britain. It was during the transitions – in and out of glaciations – when this landscape was both accessible and attractive to large herbivores and the humans that hunted them.

Two hundred and thirty thousand years ago, then, the landscape of Britain was reachable – and open enough – for pre-Neanderthals to thrive here, as shown by their presence in Pontnewydd. But then it got steadily colder as the next glaciation cycled in, and by 180,000 years ago, Britain had emptied of people. An interruption to this land of ice and snow came along 130,000 years ago, when temperatures rose and Britain basked in a balmy interglacial period. It lasted 15,000 years and was even warmer than today. An eclectic mix of animals inhabited the British Isles back then – red deer and fallow deer, brown bear and wolves, but also lions, hyenas, elephants and hippos. But – no humans, of any kind. Perhaps the Neanderthal population bordering northern Europe was just too sparse to bounce back, and so they were too slow off the mark to follow the herds across to the greening grasslands of southern Britain before the sea levels rose. Horses also failed to make the journey to the British Isles at this time.

By 60,000 years ago, Neanderthals had made it back to Britain, during another warm period punctuating the glacial conditions. But still, it wasn't all that warm – once again, the landscape would have been open, as Neanderthals seem to have preferred. With few trees, those people must have been burning other material as fuel, perhaps dung and bones – real 'bone-fires'. We know that Neanderthals were definitely here at that time, from traces such as stone tools, butchered bones and buried hearths, but we don't have anything of the people themselves – no bones; no burials.

Then, around 40,000 years ago, a range of new types of stone tool appear in Britain: thin blades of flint and long spearpoints. These were long thought to be hallmarks of a new group of people: modern humans, *Homo sapiens*. But palaeoanthropologists like Chris Stringer are more cautious – we have to be open to the possibility that some of these blades and spearpoints could have been made by the last Neanderthals to live in Britain. Or indeed, they could have been made by a hybrid population – as this is the time when modern humans were spreading across Europe, coming into contact – we think – with the longstanding indigenous people of the continent.

But by this time, around 40,000 years ago, the Neanderthals – whether through processes of local extinction, or assimilation into modern human populations, or even perhaps a bit of both – were essentially extinct as a clearly recognisable and separate type of human.

There's a humble fragment of upper jaw and teeth from Kent's Cavern in Torquay – just enough to be sure we're looking at the remains of a modern human – that has been dated to about 41,000 years ago. If the date's correct, this would make it the earliest evidence of *Homo sapiens* in Britain. The radiocarbon dating is a bit tricky, though; it's based on animal bones apparently found close to the jaw, in a fairly slapdash excavation in the 1920s – not the jaw itself. But there were modern humans around in central Europe by this time, and they produced some wonderful early art. There are extremely ancient ivory carvings of animals and weird human-beast mash-ups like the Lion Man of Ulm (which may actually be a rearing bear) dating to around 40,000 years ago (though possibly somewhat later), as well as bone flutes. And by 37,000 years ago, we start to see naturalistic paintings and engravings of animals on the walls of caves and rock shelters. And then, of course, there are the burials – also rich with symbolic meaning – like the Red Lady of Paviland.

There are always questions about why modern humans survived, and Neanderthals didn't. We've seen so much evidence of Neanderthal culture emerging in recent years that the answer can no longer be simply tied to a difference in sophistication. And let's remember, the Neanderthals had already survived through adverse conditions in Ice Age Europe for hundreds of thousands of years. Clive Gamble has suggested that modern humans were more mobile in the landscape – at least, as far as we can work out, looking at the distances that certain materials such as flint travel from where they were first picked up. Perhaps a combination of longer regular journeys and exchange of goods with neighbouring groups – a dependable support network – meant that modern humans were able to survive through to the end of the Ice Age and beyond, while

Neanderthals did not. In reality, we may never get at the real answer to this question. And something we tend to overlook or downplay in our reconstructed histories is the role of chance. Just happening to be in the right place at the right time can be crucial – as we all know from chance events in our own lives.

Still, modern humans were only ever fleetingly in Britain in the run-up to the peak of the last Ice Age, between 40,000 and 30,000 years ago. We catch occasional glimpses of them – just a few bone or stone tools here and there, mostly in caves, hidden away from the advancing glaciers. And, of course, that extraordinary 34,000-year-old burial at Paviland. The stone tools of this period show a connection with sites in Belgium – which was linked to Britain by the vast expanse of 'Doggerland' – now submerged under the waves of the North Sea. Hunters were using a different kit now: rather than large spears tipped with leaf points, they had adopted a lighter, flexible set of weapons. It's difficult to tie such trends to changes in subsistence – after all, humans are great at inventing new fashions. But it may be that this new hunting kit was well suited to opportunistic hunting – going after a wide range of prey, whatever you could manage to catch – in an increasingly unstable climate and unpredictable environment. And it could be that, during this time, human hunters were only visiting what is now Britain sporadically, during summer months.

After the Red Lady was interred, the climate deteriorated further. Winter was coming – eclipsing anything that could ever have been called summer. By about 30,000 years ago, humans and pretty much everything else – apart from the most committed Arctic species, like musk ox, hare and lemming – were well on their way to disappearing from the British landscape. And it would be a chilly 15,000 years before anyone came back.

Human hunters survived through the peak of the Ice Age in southern Europe – where we find not only their stone, bone and antler tools, but even more extraordinary examples of artistic creativity, from evocative ivory carvings to the mesmerising cave paintings in sites such as Lascaux.

The warming of Britain after the Ice Age happened fairly rapidly, and by 15,000 years ago, the ice sheets had retreated, and the tundra of southern Britain grew green, transformed into wide grasslands colonised by saiga antelope, horses and deer – swiftly followed by bands of hunter-gatherers.

These post-glacial colonisers left their artistic mark on the British landscape – nothing quite as spectacular as Lascaux, but beautiful and enigmatic nonetheless – in the form of engraved shapes in the caves of Creswell Crags, in Derbyshire. Adorning the high ceilings of caves dug out by enthusiastic Victorian antiquarians, these engravings were completely missed – until 2003, during a determined search for the 'missing art' of Ice Age Britain. The quest was led by Paul Pettitt. He said, 'If I was a betting man I'd have had a lot of money staked on us finding nothing! When I organised the trip I just thought it would be a pleasant few days with two colleagues.' But instead, on the first evening of the research trip, they had reason to order a bottle of champagne. For on the walls of a cave at Creswell Crags, they'd found the earliest art in Britain: flowing lines describing the shapes of animals, and other shapes that could be representations of vulvae. More abstract engravings deep inside one cave have been interpreted either as birds or, possibly, outlines of female bodies.

But further south, in a cave in the Mendips, we catch sight of the humans themselves.

Gough's Cave

The Mendips are a wedge-shaped range of hills, wide in the east, narrowing to a slender ridge in the west. These uplands cover an area of some 200 square kilometres, stretching from Midsomer Norton in the east to Crook Peak in the west – although, in fact, the spiny ridge continues beyond Crook Peak, undulating like the back of a sleeping dragon, in the form of Bleadon Hill, and then – projecting out into the tidal waters of the Severn Estuary – Brean Down. The highest point of the Mendips is marked by a trig point at Beacon Batch, on Black Down, 325 metres above sea level. Despite their relatively modest elevation, the Mendips always seem to have their own climate – a few degrees colder than the lowlands of the Somerset Levels, or Bristol, nestling in the Avon Valley to the north.

Geologically, the Mendips are mainly limestone, laid down at the bottom of an ancient sea more than 300 million years ago. These rocks were raised up by tectonic movement, which threw up ripples in the earth's crust, building many ranges of hills and mountains. And then, over millions of years, the steeply raised-up rocks of the Mendips were ground down by the action of wind, water and ice, leaving the more undulating topography we see today. The successive Ice Ages of the Pleistocene left indelible marks on the Mendips: torrential rivers of meltwater gouged out gorges, while subterranean rivers leached away limestone to sculpt out huge, labyrinthine cave systems. The ice sheets themselves never reached this far, but the thin soil over the hills would have been frozen into rock-hard permafrost, and capped with snow, at the peak of the Ice Age. Now that the snowcaps have melted away, the gorges are dry – instead, precipitating water easily finds its way off the high ground through underground streams and rivers.

Today, the Mendips are draped in close-cropped, sheep-grazed fields divided by drystone walls, with wooded slopes, gorges and combes around the edges. The hills are frequented by walkers, while intrepid cavers and cave-divers endlessly explore the underground caverns. In 2018, twelve young boys – part of a football team on a day out gone badly wrong – were stranded deep inside a cave system in Thailand, when the monsoons came early and the cave flooded. Spearheading the international rescue effort were three British men – all part of the Mendip Cave Rescue team.

But while more demanding potholes require suitable protective clothing and expertise to navigate, several impressive Mendip caves are more accessible and open to the general public – including Wookey Hole and, in Cheddar Gorge, Cox's Cave and Gough's Cave. Wookey Hole and Cox's Cave have been transformed into visitor experiences which – for me – detract somewhat from the natural beauty and aura of these ancient places. On a recent visit, I found myself following a disembodied voice around the twists and turns of Cox's Cave, being told of the ingenuity of Ancient Men (while wondering where all the women and children were) and watching projections of two men clad in furs as they knapped flints and jabbed with their spears, pretending to kill first a wolf, and then a stag. In the last cavern, the voice-over – which had dropped to an almost inaudible whisper for some of the more mystical passages – now developed an exultant tone. As red, green and blue points of laser light danced over the cave walls, the voice told us how Man (again) had eventually emerged victorious, having vanquished the beasts, becoming the most successful predator the world had ever seen. That old trope of human exceptional-ism, triumph over nature, was still ringing hollow in my ears as I emerged out of the cave into the twenty-first century. Man had emerged from the Ice Age to become a weapon of mass extinction. Here we were, divorcing ourselves from Nature, wreaking havoc with the climate, and crucifying biodiversity.

We don't really know how our prehistoric ancestors viewed themselves in the world – we have so little to go on. But perhaps those images of animals that persist from the Ice Age – and the curious human–beast icons like the Lion Man of Ulm – sug-gest that Palaeolithic people saw themselves as part of Nature, rather than separate from it. They were certainly closer to the source of their food than most of us are, in developed countries today, where we buy our industrially produced food, cut up and packaged, rather than hunting it and gathering it.

Gough's Cave had escaped being quite as thoroughly theme-park-ified – though its entrance is sadly hidden behind a monstrosity of a concrete building from the 1930s. The Caveman Restaurant, as it was, now stands mostly empty. It confers on this part of the gorge a strange quality – ugly, industrial and utilitarian. You have the sense of arriving at a particularly dilapidated motorway service station. Inside, it gets better. A flat concrete floor and metal steps make the first 800 metres or so of the cave accessible to casual visitors. This 'show-cave' part of the cavern, open to the public, has been fairly flooded with light – so that algae, mosses and ferns now grow deep inside its naturally sunless crevices. But the lighting is a warm white – no lasers here – and is carefully placed to illuminate particularly spectacular clusters of sta-lagmites, stalactites and terraced steps of flowstone. There are several beautiful, mirror-like pools of water that reflect the stalactites above – but a quick examination reveals them to be quite unnatural. They are part of the touristic enhancements that have been added to the cave over the years. The pools are artificial – contained within walls of what look like Pulhamite, the go-to concrete used by Victorians wanting to add a touch of drama to natural landscapes – both above and below ground.

The caves of Cheddar Gorge have attracted visitors since at least the eighteenth century, when women living in cottages in the Gorge – some even inside the caves themselves – would act as guides; they supplemented their income by selling specimens of minerals, and flowers. Today, the caves are flanked by shops selling cakes, cheese (of course) and sweets, wood-carvings and teddy bears.

By the 1860s, tours of one cave, which had become known as the 'Great Stalactite Cavern', were being conducted by John Weeks, whose property in the gorge included – according to a tithe record book of the era – a 'garden with hut and cavern'. A man who may well have been that particular John Weeks was described by the diarising Rev. Frank Kilbert, curate of Clyro:

> . . .a ghastly old man, with his jaws bandaged white like a corpse and an enormous nose, conducted us solemnly into a cave in the cliff as black as pitch . . . he gave each of us an end of a tallow candle, lighted and fastened to the end of a short stick held horizontally, and we went to our doom. The corpse led us over the slippery, rough streaming rocks and up rude steep steps into an inner cave . . . All around in the darkness and solemn silence we could hear the dripping and splashing of water from the roof of the cave at a vast height above. Every now and then the corpse stopped suddenly at some specially awkward and inconvenient place

when we were balancing on a slippery rock face or crawling painfully with cramped and bended backs down some devil's staircase . . . and solemnly elevating his frame of flaring and guttering candles to some monstrosity water-sculptured in the face of the rock . . . in a loud harsh voice emited [*sic*] such cries as these: 'Call that, a turtle.' 'Call that, a pulpit.' 'Call that, a parson.' 'Call that, an alligator.'

The corpse appeared to have a certain grim and ghastly humour of its own, and gave a horrible grin when any of these cries had excited peals of laughter.

By the end of the 1860s, Cheddar was becoming a popular tourist destination, helped along by the opening of its very own station on a Great Western Railway branch line. In 1868, a retired sea captain by the name of Richard Gough arrived in Cheddar. Nine years later, he'd taken over as the manager of the Great Stalactite Cavern, leasing it from the Marquis of Bath. At this time, Cox's Cave was considered a much more impressive tourist attraction, but Gough was sure that his cave had more to offer. Water would sometimes flow in at the back of the existing cave, and this is where he set about digging in the hope of finding a further extension. He was extremely determined, describing himself 'cutting through 17 feet of Stalagmite, and excavating 40 or 50 tons of boulder stones'. And he wasn't disappointed. In November 1877, he broke through to 'a pond of water, and thence into the New Cave'. The *Wells Journal* duly reported that Mr Gough had discovered a 'large and handsome Chamber, the Stalactite formations in which are extremely beautiful'.

In 1883, Gough was hauled up before the court at Axbridge to explain why he'd illuminated the cave using gas evaporated from gasoline – for which he lacked the requisite licence. He had his gasoline confiscated and was fined 10 shillings. He baulked at the fine, but it didn't hold him back. He was determined to make his cave a successful tourist attraction – and he continued pushing its boundaries, discovering a further two chambers in 1887. The *Weston-super-Mare Mercury* announced the 'newly discovered caverns', opened up 'by the aid of drill and dynamite'. The two deepest caverns are accessible through a manmade tunnel today – with Gough's drill-holes still clear to see.

Richard Gough was an entrepreneur and a showman. He is said to have travelled everywhere with a small menagerie – a donkey, a monkey and a talking jackdaw. And his showmanship extended into the caves. He created several 'fountains' at different spots in the caves, using Victorian concrete to build up walls, mimicking natural gour or rimstone pools. He is also said to have brought cartloads of extra stalagmites from another cave near Weston-super-Mare, to enhance the display in his cave at Cheddar. The natural elements in Gough's Cave are wonderful, but it is, as a survey by the British Geological Society reported, 'a show cave which suffered considerable damage during its development in the 1880s'.

And yet, for the Victorian tourists, Gough's Cave was ticking a lot of boxes. With its walkways, impressive displays (if not all home-grown) of stalactites and stalagmites, and aesthetically pleasing fake pools, it was starting to out-compete the neighbouring show-cave, run by Gough's cousins – the Cox brothers. The rivalry between the cousins spilled out into local newspaper adverts, and broke out into physical confrontations between carriage drivers fighting over punters at Cheddar station.

After all those 'improvements' Gough had made to his cave, he was brazen in his adverts. One from the *Weston-super-Mare Mercury* in 1887 read:

If you want to see a
NATURAL CAVE
GO TO GOUGH'S

Gough continued the expansion of his underground empire, now helped by his sons, breaking through into even more caverns in 1898. Switching from gaslight to electric lighting was another masterstroke, and by the early twentieth century, people went to Cheddar to see Gough's Cave, not Cox's Cave. The fate of the latter as a sideshow – a convenient dark space for projected images of fur-clad cavemen, laser light shows and echoing pan-pipes – was sealed.

Richard Gough died in 1902, aged seventy-five, safe in the knowledge that he'd built up a successful tourist business from scratch, and was passing that business on to his sons. The following year, those Gough brothers were dutifully continuing their father's project, and carrying out some work to mitigate the recurrent problem of winter flooding, digging a drainage ditch in the vestibule, just inside the cave's entrance. Sealed within a bank of cave earth and boulders, under a six-inch-thick stalagmite crust, they came across flint tools, a bone rod with a hole in it – and something wholly unexpected: human remains; and not just a few bones – most of a skeleton. Around the human bones were many flint tools, a fragment of horse bone, and a piece of worked reindeer antler. Bones of ancient cattle and cave bear had been found in a nearby pit. These finds suggested a late Ice Age date – right at the end of the Palaeolithic or 'Old Stone Age', around 12,000 years ago. The ancient skeleton quickly became known as 'Cheddar Man'.

Entering the vestibule of Gough's Cave today, a plastic skeleton lies on a sheet of plastic netting in the area where Cheddar Man was discovered. (The completeness of the ribcage and pelvis in displays like these – and indeed in any number of horror and adventure films – always irks me. When bodies rot, soft tissue – including cartilage and ligaments – decay. The ribs, once bound to the sternum by long rods of costal cartilage, then exist as separate bones, and collapse in a heap. The two bones of the pelvis eventually fall apart from each other at the front, where they were once joined by fibrocartilage, and away from the sacrum at the back, where the sacroiliac joint once existed. Plastic skeletons, with costal cartilages helping to keep the thorax three-dimensional, and complete pelves, abound in films, standing in for skeletons

which really should be just bones. Now you know about this,
it will irk you too.)

Just outside the cave, as you leave, there is a small display
including a black-and-white photograph of the real bones of
Cheddar Man. It shows the Gough brothers with their find in
1903 – the skull sitting atop a pile of stones like some strange
trophy. And of course it was – it helped to raise the profile of
Gough's Cave even further.

The physician and anthropologist Charles Gabriel Seligman
and the anatomist Frederick Gymer Parsons examined the
remains of Cheddar Man. The skull was coated in a layer of
stalagmite, they reported, suggesting that it may have lain,
unburied, in the cave for some time before becoming naturally
covered up with cave earth and another layer of stalagmite. The
face was badly damaged, with one of the cheekbones missing,
but key features were preserved – a large mastoid process (a
bony protrusion for muscle attachment just behind the ear) and
a suprameatal ridge (over the opening of the auditory meatus –
or ear-hole) – suggesting this individual was male. The teeth
were intact in the mandible, and showed very little sign of
wear, suggesting that the man had been young – in his twenties – when he died. A line of fusion along the crest of the hip
bone was still evident, in keeping with this young age. The left
femur was very well preserved, and once Seligman and Parsons
had broken the stalagmitic crust off its ends, they were able to
measure its length – 44cm – which allowed them to calculate
the stature of this man at around 5ft 4.

In 1928, the cave entrance was enlarged, and more finds
emerged – this time, archaeologists excavated more carefully
and recorded their finds more systematically. They dug down
through occupation layers dating to the Roman period, the Iron

Age, and then – the Bronze Age and Neolithic were apparently missing – right back to the Palaeolithic. A total of 1,749 flint artefacts were recovered, from thin, knife-like blades to round scrapers and pointed burins and borers. Another one of those rods with a hole in it turned up as well. This is a well-known Palaeolithic type of artefact, once classified – somewhat fancifully – as a '*baton de commandement*' – a command baton, or swagger stick: a symbol of authority; perhaps also a magic wand. Each era imposes its own ideas on the past, and now we veer away from such militaristic, imperialistic or mystical interpretations, preferring a more utilitarian explanation. 'Spear-straightener' has been one suggestion, but still a little odd. It seems more likely from the wear on them that these rods were used in conjunction with twine – possibly for plaiting or twisting rope – or as something more like a fish bat, or 'priest', for killing fish. Or they could even have been parts of a weapon similar to nunchucks. The perforated baton from Gough's Cave was made of antler, with a simple decoration of incised lines along the shaft. (And two similar objects emerged in subsequent digs – meaning three of only four of these artefacts found in the whole of the UK have come from Gough's Cave.)

Other artefacts were less mysterious – two fox canines and a periwinkle shell, all pierced for suspension – presumably for a necklace or sewn onto clothes. This dig also turned up animal bones – wolf, bear, Irish elk, Arctic fox and hare – and parts of two human skulls, thought to date to around the same time as Cheddar Man himself – 12,000 years ago. More digs, into the 1930s, resulted in a great haul of archaeological artefacts – the largest Palaeolithic collection from any single British cave.

In 1986, Roger Jacobi, then based at the University of

Lancaster, did a small dig in Gough's Cave, just inside the cul-de-sac on the left in the vestibule. He opened up a trench just 1.5 metres long, in an area protected by a fallen boulder. He didn't know if he'd just find backfill – disturbed sediment from previous digs – but in the end he realised he was digging down into pristine layers, undisturbed since the end of the Ice Age. He found plenty of archaeological material – fragments of flint, animal bones and human teeth. Enough to prompt a return visit the following year, with colleagues from the Natural History Museum. They found interesting pieces of bone and ivory, with scored patterns or 'notations' on them. And, randomly mixed in among animal bones, they discovered the fragmentary remains of at least three human individuals: a skull-cap of an adult, a piece of frontal bone, and the upper and lower jaws of a child, as well as numerous fragments of other bones. These new finds – together with those from the previous excavations – meant that the remains of at least five individuals in total had now been recovered from this particular side chamber of Gough's Cave. But when the researchers looked carefully at the new skeletal material they'd dug up, they discovered something that hadn't been picked up in the earlier discoveries – cut-marks on the bones.

The bones had been marked by a sharp knife around sites of muscles attachment on the mandibles, and there were more cut-marks on ribs. News of these apparently butchered human bones quickly reached the press – excited by a potential story of ancient cannibalism. The researchers were more circumspect. 'Careful study of the cut marks and their distribution is required,' they wrote in an article in the journal *Antiquity*, ' . . . before further conclusions can be drawn.'

Meanwhile, they set about examining the skeletal material

in other ways – testing samples for isotopes of carbon and nitrogen, to reveal what sort of diet these Palaeolithic people had eaten. They knew from pollen analysis from other sites nearby that the landscape of the Mendips 12,000 years ago was open and steppe-like up on the hills, with alder, willow and hazel woods nestling down in the valleys. The bones from the cave help us to populate that landscape with animals – with a weird mixture of more temperate species, like beaver, horse, red deer and wild cattle or aurochsen, together with Arctic species such as ptarmigan, Arctic fox and lemming. Many of the animal bones bearing cut-marks were from horse and red deer – but just how important was meat in these people's diets? Very, it turned out – with the isotope analysis turning up an even stronger signal for meat in the humans' diet than in a sample from a bone of Arctic fox in the cave. But the burning question remained – was some of the meat they were eating from fellow humans?

More recent analyses focused on the timing of the events represented by the late Palaeolithic assemblage in the cave, refining the date when human hunters were there. Animal bones with cut-marks were crucial here, as they clearly record a human presence. Based on radiocarbon dating of cut-marked animal bones, the occupation of the cave could be pinned down to a time when the climate had warmed up rapidly, 14,700 years ago, when big herbivores including horses had returned to the landscape. Gough's Cave provides us with some of the earliest evidence we have for human recolonisation of Britain after the peak of the Ice Age – these hunters were among the first people to return to these lands after the ice sheets shrank and melted. And they seem to have mainly used this cave as a camp while hunting wild horses. But the human presence at Cheddar seemed very brief. The range of the radiocarbon dates indicated that the cave had been used over quite a short time span – just a few generations, a couple of hundred years, at the most. The end of the occupation also didn't seem to match with ecological changes. Some time later, further warming would have seen an increase in birch woodland, and this is when horses would have disappeared from the landscape. But the hunters who used Gough's Cave vanish too early – before the horses do – and it's not at all clear why. There's evidence of people continuing to use other caves in Britain (and I dug at one of them, briefly: King Arthur's Cave in the Wye Valley), although archaeologists have also found a growing number of open-air sites towards the end of the Ice Age, across northern Europe. The pattern is complex. What was clear from the recent analysis, though, was that the cut-marked human bones from Gough's Cave were the same age as the cut-marked animal bones.

The cannibalism debate rumbled on. No one could deny the presence of cut-marks on the bones – people had clearly used stone knives to separate flesh from the bones – but while some experts argued that this was evidence for cannibalism, others suggested that some sort of 'ritual defleshing' could have been the aim. The difference seems subtle – but it's important. If it was cannibalism, the whole point of the exercise would have been to cut meat away from the skeleton – to eat. If it was ritual defleshing, the ultimate aim would have been to clean and isolate the bones themselves. Of course, there could also be a half-way house here, if the defleshing was somehow rit-ualised and designed to produce cleaned bones, for whatever use or reason, but then the stripped-off flesh was also eaten. When you start thinking about the possibilities, you realise how little of the process we are seeing in just those cut-marks on the bones. Which is why it's so important to extract as much information from them as we can.

In 2011, I was making an archaeology series for the BBC, looking at new finds dug up in fresh excavations across Britain and novel discoveries emerging from re-examination and analysis of old finds in museum archives.

I went to the Natural History Museum in London to meet up with Dr Silvia Bello, who had been carrying out a new, painstakingly detailed analysis of the human remains from Gough's Cave. She'd examined every single fragment of bone, all 205 of them, using a microscope to focus in on those cut-marks, and she'd 3D-scanned them as well – all in the service of trying to work out *why* those cuts had been made.

Silvia met me by the giant sloth skeleton at the end of the long 'Mary Anning' corridor – its walls festooned with so many fossils of ichthyosaurs and plesiosaurs collected by that pioneering palaeontologist. I followed Silvia through the door behind the huge sloth into the Palaeoanthropology Department, and on to an office where she'd laid out some of the skeletal material from Cheddar, including the calvarium or skull-cap. The bones lay on a table, well-cushioned on a sheet of green cloth draped over bubble wrap.

Silvia's careful analysis had allowed her to piece together fragments that had come from the same bone – in the end, she managed to find such matches for seventy fragments, making up parts of twenty-four different bones between them. Some of the matches were between fragments found at different times, in different campaigns of excavation in the cave. Then she could work out the minimum number of individuals represented by the remains. There were six, she told me: three adults (because there were three complete adult clavicles – two right clavicles, and a left clavicle that was clearly not one of a pair with either); two adolescents (based on duplicated immature bones from the feet); and one young child (represented only by fragments of skull).

It was more than twenty years since the cut-marks had been remarked upon and people had started to seriously whisper about cannibalism at Cheddar. But would Silvia's re-assessment of the evidence bolster those claims or finally lay them to rest? She was brutally direct:

'We now have clear proof of cannibalism in this site.'

Signs of butchery were everywhere – not just on the odd bone. Almost two thirds of bones from post-cranial parts of the skeleton (any bone other than the skull and mandible) bore cut-marks. And in many places, the cuts were grouped, in parallel, at key sites of muscle and ligament attachment. They were exactly the sort of marks you'd expect after a stone knife had been used to cut away skin and muscles – filleting, scalping and skinning – and to take the body apart at the joints. A third had been cracked open – many bearing the clear marks of a stone hammer – to access the marrow. This is very significant – rather than ritual defleshing, it strongly suggests 'nutritional' cannibalism: smashing long bones to access the rich, fatty – and undoubtedly delicious – marrow inside them. The nature of the fractures, with curved or spiralling edges to them, reveals that they were created when the bones were still fresh. Breaks in old, dry, brittle bones look very different – blocky, hard-edged.

But the evidence for cannibalism didn't stop there – because it wasn't just stone knives and hammers that had left their traces on these bones. Silvia had found – on eighty-seven separate fragments – the unmistakable marks of human teeth.

Those bones had been *gnawed*. Bitten, crushed, scraped with incisors. The ends of some ribs had been completely chewed off. Only one specimen in the sample had been chewed by a sharp-toothed, non-human carnivore – in all the other gnawed bones, it was human teeth that had done the damage.

The cannibals had comprehensively devoured whole bodies – skinning them, then dealing with meatier parts where flesh had been cut away with stone knives before the bones were chewed; smashing open long bones to get at the marrow; right down to fingers, which also showed signs of having been chopped off and munched on. The pattern of cut-marks also showed the tissues of the bodies had been fresh when they were butchered. If they'd been left to rot before being dismembered, the picture would have been different.

The way that all the different bodies had been butchered was consistent, and very similar to the way that other large mammal remains from the cave had been cut up. But there was something unusual about the way the human remains had been treated – when it came to the head.

'We had three skulls which were perfectly preserved,' Silvia told me. 'So there was a question – why were they saving them?'

The skulls had escaped the vigorous fragmentation that characterised the rest of the skeleton, but they had still been cut into and modified. There were cut marks and evidence of disarticulation from the neck and careful defleshing – removing tongue, cheeks and other facial muscles – but no sign of chewing. Instead, once the flesh had been cut away, the bones of the face had been broken off the brain-case or cranium, using stone tools. The cranium had been broken open – but it seems that this wasn't just aimed at extracting the brain.

'The way that they modified it – it's not just to extract the brain,' explained Silvia. 'There are easier ways to break it. But here we have a very clear process of complete defleshing.'

I held the most complete of the skulls – which was really just the upper half of a skull, with most of the base missing. I looked at the sides of it, tracing the cutmarks on it with my fingers.

'You can almost imagine somebody peeling off the tissues, and then cutting down underneath – separating the muscle from the underlying tissue.' Even I, as an anatomist and osteo-archaeologist, was finding this a little gruesome.

'Exactly,' agreed Silvia, 'this is a classic example of scalping. And then when we analysed the face and other parts, there are clear signs that they're doing this in a very detailed way. They were cutting the eyes; they were cutting the cheeks; they were cutting the lips.'

'Why do you think they would want to do that?'

Silvia took the skull from my hands and turned it over it hers, the top of the skull resting on one of her palms. She pointed out where the edges of the skull had been carefully chipped away with a stone tool – to create a fairly level brim. Whoever had done this, had done it quite intentionally – to create this bowl shape.

'We think that it was to produce a container,' she said. 'It was a cup.'

This was deeply strange. I wanted to question it, to doubt it. But there was the evidence in front of me, and I couldn't think of any other explanation for the way this skull had been carved, sculpted. It certainly didn't seem to be purely functional – it wasn't just about extracting food from a human body. Those Ice Age hunters had gone to great lengths, scrupulously cleaning the skull and transforming it into a cup.

For Silvia, this was the key piece of evidence which proved that the cannibalism at Gough's Cave wasn't simply nutritional – it wasn't just about survival. It had a ritual element to it as well. An additional piece of the puzzle emerged recently: a fragmented radius from the cave has been deliberately smashed into and bears human tooth marks, but there's also a strange zigzag line inscribed on it as well – clearly not just functional.

When it comes to the skulls, there are many ethnographic accounts of crania – or even whole heads – being used in ritual ways in various societies, during historical times; heads taken as trophies in battles, displayed as symbols of power or prestige, or to instil fear into enemies. There are also recent examples of some communities keeping and curating body parts or even entire mummies of the deceased. Those examples can open our minds to the possibilities, but in truth we won't ever know what those skulls meant to the Palaeolithic inhabitants of Cheddar. But we know they meant *something* – and more than just 'food'. (Although Paul Pettitt jokes, in the worst possible taste, 'If you're devouring a human body you need something to drain the blood into and drink it out of!')

It seems strange to our modern sensibilities that our ancient ancestors would make such macabre objects. But we have to try to escape from our own cultural lens when we peer back into the past. Eating people and making their skulls into cups seems gruesome to us. What were those cannibals thinking as they did these things? We can now be very clear – thanks to Silvia's painstaking analysis – that the human remains at Gough's Cave really do represent victims of cannibalism. But perhaps 'victim' also carries too many unfounded implications. After all, we don't know *who* was eating *whom* at Cheddar – or indeed, why.

It could have been a brutal way of marking superiority over a conquered tribe or caste – symbolising victory and reducing the victims to the status of prey. Or perhaps – however hard this is for us to imagine – consuming the dead could have been seen as a perfectly respectful way to treat dead, dear friends and relatives. Were the cannibals driven by hunger – or by their beliefs? Or both?

But then again, maybe we're overthinking this, imbuing our ancestors' actions with more thoughtful intent than was actually there. Perhaps it was all very functional – and they simply did not make the distinction between humans and other animals that we do. Then the questions would become not 'Why eat a human?', but 'Why not?'; not 'Why make a skull into a cup?', but 'Why not? Here's this round thing that looks like it could be useful with a bit of shaping.' Animal bones and antler were always being made into tools, weapons and other useful objects – why should human bones be any different?

Whatever the motives, it seems the late Ice Age hunters at Cheddar were not especially weird in the way they approached the dead. The finds from Cheddar are particularly dense, and have been more thoroughly scrutinised than other collections, but they do fit with what we know of mortuary practices around this time elsewhere in Europe. This period, right at the end of the Palaeolithic, between 15,000 and 12,000 years ago, is known as the 'Magdalenian' – or in Britain, the 'Creswellian' (after Creswell Crags). Fragmented human bones, often with cut-marks on them, have been found at Magdalenian sites along the Dordogne Valley in France and the Rhine in Germany. And yet, if you take all the skeletal evidence of humans in Europe from this period, we have fragments of around only 200 individuals in total. That's not many – we're clearly only seeing a fraction of the dead. Perhaps the remains that have been preserved were treated in an unusual way – or perhaps it's because of a quirk of preservation in caves, when other remains could have been more easily scattered and lost in open-air environments.

Among those fragmentary remains, bits of skull are dispro-portionately represented. And although the skull cups from Gough's Cave are unusual – they are not unique. There are at least three other sites where crania seem to have been modified for use as cups. Most are from France, dating from very close to the peak of the last Ice Age, but some appear right through to the Neolithic and Bronze Age. So it may be that whatever was happening at Gough's Cave could have been an expression of widely held beliefs and practices in Europe at the end of the Stone Age. (Beliefs that may somehow have ended up getting woven into Christianity, much later – in a ritual where the 'body' and 'blood' of a deity is consumed.)

We are left with a picture of mortuary and funerary practices where most of the dead have disappeared, leaving no trace of the rites, if any, that accompanied their passing. Then, we have this evidence that some individuals were butchered and eaten, their bones fragmented; a few skulls were made into receptacles. It is extremely unusual for more complete skeletons to survive from this period – fewer than ten are known, from right across Europe in the Magdalenian.

And Cheddar Man himself – it turns out – is *not* one of those.

When the Gough brothers dug out the bones of Cheddar Man with their picks and shovels, they paid scant attention to the archaeological layers they were digging through. When Seligman and Parsons came to look at the skeleton, ten years after it had been excavated, they were told that the skeleton had been found buried under a couple of feet of cave earth, and apparently in close association with the flints and pierced baton. They didn't seem to question this – despite the fact that the surfaces of the skull and long bones were covered in a stalagmite crust, suggesting perhaps that the skeleton had been quite shallow, on top of the deeper, older deposits. Cheddar Man continued to be thought of as Palaeolithic in date until 1970, when the bones were radiocarbon-dated – producing the surprisingly late date of around 9,080 years before the present. This meant that Cheddar Man had lived and died in the Mendips around 5,000 years later than those other individuals whose remains had been disarticulated and devoured, their fragmented bones surviving in Gough's Cave to tell the tale. And in fact, more recent, careful analyses of finds from the site have revealed other clues to Mesolithic use of the cave, with stone tools, and a piece of reindeer antler radiocarbon-dated to around 10,000 years ago.

At around 10,000 years old, Cheddar Man is still Stone Age, still a hunter-gatherer. He comes from a time we call the Mesolithic – 'the Stone Age in the Middle' – sandwiched in between the old Stone Age, the Palaeolithic, and the new Stone Age, the Neolithic. The landscape, and the way that humans lived in it, had changed since the tail-end of the Ice Age. Britain had become more temperate and more wooded, and the large herds of animals that had once roamed the open grassy plains of Late Glacial Britain had disappeared, replaced by species more at home in woodland.

In the Mesolithic, we find traces of more permanent – or at least, less ephemeral – buildings in the landscape. This is the point in time where we find evidence of what may reasonably be called Britain's first houses – robust huts or tipi-like structures that were permanent in the landscape and used over several generations – where, previously, people had tended to camp out in caves and in temporary shelters, more like tents. The Mesolithic hunters were probably not living in such houses all year round, but coming back to seasonal camps year after year. There's a change in hunting technology too – we see more evidence for the use of bows and arrows, for instance.

In the rest of northern Europe around this time, when human remains turn up they are usually in the context of burials rather than fragmented remains. And often those burials are clustered, in cemeteries – out in the open. Mesolithic burials in Britain are vanishingly rare, but Cheddar Man may be one such burial. Others have been discovered in the Mendips. Just a mile away from Gough's Cave, Aveline's Hole in Burrington Combe proved to be a veritable Mesolithic cemetery – contained within a cave – with around fifty people buried there over a century or two. So if Cheddar Man was buried, that makes sense for the Mesolithic, fitting with the pattern seen in Aveline's Hole and across Europe more widely. In the end, though, this is all conjecture. The way that Cheddar Man was excavated means we'll never know for certain now if he was laid to rest in a grave or whether he died in the cave and became naturally entombed in the cave sediments.

The story of Cheddar Man has taken twists and turns, and left us with some questions that we'll never be able to solve, as the evidence is simply no longer there. But analysis of his bones has provided us with some more details about who he was – and Tom Booth was part of the team that extracted and sequenced Cheddar Man's DNA.

That ancient DNA yielded some interesting findings, allowing us to – cautiously – put some flesh on those old bones. His eyes were probably blue, while his skin is likely to have been fairly dark. A striking combination. Reconstructions of skin colour based on DNA always come with a warning – we're very much dealing with probabilities here, rather than definitive answers. But the results suggested that his skin colour was likely to have fallen into one of the two darkest of five categories, appearing 'dark or 'dark to black'. He certainly lacked the genetic variants linked to lighter skin colour that become more widespread in later European populations. Those variants have also been found to be absent in DNA from individuals from Spain, Luxembourg and Hungary, at this time in prehistory. The genetic basis for the pale skin that was to become characteristic of western European populations seems to arrive later, with populations expanding across Europe in the Neolithic – as farming spreads – and again, in the Bronze

Age – with a population boom and spread that starts in the Pontic steppe then ripples out.

This late development of pale skin in Europeans is a new and surprising revelation emerging from studies of ancient genomes. Our species arose in Africa, more than 300,000 years ago, and it was hypothesised that early modern humans, and indeed their ancestors, possessed dark skin pigmentation – protecting underlying tissues from damage wreaked by UV radiation. But as humans expanded out of Africa, and eventually into more northerly latitudes, they didn't need so much natural sunscreen and, in addition, may have struggled to make enough vitamin D – as we make a precursor to this vitamin in our skin, using sunlight energy to power the process. So, the hypothesis suggested, this colonisation of the north would have been accompanied by paling of skin, as the selection pressure for dark skin to protect against sun damage was relaxed, while pale skin mutations would have been favoured by natural selection. But – as so often in biology – it's not that simple. Darker skin tones were clearly not that much of a disadvantage in northerly latitudes, as they persisted as the predominant form for tens of thousands of years after modern humans first trekked to northern Europe – as Cheddar Man and others demonstrate. (Other recent studies have also showed that archaic skin tones were far more varied than we've previously suspected – suggesting the association between latitude and skin colour is nowhere near as straightforward as we'd thought. There probably is selection pressure at the extremes – for dark skin in the tropics, for pale skin in the high Arctic – and the mid-tones in between may be due to population movements and mixing.)

Until the recent ancient DNA study, Cheddar Man had always been reconstructed with pale skin, but that was just based on what we see in populations today. It seemed liked the best guess – but it was just that: a guess. A new reconstruction was commissioned at the same time that Cheddar Man's DNA was being analysed, for a Channel 4 television programme. The bust was created by the wonderful Dutch palaeoartists, twin brothers Adrie and Alfons Kennis, with whom I have had the pleasure of working on several occasions, creating television programmes and books together. And they produced a new, life-size, scientifically informed sculpture of Cheddar Man – in all his blue-eyed, dark-skinned glory. The reconstruction caused a sensation when it appeared in the Channel 4 documentary about those new genetic insights, in February 2018.

But then some commentators began to question the validity of this prediction of skin and eye colour based on DNA. The study was based on looking at thirty-six genetic variants, spread across sixteen genes, examining these particular sections in over 1,400 modern genomes. The geneticists then used this data to create a model that could predict skin colour from a genetic code. When they tested their model on modern people, it performed very well, predicting skin colour quite accurately. But could it accurately predict the tone of Cheddar Man's skin? Tom and his colleagues were cautiously robust about their methods. They were up front about the fact that Cheddar Man's DNA had been, unsurprisingly, quite badly degraded – so there was a process of patching it together even before they could apply their predictive model. But they were sure they'd correctly reconstructed and then interpreted the genetic sequence.

Other researchers have urged more caution – emphasising that the genetics of skin colour are turning out to be much more complicated than previously thought, involving many more than just sixteen genes. It's difficult to make predictions *today*, they say, let alone being able to project a prediction 10,000 years into the past. Nevertheless, there's broad agreement that Cheddar Man's skin tone would certainly have been darker brown than that of most northern Europeans today. And for the reconstruction, the geneticists suggested going for a skin tone in the middle of the range predicted from the DNA analysis – a conservative approach based on the best available evidence. The response to the bust of Cheddar Man perhaps says more about identity politics today – and indeed, racism – in a world where people are still too often judged on the basis of their skin colour.

I asked Tom about the controversy around the reconstruction when the Channel 4 programme aired. 'Skin pigmentation is so often taken as a reflection of ancestry,' he said. 'But the bust does reflect a truth – that Cheddar Man comes from a population that doesn't really exist anymore and was genetically outside the variation that we see in Europe today. And I think this is at the heart of why the bust was so impactful; nothing says "my ancestry is different from yours" more than that combination of dark skin and light-blue eyes.'

As one individual from Britain's past, coming into focus so clearly in the era of ancient genomics, Cheddar Man urges us to look at human diversity differently – and to embrace it. There is nothing, ever, that can be construed as 'racial purity'. There are different populations, and they split and fuse through time. There are populations – we know from ancient DNA analyses – that have left no appreciable trace in humans alive today. They are no less 'human' for it. There are, and there have been, many different ways of being human – and none is any more valid than any other.

Let yourself imagine this young man, then. Peer back

through the millennia and catch sight of him, standing on the rocky crest of Cheddar Gorge. It's wintertime and he's spotted movement down in the wooded ravine, through the tracery of branches. A group of red deer are making their way up the gorge. The afternoon sun gleams off the wetlands of the Somerset Levels beyond, as the gorge itself is plunged into darkness. The young man holds a spear, fitted with vicious-looking stone barbs at the tip. He has a bow and arrows, slung over his shoulders. He's about 5ft 5, slightly built. He wears clothes made from animal skins – carefully made clothes, well-fitted and warm. He has dark skin, long black hair – and piercing blue eyes.

Then he is gone, dropping over the edge of the gorge and deftly clambering down. Perhaps he is heading down to stalk those deer in the gloaming, then heading to the cave to camp there for the night. Does he fall? Does his family find him and carry his body into the cave to bury him there? Science takes us so far, then we leap off into the realm of storytelling. Because we're human, and that's how we understand the world. That's how we connect.

Perhaps we want something more. A connection that seems more real, somehow – a genetic connection with this ancestor. Are our family trees interwoven? Are we part of his story, and he of ours?

Comparing genomes of modern British people – at least, those whose ancestors are mostly from this corner of the globe – to that of Cheddar Man, there seems to be a connection. The comparison shows around 10 per cent 'shared ancestry'. But that shared ancestry doesn't mean that DNA has been inherited directly from the Mesolithic population here in Britain. We know that there were later migrations – in the

Neolithic and the Bronze Age particularly – that mixed things up a lot, introducing new genes but also bringing in DNA from other Mesolithic populations in Europe. This may be where that 10 per cent similarity comes from: a later import, not a direct connection.

Attempting to make those connections shows how foolish it is. Genetics, like epidemiology, is at its most powerful when operating at a population level. At the level of the individual, at least when considering ancestry, it is much less interesting. It can say: people with similar bits of DNA to you are now found here – and there. As we do more DNA studies, we'll be able to see how those similarities relate to ancient population mobility and migrations. But how does that feed into ideas about individual identity? Or – perhaps more pertinently – how *can* it, when you only have to go back ten generations – so around 300 years – to gain over a thousand theoretical, direct ancestors. Can you possibly, in any meaningful way, identify with all of them? It's surely individuals, and individual stories, that we identify with most – even if (perhaps because) there is no way of demonstrating a direct genetic connection to them, other than: they were a human, like you.

Anyone, then – I think – can feel a human connection with that 10,000-year-old man who lived and died on the Mendips.

Ancestors belong to everyone – and no one.

5.

THE FOUNDING FARMERS

The Rock of the Plough

I'm walking on a high hill above Balranald in North Uist, the Outer Hebrides, the edge of the world. The hill is called Cleitreabhal a Deas (which is pronounced, in the local Gaelic dialect, 'Klee-ah-trah-val uh jayss').

I've been camping behind the dunes of Hougharry Bay, watching short-eared owls hunting in the evenings, on the machair beneath a burial ground on a low hill. Nearby

Kilmuir cemetery seemed, more often than not, to be picked out in bright sunshine against a dark purple sky, or wreathed in rainbows.

I'd already explored that graveyard – with its ruined, roofless eighteenth-century church, a shed in the corner containing – a glance through the window revealed – a wheelbarrow and several spades. Up on the low hill in the cemetery, imposing stone-walled enclosures housed the tombs of the local elite. The Macdonalds of Balranald were settling down into their graves, with voids collapsing in and hollowing out the turf above; '1768' just visible, engraved on the stone lintel over the doorway to that open-air crypt. This tomb may occupy what was the site of the earliest (or at least, the earliest recorded) church here: the church of St Mary, Cille Mhoire, or Kilmuir.

The most peripheral graves, in various extensions to the graveyard beyond its original (once circular) enclosure, were the most recent – sharp-edged, clearly legible. Then there were a few graves of anonymous men from the First World War – washed up on beaches, perhaps? Would their mothers ever know where their sons' bodies had ended up?

Among the more obvious gravestones, a few strange, low stones – some apparently natural, others bearing obscure traces of shaping or carving. A visitor to the cemetery 100 years ago noted that one grave was marked with a saddle quern as its headstone; the mundane becoming sacred: a household object used daily in life becoming a marker of identity in death, perhaps. The oldest here date to the tenth or eleventh centuries, when North Uist was part of the Norse-originated Kingdom of the Isles.

But I was after more ancient ancestors. Not the people who

had lived here a thousand years ago, or two thousand. Five thousand would do.

I drive up the road towards the domes on the hill – which is so prominent in the landscape, though only just over 100 metres high. Cleitreabhal a Deas, or South Clettravel, is the site of a radar station. It used to be known as RRH Benbecula; RRH stands for Remote Radar Head, and Benbecula is the island immediately to the south of North Uist, which used to accommodate an RAF base. The domes here are part of an 'early warning' radar station, the locals tell me. Officially, it's part of the UK Air Surveillance and Control System (ASACS). Today, the station affords me a convenient opportunity to park up my camper van and climb over a gate onto the southern slope. I'm wearing sandals; a poor choice, I realise, as what looked like dry heath becomes sodden moor and I sink into the oozing wet sphagnum moss. I don't really mind; my sandals are used to this, as I am. I just need to get down to those rocks sticking out of the hillside.

It gets boggier – feet thoroughly wet now – before the land rises up again, more heathered than mossed, and I'm next to the stones: a series of orthostats, or stones set upright in the ground. They flank a narrow corridor, leading into a larger space. Open to the elements now, these vertically positioned stone slabs would have formed the walls of a tunnel, leading into a chamber. Both would have been roofed with stone, and buried under a mound that has long since disappeared. In this burial chamber, the bones of the dead would have been laid, 5,000 years ago. Now it is empty, and has been for a very long time.

The western part of the tomb has become incorporated into a later monument. I can make out the ruins of a circular building – an Iron Age wheelhouse – a type of roundhouse with spoke-like divisions inside. Again, it is roofless now and much reduced, but it would have been covered with a corbelled stone roof. Excavations up here in the 1930s filled in the gap between Neolithic and Iron Age, with evidence of Bronze Age 'Beaker' pottery turning up.

These remains together – from chambered cairn to wheelhouse – represent a much longer continuity than Kilmuir burial ground, with its mere thousand years of use. Here, at this lofty site up on South Clettravel, people were burying, living, being part of the landscape for at least 3,000 years. Was occupation here on the northwest corner of North Uist continuous for all that time, and beyond, I wonder? Did the church and burial ground on the low knoll at Kilmuir respect and replace these earlier tombs and habitations up on the hill?

Whatever played out here, over the centuries and millennia, the Neolithic tomb is part of a much wider story. It's a type of monument that appears right across Britain at this time – between 4000 and 3000 BCE. However remote the Outer Hebrides seem today, they were a linked-up part of that story, part of that culture.

Further down the hill, on the southern slope, I find a standing stone – perhaps a waymarker to the cairn for someone ascending to the hip of the hill, heading for this blind summit, on their way to the tomb.

Back down at Balranald nature reserve later, two crofters, a young woman and a young man, are baling up the rich mix of machair hay. Before it was mown, I spotted among the grasses the small white stars of little mouse-ear, yellow tufts of smooth catsear, and purple Devil's-bit scabious. Dry, brown pods of yellow rattle clattered in the wind. The field was mowed two days ago, from the middle to the edges, to allow the corn-crakes to escape. Gulls circle, darting down now and then to pick up the remains of less fortunate former inhabitants. One John Deere tractor follows the heaped-up ridges of hay with a machine that engorges itself with the cuttings, swallowing them into its metal stomach, then pausing to disgorge a per-fectly round barrel of hay before starting again. The other tractor trails an ingenious mechanical device that picks up a bale then rotates and rolls it, stretch-wrapping it in black plastic. Inside these tight packages, the machair grasses and flowers – all that rich, wet goodness – will pickle themselves into baleage for winter forage.

Across the Outer Hebrides, a once densely populated and farmed landscape has been left fallow for around two cen-turies – following the eviction of tenant farmers from the landscape by landowners keen to create more room for grazing sheep, as well as famines and emigration. Modern OS maps preserve some of this history in the form of ruined homesteads, but satellite images of the islands of the Outer Hebrides are even more striking. Zoom in and you can see that almost every suitable patch of land is still marked with bands of ridge and furrow – an arable farming system common across Britain in the Middle Ages, and persisting in Scotland and Ireland until the nineteenth century. But there are still areas that are under the plough. Around the Balranald nature reserve, crofters make hay but also plough the machair and sow mixed crops of wheat, barley and oats on a rotation. I had walked past such fields there, on the westernmost tip of North Uist. The feathery heads of oats shimmered among the stouter ears of barley and wheat. Wilderness was allowed to permeate these fields, too, with corn marigold – extinct across most of Britain – painting swathes of bright yellow. This flower is thought to have arrived in Britain with the first crops, the first farmers.

Names in the landscape speak of the agricultural past: Clettravel – Cleitreabhal in Gaelic – is *cleit treabhal*: the rock of the plough, or the rock of the farm. The crofters at Balranald are continuing the work of the first farmers on the Hebrides: the Neolithic people who entombed their dead in the chambered cairn up on that hill.

Trouble in Paradise

The British Neolithic starts around 6,000 years ago. The beginning of this era in prehistory marks a change in subsistence that I believe was the most profound revolution that human societies have ever experienced, when our ancestors started farming. Before this, for generations and generations, for hundreds of thousands of years, humans subsisted by gathering wild plants and hunting wild animals. But after the last Ice Age, as the world started to warm up, patterns of subsistence changed, with a shift from gathering to growing; from hunting to rearing; from eating wild species to eating domesticated ones. Different species were domesticated at different times, in different parts of the world. There have been many centres, or origins, for domestication, but the earliest appeared in East Asia, West Asia and in Mexico. The British Neolithic represents a ripple of influence spreading from the famous Fertile Crescent in West Asia, around the Tigris and Euphrates rivers, where the founder crops included wheat, barley, oats and rye, and where sheep, goats and cattle were first domesticated.

Domestication is a process – not a moment in time – where traits useful to humans spread through populations that were once wholly wild. It represents an evolutionary change, with humans exerting selection pressures on once-wild species, leading to changes in them and their genetic make-up over time. It's tempting to see this as 'human domination of nature', but it's something much more subtle, especially to begin with. All species live in complex webs of interaction with others – no species is an island. How populations evolve over time is affected by many other life forms. Some of those other life forms represent food; some – competition; some – mutual benefits; some – disease and suffering; some – death. The predator–prey relationship is just one of those complex interactions. And when it comes to domesticated animals, in most instances we can see that as a special case of that predator–prey relationship. It's just that the prey doesn't have the option of escape any more, and that nudges evolution in interesting directions.

When wild populations interact as predators and prey, they affect each other's evolutionary path, creating something like an escalating arms race. Foxes hunting rabbits may catch the smaller, slower bunnies more easily. Large, quick rabbits will have a survival advantage – over time, as more of them survive and pass their genes on (as rabbits do so well), those traits of large size and speed will spread more widely through the population. In domestication, farmers will also affect populations, by weeding out certain individuals or, at least, hanging onto others that possess favoured traits, and breeding from those. Over generations, those traits spread through populations of farmed animals. Traits that would be a distinct survival disadvantage among wild animals – including being relatively tame and docile – are preserved and favoured in domesticates.

The earliest farmers would not have been controlling breeding of their livestock anywhere near as strictly as we do today.

But simply by managing herds, choosing to kill some animals when young while allowing others to mature and reproduce, they would have affected those beasts, changing them over time. In a somewhat similar way, it's thought that the hallmarks of domesticated crops – which include slightly larger seeds and a tendency for grains to stay stuck to the ear in cereals – could have come about as side effects of agricultural practices, without any thoughtful intent on the part of the farmers. We can pick up on some of the changes in the skeletal remains of these animals, as well as in charred, preserved plant remains, on archaeological sites, allowing us to see that transition from wild to domesticated. We can look at the genetic basis of those changes too, and see them spreading through populations. And that's how archaeologists and geneticists have been able to pin down the origin of domesticated animals and the 'founder crops' of the Neolithic. Although there were many centres of domestication around the world, and through time, the earliest seem to be in the Middle East – in the Fertile Crescent, in China and in Mexico. Once the Neolithic Revolution took off in those places – the idea spread. Farming was a successful way of life that would fuel a population boom and expansion. By studying ancient genomes, it's been possible to show that this wasn't just a spread of ideas (and crops and livestock); it was a spread of *people*. The Neolithic Revolution that took hold between 11,000 and 8,000 years ago in the Fertile Crescent rippled out, further and further. By 8,500 years ago, farmers were growing crops in Cyprus. Two thousand years later, crops, livestock and the people who tended them had colonised the Danube Valley. By 6,000 years ago, that 'ripple of influence' had broken on the shores of Britain – a new lifestyle, seed corn and livestock had arrived.

This expansion of the Neolithic was once seen as a monolithic, megalithic juggernaut – with a fully formed package, including farming, pottery and permanent settlement in the landscape, sweeping through and replacing earlier lifestyles. Now, this fascinating period in prehistory tends to be seen as an immensely complex, transitional stretch of time. A whole range of transformations were taking hold, at different rates and in different ways. New technologies were being adopted, with tools for farming appearing in lithic assemblages, and new methods of storing food – including pottery. Across centuries, societies and lifestyles were changing. We can view the Neolithic as a period of change – away from the mobile, hunting and gathering societies of the preceding Mesolithic, towards the settled, farming populations of the early Bronze Age. But while those terms help us frame the past, divide it up and see trends over time, we must remember that they are constructs. Categories are hugely, undeniably useful as we set out to analyse all sorts of phenomena, from tombs to turtles, stone spearheads to snakes, people to planets. But we must guard against letting categories expand to become archetypes, clouding our vision and obscuring important details. Nearly seventy years ago, British archaeologist Stuart Piggott expressed his concern 'that such phrases as "Neolithic" or "Bronze Age" periods have a rather dubious validity'. The terms certainly don't represent cultural identities – all those thousands of years ago, people across Europe would not have thought of themselves as 'Neolithic' or 'Bronze Age'. But Stuart Piggott continued to employ those terms, with caution, as nothing better existed then – or indeed, now. So we can do the same, as long as we remember that this is *our* way of parcelling up and understanding the past.

Through that time of change that we define as the Neolithic, then, we can imagine a patchwork of evolving communities. And then we wonder about the interactions between those farmers, expanding into new territories (for them) and the hunter-gatherer groups who were already there. Did the hunters see the farmers as invaders? Was there animosity and antagonism, or peaceful co-existence? Were the two groups – whether viewing each other with suspicion or toler-ance – hermetically sealed from each other, sharing landscapes but operating a form of apartheid?

It's very difficult to find answers to these questions. We can see the spread of *farming* so clearly in the archaeological record, but in the end we're surely more interested in the *farmers* themselves. We want to understand those societies, to learn something about the human experience during this time of important transition. Archaeology can provide many clues, showing us that goods were being exchanged between hunters and farmers, for instance. North of the farmed Danube Valley, we can see that hunter-gatherers were acquiring pottery, antler axes and bone combs from their new neighbours in the south. They may have traded fur and amber in return. But it's difficult to know the real nature of that exchange. If we use the word 'trade', that suggests a friendly, or at least tolerant, contact. If objects were moving between those communities – were people? There are so many possibilities. Disenfranchised teenagers could have run away from farms to join the hunters. Hunters facing a lean year could have come down to help work on the farms, to join that community. Women may have left to marry into another group. Slaves could have been bought and sold. And then, perhaps there was no exchange at all. Materials, goods – and people – could simply have been taken, plundered in raids.

To begin exploring this interaction between farmers and hunters, we can look for signs of violence among human remains from this transitional time, which might indicate a less-than-congenial co-existence.

One of the most obvious and undeniable signs of interpersonal violence, ancient or modern, is a weapon or projectile lodged in a body. Today we'd look for a bullet tearing through flesh. In the Stone Age, we look for stone arrowheads and spearheads lodged in ancient bones. The earliest examples in Europe come from two sites in Italy, around 13,000 years ago. After that, there are many examples of stone and bone points penetrating human bones, right through the Neolithic and beyond. But there are also many, many sites where such weapon-tips have been found associated with human remains – and have been interpreted as grave goods. We should be extremely cautious about this: it would be a rare occurrence for a stone point to hit a bone; we should expect more to have penetrated and stopped within soft tissue. Careful excavation and recording is absolutely essential if we are to identify such weapons lodged *in a body*, as opposed to weapons buried *with a body*.

Crania from Denmark and Britain have been examined for signs of trauma, and many – around 10 per cent – show signs of injury. Often, these injuries have healed, so they are not related to violent deaths, but to violence experienced within a lifetime. Some people may have suffered injuries in ritualised combat; some may have survived what were intended to be lethal attacks. We cannot differentiate between those intentions, so we should neither assume that all injuries result from ritual combat or from genuine conflict – or indeed, punishment – and instead bear both possibilities in mind as we examine each case. It's also important to consider that some injuries, particularly those involving other bones in the skeleton apart from the skull, could have been accidental.

There are sporadic cases of violence leading to injury and death in the archaeological record, but then, a few centuries into the Neolithic in Europe, there are some sites that bear witness to an astonishing explosion in violence. At three sites in central Europe, in particular, archaeologists have uncovered clear signs of large-scale brutality and violence. Human remains from the early Neolithic sites of Talheim in Germany, Asparn/Schletz in Austria and, most recently, Schöneck-Kilianstädten in Germany, present us with unequivocal evidence of ancient massacres.

These three sites are all classified as 'LBK'. The earliest farmers in central Europe made a distinctive type of pottery, decorated with striking geometric patterns. The German name for this pottery – which then gets applied to the whole of this Neolithic culture – is *Linearbandkeramik* or, more briefly, LBK. The culture appears around 5600 BCE and spans seven centuries, until 4900 BCE.

In general, burial practices for this period are quite varied – including inhumation and cremation – but tend to be individual. Formal burials often contain grave goods: shell ornaments, pottery, and – particularly in male burials – stone adzes or arrowheads. These stone artefacts could both be used in subsistence, but potentially also against human targets. The adze is a woodworking tool, but could be an effective weapon as well, as injuries preserved in ancient skeletons show all too clearly. Stone-tipped arrows could also be aimed at game – or people. Some archaeologists believe that these grave goods indicate a hunter-warrior identity.

But archaeologists found something very different within the

LBK settlement site at Schöneck-Kilianstädten: a mass grave. In a long pit, they unearthed the jumbled remains of at least twenty-six individuals. Half were adults; half juvenile. Of the adults, most were male, with just two skulls from older individuals recorded as possibly female. Of the juveniles, most were less than six years old. One was an infant, around six months of age. Two stone arrowpoints were found among the bones.

The skeletons bore the stigmata of various diseases common in the Neolithic, from probable TB to signs of vitamin C deficiency, the odd healed fracture, and bone infection. Arthritis and dental disease were rare in the sample. The general health status was 'as expected for an LBK group from Central Europe'. But against that background picture of health and disease was unequivocal evidence of violent injury around the time of death. Skulls had been smashed in with blunt weapons – probably adzes; legs had been hacked at, fracturing fibulae and tibiae. That focus on the legs suggests the attackers were not only interested in dealing fatal blows to their victims. They were terrorising them – demonstrating the futility of trying to escape, finding physical expression, perhaps, for their hatred and disdain. That contempt, that wrath, extends to the way those dead bodies were finally disposed of – unceremoniously dumped in the long pit.

The picture is similar to that seen at Asparn/Schletz in Austria, where a comparable distribution of ages and sexes was seen among the human remains of bodies thrown into a ditch. The archaeologists have suggested that teenagers – who are largely missing from those mass graves – may have simply been more agile, better able to escape than either the older adults or the younger children. Alternatively, the youths could have been viewed as a valuable commodity, and taken away by their attackers. Young women, too, are rare among the remains – perhaps they were taken as captives rather than being slaughtered like the rest. That's a familiar theme, once we have records of warfare. It seems to have its roots in prehistory.

Once you account for the missing sections of the demographic in those mass graves – the young people, the women – then both Schöneck-Kilianstädten and Asparn/Schletz appear to have been communities of around thirty to forty people, suggesting that, in each case, a whole hamlet was wiped out by a vicious, lethal attack. The scale of the violence at these places must surely have left deep psychological scars. Professor Rick Schulting of Oxford University has spent many years studying Mesolithic and Neolithic life-ways – exploring that transition to agriculture and the evidence for changing diets, as well as violence in those societies. Sometimes it's too easy to identify violent injuries on bones, count them up, and leave it at that. But he urges us to think about the wider effects of such atrocities on societies and culture.

'Events on this scale', he writes, 'can resonate through space and time, through the telling and re-telling of incidents of violence so that they become part of cultural memory, creating a climate of fear and mistrust, and instigating cycles of revenge . . . Specialised war leaders are likely to emerge . . .'.

In the past, scholars have been cautious, even reticent, about talking about 'war' in the Stone Age – because it presumes a certain level of social organisation, perhaps. But given the scale of these violent attacks, it seems reasonable to characterise them as examples of prehistoric warfare – which, with at least three examples from widely separated sites, seems to have been on the rise among those late LBK societies in Europe. We'll never know what sparked each of these atrocities, but competition between different groups of farmers could have been the stimulus. Population numbers had been rising, and then a downturn in climate could have led to drought and famine – still powerful drivers of violent unrest even today. And while hunter-gatherers can avoid conflict by moving away from a source of friction, settled farmers have fewer options.

Because we use that overarching LBK label, it's tempting to think of all those early farming communities in central Europe as one big happy family. But the evidence suggests they did not see themselves in that cohesive way at all. Archaeologists think that this is farming communities pitted against each other, rather than attacks by any remaining hunter-gatherers on the farmers who are taking control of more and more land, as each generation passes.

So, long before anything we could sensibly label as a 'state', people were engaging in collective violence. Those farmers could identify as belonging to a group – and they could turn that in-group identity outwards, engaging extremely effectively in – to use the modern vernacular – 'othering'. Once you've thoroughly dehumanised another human group, there's nothing to stop you seizing their territory, their women, their young people; there's nothing to stop you swinging your woodworking adze into the side of the other's skull; there's nothing to stop you smashing the other's legs, even if they're already dead. The others could never run away. There was no escape.

This picture of Neolithic Europe, wracked by violence, stands in stark contrast to the more rosy view of prehistoric societies that has often prevailed in both popular and academic circles. Cases of unequivocal violence have been accommodated, or dismissed, as unusual cases, isolated events. But with examples mounting up, together with sites that show the extremes of collective violence that were perpetrated, it becomes harder and harder to create a universally peaceable reconstruction of these Stone Age societies. And it looks like the end of the LBK in central Europe was a bloodbath – a widespread crisis – with whole communities massacred and their bodies disposed of in mass graves, with no signs of reverence. The evidence is mounting up that, as the authors of the new report on Schöneck-Kilianstädten put it, 'massacres of entire communities were not isolated occurrences but rather were frequent features' of the early Neolithic in central Europe.

These outbreaks of violence provide us with a picture of the Neolithic that is not always a rural idyll. As the idea and practice of agriculture spread across Europe, it wasn't always peaceful. As populations expanded, pressure on resources may have sparked violent clashes. The first Neolithic colonisers of Britain, loading their families and their livestock onto boats to cross the sea, may have been driven by a spirit of adventure and pioneering zeal, but they could equally have been fleeing from the threat of violent confrontations. And of course, a combination of factors could – and most probably did – play out over decades and centuries.

Once farming communities settled in Britain, there are some examples of people having met violent deaths. There are several examples of decapitated skulls, found in pits and ditches at Neolithic sites in Britain, some with tell-tale signs of injury.

There's nothing comparable to those early Neolithic, LBK mass graves in Britain – though there are some multiple burials where one or more skeletons bear signs of violent injury. One example is Fengate in Norfolk, where a Neolithic grave was found to contain four individuals: a man, a woman and two children. A stone arrowhead was found between the ribs of the man and may have been the cause of his death. But – even if all four individuals were killed – this is violence on a very different scale from those LBK sites in central Europe. At another site, Hambledon Hill in Dorset, just two skeletons were discovered, again with arrowheads among their bones. But the context of these human remains suggests their deaths may have been part of a large-scale violent event. The skeletons were discovered among charred remains of a burnt palisade and the rubble of a collapsed bank of a Neolithic causewayed enclosure.

These glimpses of aggression are important – but rare. They tell us something about the levels of violence in those societies, but they are set apart from standard mortuary practices in the early Neolithic. Those practices – or at least, the ones that leave a trace in the archaeological record – are focused on monuments that are found right across western Europe, including the British Isles: the long barrows.

The first three or four centuries of the fourth millennium BCE were a time of great change in Britain. Clues that a new type of subsistence was taking root appear in the form of sheep teeth and charred cereal grains from archaeological sites: farming had arrived. It's also during these centuries that we see the earliest pottery to be found in Britain, and the appearance of new monuments and architectural features in the landscape: long barrows and, a couple of centuries later, the first causewayed enclosures. These monuments first appear in France and Iberia, around the middle of the fifth millennium BCE, before spreading to Britain. Causewayed enclosures also seem to be an idea imported from mainland Europe. They pop up in Germany, Scandinavia and France – then very quickly spread first to Ireland, and then Britain. They're large enclosures, encircled by a bank and ditch that's interrupted by sections of intact ground – the causeways – that presumably acted as gateways into the enclosure. They're thought to have been used as places for seasonal gatherings – bringing together people who were widely scattered across the landscape – but also, occasionally, for defence. There are around eighty of them in Britain – including that one at Hambledon Hill. And many are associated with long barrows – containing tombs.

Tomb of the Otters

In 2011, I flew up to Orkney – to the island of Ronaldsay, to see a newly discovered Neolithic monument. Just the previous year, at Banks Farm, some construction work near the farmhouse had revealed a previously unknown and undisturbed Neolithic tomb. This new find was just a little over a mile away from the now world-famous 'Tomb of the Eagles' – discovered by another local farmer, back in 1958. When excavated, it was found to contain 16,000 fragments of human bone, representing hundreds of individuals – the largest collection of human remains from any Neolithic tomb in the UK. It also contained hundreds of bones of white-tailed sea-eagles, giving it its evocative name.

The new tomb contained otter bones, and had quickly been dubbed 'Tomb of the Otters'. I was very keen to see this new discovery – it really was a once-in-a-lifetime opportunity to be one of the first to see inside a Neolithic tomb. I drove down to the southern tip of Ronaldsay, to Banks Farm, where I met farmer Hamish Mowatt and archaeologist Dan Lee of the Orkney Research Centre for Archaeology.

Hamish had always thought that the low mound – about 18 metres long and a couple of metres tall – close to his farmhouse was a natural feature. He'd been planning some building work, and was just starting to take down the bank with a JCB digger, when the bucket jarringly scraped against stones. There were large, flat slabs concealed in the top of the mound. When Hamish used the JCB to remove a large stone from the western end – there was a well-like cavity under it.

'I got a torch and shone it in,' said Hamish, ' . . . then you could see the rock face. At that point, you're looking into something that hasn't seen the light of day for thousands of years. The old heart starts to pound a bit then.' Hamish patted his chest and smiled.

'You can't leave it at that point,' he said. 'And then, when I shone the torch around, I saw this eerie, white object – with two holes looking back at me. So I sat back. Then I looked again – and yes, it was definitely a skull.'

'It's a remarkable thing to find – just metres away from your house . . . Yes, it's basically 10 metres away – right by my front door.'

Hamish had wasted no time in contacting local archaeologists, who arrived to inspect the site. As it had been opened, exposing it to the elements and liable to flood – they decided that it was best to excavate. Dan Lee would lead the project. 'We had to move quite quickly as we weren't sure how much the conditions had changed within the tomb,' he explained, 'but we could see that the whole thing was full of water.'

They had to get on with it despite driving rain and gale-force winds. Removing some of the huge slabs that formed its roof, and digging down into the backfill inside the tomb, they could appreciate the full extent of it. And it was big – with an entrance passage leading to central chamber and five cells leading off that.

Eventually, as they dug down close to the original floor of the tomb, they found a jumbled mass of human bones in the central chamber. They partly excavated two of the cells, where skulls and some long bones seemed to have been placed on top of the rubble, perhaps as a final offering or gesture before the tomb was sealed. They dug down through the layers of mud-covered bones – carefully recording the position of each fragment as they lifted it. This was incredibly important – we don't have this sort of information from Neolithic tombs that were excavated by early antiquarians and archaeologists; they removed bones but didn't keep them all, and certainly didn't record precisely where they'd come from in such passage graves. The archaeologists also found that slabs had been laid into the entrance passage as part of the process of closing the tomb, in antiquity. There was otter spraint on the slabs, suggesting the tomb had remained accessible for a period of time – perhaps they were just waiting to place those final bones in the tomb – before being completely sealed off. Layers of grey silt – containing fragments of fish bones, formed from otter spraint – were found inside the cells too. It seemed that otters had made good use of this ready-made holt. Banks Tomb quickly became known as the 'Tomb of the Otters'.

Walking over to the tomb itself, Dan lifted away a heavy stone slab that the archaeologists had lain against the entrance to seal it.

'This is pretty similar to what it looked like when we first saw it,' said Dan, 'with bits of skulls tucked in amongst these stones, almost as a final offering, before this doorway was closed up and the tomb sealed up for good.'

'Amazing to have the opportunity to excavate a pristine site like this,' I said.

'It was amazing. As I excavated, carefully removing each piece of bone, I had this sense of carrying out in reverse those actions carried out five thousand years ago. The wealth of information that we'll learn from this is incredible.'

After the excavation, the skeletal material was taken to the Orkney Research Centre's labs in Kirkwall for initial analysis, and I travelled there with Dan to look at some of the human remains themselves. Knowing that around a quarter of the skulls from the Tomb of the Eagles had shown clear signs of violence, he'd been interested to see if the Tomb of the Otters would turn up anything comparable.

'How many individuals do you think were there, in the tomb?' I asked him.

'So far, we think at least fourteen,' he replied. It looked like a communal burial place for a whole community. That number grew when all the bones were carefully analysed and counted up.

The human remains were extremely well preserved. Dan had set out a few of the skulls, suitably cushioned on bubble wrap, on a bench in the lab – and they were remarkably intact. 'That's perhaps the last skull that was laid in the chamber,' said Dan, pointing out an almost complete skull. I picked it up – it was stained dark, peaty brown. The top of the skull was complete. The upper jaws or maxillae were a little damaged, and the teeth missing, but the orbits – the eye sockets – were intact, and arched over by an impressively jutting brow ridge. Every skull is different, unique, and our faces are built on that underlying framework of bone. I could imagine the face of this person who'd lived and died in Neolithic Orkney.

'Is there any evidence of violence in these remains?' I asked.

'Well, we seem to have less evidence for that here at Banks

than we have from the Tomb of the Eagles, but we need to look more closely at the cranial fragments.'

I looked at the skulls – some were broken, certainly – but those breaks looked like they'd happened some time after the person had died. There wasn't anything that looked convincingly like a fracture.

The close proximity of the two tombs was interesting. Were these two neighbouring farming communities, or was one tomb opened after the other was sealed? Radiocarbon dating should help to resolve such questions. But the human remains from the tomb potentially hold even more information: if the DNA is well preserved in those bones, they represent another opportunity to find out more about who these very early farmers were – and where they'd come from.

It was only early days, but the team was starting to find interesting signs of burial rituals.

'At this stage of the analysis, do you have any idea about whether these remains were placed in the tomb as bones – or as whole bodies?' I asked Dan.

'It's possible we're looking at bodies being taken into the central passage, and being allowed to decompose, before at some point the disarticulated remains get moved into various cells – and become intermingled by later activity. That's what it looks like – all mingled together, a mass of bones, a mass of the ancestors.'

This is a familiar pattern in early Neolithic tombs. The presence of disarticulated skeletons may seem odd to us – but it may have been incidental to the ongoing use of the monument: earlier bodies placed in the tomb get disturbed as later burials are brought in. You often see something similar in medieval cemeteries, where the last interments comprise complete skeletons, with the bones from earlier burials jumbled up and pushed out of the way to accommodate the new arrivals. In a similar way, some long barrows have produced evidence that bodies which were first laid in a passage or entrance may have been moved deeper, or into side chambers, to make room for newer burials. There are particular tombs in Orkney – which do seem to replicate the pattern of domestic dwellings – sub-divided into stalls. Dead bodies seem initially to have been placed, tucked up in a crouched position, on stone or wooden benches in each stall, as though sleeping there. When a new body arrived in the tomb, the remains of the earlier one were pushed to the back of the bench, or swept underneath it. That might have held symbolic meaning, as some archaeologists have suggested – moving the more ancient dead into deeper, colder, darker, more hidden recesses of the tomb. There are a number of ethnographic and archaeological analogies for this type of mortuary practice – from Iron Age 'bench tombs' in Judah to more recent examples from East Africa, Madagascar and China. In those cases, the interaction with the corpse, and its changing state, means that death is seen not so much as a singular event, but as a process. The attitude towards the dead also changes: the recent dead, and their decomposing bodies, are feared; the long dead, reduced to bare bones, revered. Ethnographic comparisons can open our minds to possibilities, but they are not prescriptive. We can't know what was in the minds of those Neolithic people as they moved bodies around inside long barrows. It could have been deeply ritualised and heavy with symbolism. Or it may have been much more practical – and more like those medieval cemeteries. It always reminds me of the University of Birmingham train station, which gets very crowded after the last lectures of the day, with a disembodied voice over the loudspeakers urging us all to MOVE ALONG THE PLATFORM!

Most of the human remains placed in these early Neolithic tombs – from Orkney to southern Britain – appear to have started out as whole bodies, with bones later moved around. But some remains bear witness to corpses having been defleshed – some deliberately cut up with stone knives, leaving tell-tale cut marks; some left to decompose naturally. We need to remind ourselves once again that although this practice seems deeply strange to us – it was most likely business as usual. And there are modern examples of cultures where exposure of corpses is still practiced: the 'sky burials' of Tibet, and Parsi 'Towers of Silence' in India. In both those examples, the primary agents of excarnation are carrion birds. There are some examples of raised, timber structures that have been interpreted as excarnation platforms in Britain, some associated with funerary monuments, others with water. But there's also evidence that some bodies were left out at ground level and scavenged by animals such as wolves. There are many sites with bones that have been gnawed by carnivores, and it's possible that this was even encouraged. There's a curious (again, to most of *us*) ethnographic example of something similar to this among the Nandi of Kenya, who used to leave dead bodies out to be eaten by hyenas, in the belief that this would release the heart of the deceased to travel to the land of spirits.

A striking example of carnivore scavenging comes from a chambered monument in the Cotswolds, Adlestrop Barrow, excavated in the 1930s. Around a fifth of the bones have been punctured, gnawed or scraped by carnivore teeth. Looking at the material in a different way, it represents at least three adults and four juveniles – and every corpse showed some signs of having been scavenged. Using evidence from experiments where wolves were observed consuming deer carcasses, archaeologists have been able to interpret these remains from Adlestrop. The pattern is what you'd expect if bodies were left exposed for just a limited time – before they were completely broken up and scattered, and before the bones became at all weathered by the elements. After that exposure and excarnation, it seems the remaining body parts were collected up and transferred to the barrow. At some sites, a different method of defleshing has been suggested, involving burying bodies and then, later, digging them up to be re-interred in long barrows. This interpretation comes mainly from a conspicuous absence of extremities – hand and foot bones – in some skeletal assemblages, and also from a lack of weathering on the surface of the bones. But once again, it's hard to be secure about such an interpretation if it's based on material excavated before more modern standards of digging and recording came along.

Once human remains ended up in a long barrow – whether as whole bodies or individual bones or body parts – there seems to be no guarantee they'd be left in peace. Bones seem to have been cleared away to make room for new bodies, but there are many examples where something even more intriguing seems to have been happening. Bones appear to have been rearranged, taken out, and sometimes put back. Now, it's certainly true that some bones may have just got mixed up with others by accident in antiquity; and it's also true that some 'missing' bones may have disappeared relatively recently. Historical records suggest that antiquarians were not at all averse to collecting specimens, even trophies, from their sites. But the numbers and proportions of bones found in the tombs suggest that some purposeful movement of certain elements was going on. And some arrangements seem very deliberate – such as the finger bones stuck into the nasal aperture of the skull from Belas Knap in Wiltshire, or the careful arrangement of skulls around the edge of a chamber at Lanhill. Even stranger examples have emerged from Scandinavian passage graves – such as four human teeth inserted into sockets drilled into an ankle bone. These arrangements all seem very odd to us, but presumably they made some kind of sense at the time.

In some long barrows, it seems that efforts were made to keep all the parts of one individual together, with skeletons assembled into discrete piles. But at other times, it seems that bones are being taken from more than one individual in an attempt to reconstruct a generic skeleton. (This reminds me of the summers in the Anatomy Department at Bristol University, where I used to teach. The students all went away for two months, leaving us time to do research but also prepare and repair all the teaching material ready for the next term. One of the necessary jobs was always to tidy up the 'hanging skeletons' that stood at each teaching station – which were not plastic replicas but real bone. Over the year, fingers, toes and sometimes whole limbs would drop off. Sometimes it was possible to reunite the original limb or digit with the skeleton, or else it would get a repair from a box of unidentified 'spare parts'. We always thought we were doing something very practical, but it also *felt right*.) In those Neolithic tombs, it's been suggested that the creation of a 'composite ancestor' like this might represent an idea about the anonymity of the dead. In fact, there's been a suggestion around for a long time that some of this deconstruction of bodies and moving around of body parts was quite purposefully about 'anonymising' the dead and stripping away their individual identity – reducing them to elements so that they became part of an amorphous mass of The Dead, The Ancestors. Some Swedish archaeologists had suggested a similar interpretation of passage graves in Scandinavia, contending that secondary burial practice had taken place, with the deposition of dry bones in those tombs, showing that individual identities were being subsumed into an ancestor collective. But analysis of more newly excavated material – without all the problems attending tombs dug in antiquity – has suggested that whole bodies were interred, decaying and falling apart over time. In that case, it seemed that individual personhood was being preserved in death.

In the end, of course, it may not be that one or the other practice – fragmented skeletons or burials of whole bodies – held sway across wide geographic expanses and through time. Both may have pertained in different times and places. Mortuary practices are very likely to have varied from place to place throughout the time-span of the early Neolithic. (That ankle bone with teeth, from Denmark, being a particularly eclectic example of a practice seen nowhere else.)

An important note about the people of the long barrows is that we're only seeing a tiny proportion of the Neolithic population of Britain in the burials in those tombs. Estimates of the population of Britain in the Neolithic range from 10,000 to 100,000 – we're only seeing a fraction of those. Although it's those skeletons and bones contained in the passages and alcoves of chambered tombs that tended to draw the eye of early archaeologists, more recent excavations have uncovered quantities of cremated bone. Reassessment of material from those old digs has revealed cremated bone that was missed at the time of excavation. Among early passage graves in North Wales and Ireland, more contain cremations than inhumations.

Some cremated remains are definitely later additions – inserted into tombs in the later Neolithic, or the Bronze Age. But radio-carbon dating means that we can be sure that some were there from the early Neolithic.

It's possible, perhaps even likely, that cremation was in fact a much more common burial rite than whole-body deposition in long barrows in the Neolithic. If it was normal for cremated remains to be scattered or placed into water – as well as excar-nation rites without secondary burial, perhaps – that would explain where all those 'missing dead' might have disappeared to. Perhaps only certain individuals were accorded the special treatment of being interred – either as cremated remains or as whole bodies.

Many archaeologists have suggested that long barrows may have been 'family plots' for elite members of Neolithic soci-ety. Some in the early twentieth century believed that they could detect family resemblances in the skulls from several long barrows. But more recent analysis has cast some doubt on those interpretations. Shared occurrences of congenital pathology – such as premature fusion of cranial sutures, cleft palate and spina bifida – have also been put forward as suggest-ing familial connections between individuals buried together in the same, or nearby tombs. These are more persuasive, but still not conclusive.

It's difficult to be sure of ratios of men and women buried in these tombs, as the remains are often so fragmentary, but it looks like males may outnumber females, by around three to two. Youngsters defined as 'subadults' (aged twelve to twenty) by biological anthropologists make up around a fifth of the skeletal dead. So – we could be looking at families.

This is certainly a question that ancient DNA holds the

power to answer. It shouldn't be long before we know whether most long barrows really were family tombs. Some results have already been forthcoming. One very recent study presented the results of genome analyses on twenty-four individuals from five megalithic burial sites. The genetic data supported a higher male-to-female ratio in those tombs. The diversity of mitochondrial DNA was greater than the variation in Y chromosomes. This is what you'd expect to see in a society which tended to patrilocal – where sons tend to stay in the group of their birth, while daughters leave and join other groups. But there's an important note of caution to be sounded here – as this pattern might reflect a social system deeper in the past, rather than the one operating at the time these individuals were alive. We inherit our DNA from earlier ancestors, after all.

The fine detail is where it starts to get really interesting, though. Two individuals buried at Primrose Grange in Ireland were revealed to be a father and daughter. And there was another close relative in that tomb – either a half-sibling or double-cousin of the daughter. But there was also a genetic connection between two males buried in separate tombs – Primrose Grange and Carrowmore – 2 miles apart. The two men were most probably father and son. A link between two other males from a tomb in Gotland probably represents a grandfather–grandson or uncle–nephew relationship. And recent DNA analysis of two individuals buried in an earthen long barrow at Trumpington Meadows, Cambridgeshire revealed that they were brothers, their DNA also telling us something about their appearance as well: they both had brown eyes, brown hair, and quite brown skin. Hot off the press, analyses of ancient DNA from individuals buried in Fussell's Lodge long barrow, in Wiltshire, and Hazleton North long barrow, in Gloucestershire, have also revealed kinship ties between individuals in those tombs.

Even hotter off the press is the extremely intriguing new genetic revelation from the iconic Neolithic tomb of Newgrange in Ireland – where a family seems to have collapsed in on itself. The genes of a middle-aged man laid in the centre of this huge tomb in 3200 BCE bore witness to his parents having been first-degree relatives – either parent and child, or brother and sister. His genetic heritage is also, very clearly, linked to that mass migration that brought farming with it, arriving in Ireland around 3700 BCE. The geneticists who produced this evidence of incestuous union believe that it could point to the existence of a hereditary elite: a ruling dynasty. Incest is an almost universal taboo across human cultures – with the important exception of political, religious elites: royal families, in other words. There are examples of incest in ruling dynasties around the world – from ancient Egypt to the Inca Empire and ancient Hawaii. Incest could be a way of 'keeping it in the family' – maintaining a very tight control over inherited power and bloodlines. 'I believe we're seeing a similar social dynamic at play among colonists of Neolithic Ireland,' said Lara Cassidy, geneticist and lead author on the Newgrange paper. Remarkably, a medieval Irish myth tells of a tribe of gods who built the passage tombs – with one builder-king restarting the rising and setting of the sun by having sex with his sister. The geneticists doubt that such a story could really have lasted so many thousands of years – but mention it nonetheless, as a tantalising parallel to their new genetic story. And then there's the fact that the Irish name for the Dowth passage tomb, Fertae Chuile, literally means, 'Hill of Sin' or 'Hill of Incest'. That seems a lot of smoke, if there's no fire. But we must try not to let our imaginations run wild. The dependable science is exciting enough, on its own.

Although the headlines following the publication of that study were – of course – grabbed by that evidence of incest in one man, the study was much larger, looking at forty-one other whole genomes from many different types of Neolithic tomb in Ireland, comparing these with other data from Ireland, Britain and continental Europe. They also analysed a couple of Mesolithic genomes, showing that Ireland had been very isolated at that time – with very little evidence for coming and going across the Irish Sea. The arrival of the Neolithic was very much the beginning of a new relationship with Britain, with maritime connections being established. And whereas there's a diehard old theory about Iberian connections, the main flow of people from the continent into Britain and Ireland seems to be – on the basis of archaeology and genetics – via northern France. Once again, the Irish Neolithic appears very much as a movement of people – not the diffusion of an idea. And although one genome, from Parknabinnia court tomb in County Clare, bore evidence of hunter-gatherer ancestry – the Mesolithic genetic signature of Ireland almost completely disappeared over just a few generations.

The geneticists found no further evidence of close kinship ties in the Neolithic tombs, beyond those that had already been identified in Ireland, but what they did discover were individuals linked by more distant genetic ties, across large distances. People buried in passage tombs in Carrowmore and Carrowkeel in County Sligo were found to be distant relatives of others buried 150 kilometres away at Brú na Bóinne. This suggests a coherent community of people, who were related, across a wide landscape – once again supporting that idea of a ruling elite. They also found, in the DNA of a baby boy from Poulnabrone portal tomb, the earliest evidence for a person with Down syndrome ever found, dating to around 3500 BCE.

The genomic evidence is starting to pour in, and already we're getting glimpses of what looks like a stratified – possibly patrilineal – society in Britain and Ireland, building Neolithic, often megalithic, family tombs that continued to be used across generations. This idea of a hierarchical society, dominated by certain powerful families, stands in stark opposition to the old theory of egalitarian Neolithic communities, with the dead anonymised in communal tombs. The houses of the living in the Neolithic show apparently very little variation – no real evidence of hierarchy. And yet, in death, we seem to be learning that some families were 'more equal' than others.

Once again, though, it's a complex picture – and there are exceptions to the rule. We have to be very wary of seeking one-size-fits-all explanations for all archaeological signatures, everywhere. At a late Neolithic tomb in Isbister, Orkney, for example, there's a striking *lack* of family connections between interred individuals. As always, we should avoid looking for evidence which *supports* a particular hypothesis – submitting to a tendency we all have towards confirmation bias; it's just not a very scientific thing to do. People from particular families may have been more likely to be buried in a certain tomb – but we clearly can't extrapolate that to all tombs and all times. The era of ancient genomics, though, suddenly provides us with the opportunity to explore these questions of hierarchy and kinship in a very detailed way that has simply not been possible before: tomb by tomb, hill by hill, valley by valley.

Whoever was buried in them, though, those Neolithic tombs

had a surprising origin, as some astonishing new discoveries reveal.

A House for the Dead

Long barrows, these great mounds of stone and earth, so often contain chambers, with human remains found inside, that they have become thought of as purely funerary monuments, tombs.

In the mid-twentieth century, archaeologists were drawing comparisons between early Neolithic, LBK houses – which were large timber constructions on a trapezoidal plan – and the shape of Neolithic tombs in northwest Europe. The long barrows seemed to represent a 'petrified house' – a wooden 'House of the Living' transmuted into a stone 'House of the Dead'. Inside those Houses of the Dead, the skeletalised remains of ancestors abide – not buried or burned, but simply contained in chambers, just as living people are accommodated in their houses.

This may seem like an odd idea, but it's echoed in some modern cultures. The Serer people of Senegal bury their dead *in* their houses. They take all, or sometimes just part, of the deceased's house to the cemetery, where it is placed in a pit, along with the dead body. Everything is covered over with a mound of soil. Eventually the house rots away and the roof caves in, leaving just a slight mound marking the grave.

This theory about Houses of the Dead was doubted for a while, as there seemed to be too long a gap between the trapezoidal timber houses from LBK sites in central Europe and the appearance of the long mounds in the west. But well-dated sites from France have closed that gap, showing that similar trapezoidal buildings – which seem to be a continuation of that LBK tradition – were being constructed well into the fifth millennium, with the first long barrows or mounds being constructed very shortly after. The connection with earlier LBK houses further east in central Europe may not wholly explain the source of the idea behind the megalithic monuments, though. Mesolithic hunter-gatherers along the Atlantic coast of France sometimes buried their dead under mounds, along with 'domestic refuse' – suggesting a simple dwelling, perhaps a hut or even a tipi, may have been used as a tomb, covered over to form a burial mound. So, from a local perspective, this could have been an elaboration of an existing idea and ritual, rather than a completely new import. As a further complication in all of this, the Neolithic tombs and the buildings they were echoing may not have been simply domestic dwellings. Some archaeologists have suggested that the large buildings that the megalithic tombs replicated in stone were used as granaries. So perhaps there's also some idea of a sacred store, consecrated by the presence of the dead, ensuring life for future generations.

After the early megalithic tombs of the Atlantic seaboard, with their trapezoidal plans, building styles vary and diversify – taking in quadrangular buildings, round buildings with corbelled roofs, and very long buildings, up to 100 metres in length – but there still seems to be some correspondence between the architecture of houses containing living bodies and those containing the dead.

Recent excavations in Britain have revealed an even more direct, tangible connection between houses and long barrows. At Dorstone Hill in southwest Herefordshire, an unusual feature in the landscape was recognised as anthropogenic back in the 1960s, and has intrigued archaeologists ever since. A natural ridge between the Dore and Wye Valleys was extended by three artificial, earthen banks, potentially flanking the entrance to a causewayed enclosure on the hilltop. But there was something odd: there were banks – but no sign of the ditches which usually accompany them.

In 2011, Julian Thomas from the University of Manchester assembled a team and began a campaign of excavation at Dorstone Hill, to get to the bottom of the monuments there, quite literally. It soon became apparent that the 'banks' weren't part of an enclosure at all. Instead, they were long barrows. Long-forgotten, long-overlooked long barrows. And this was exciting, as so many of these monuments have been disturbed through time, going right back to the Romans. As cairns, they were a good source of building material, and there were probably rumours of treasure buried in them as well. More recently, antiquarians and early archaeologists attacked them with shovels, far less careful in their excavation and recording than modern standards dictate.

So the untouched early long barrows at Dorstone Hill offered a real chance to understand how and why such funerary monuments were constructed. But as the archaeologists dug down through the longest mound, they found something very curious indeed. At first, the anatomy of the barrow seemed familiar: a mound of stone, containing a stone-lined cist. But under that stone was a mound of earth, and under that – a mass of burnt clay. This was the physical manifestation of what the archaeologists had already picked up with geophysical survey and magnetic susceptibility readings, which had both indicated very intense burning. The archaeologists went on to investigate a second and third mound and found the same thing: a deep layer of burnt clay. Not only that, but pieces of charred timber as well. And in one barrow – enormous postholes. Julian realised that what they'd found were the burnt remains of a huge timber hall, from the early Neolithic.

It was a completely unexpected discovery. Starting out thinking that they were investigating a funerary monument, a burial mound, the archaeologists had instead uncovered an actual building. Dorstone Hill was unique in Britain when it was discovered, though some potentially similar examples existed in neighbouring countries. There are some French examples of Neolithic wooden long houses being replaced by cemeteries over time, and an excavation of a cairn at Ballyglass in Ireland turned up the remains of a burnt timber building underneath it. When Dorstone Hill was reported, archae-ologists wondered how many other examples might have been missed, among all the barrows that had been rather too thoroughly dug out in antiquity. But before long, something similar turned up – at another long barrow that had escaped the antiquarian's shovels, this time in Wiltshire. This second site was excavated in the summer of 2017, by a team from the University of Reading, led by Jim Leary. And a few months later, I met up with both Julian and Jim to find out how their discoveries were forcing us to think very differently about the earliest Neolithic long barrows.

'For decades, we may have been misunderstanding some of our most important prehistoric monuments,' Julian told me. 'Far from being set out as places for the dead, they were all about commemorating places of the living.'

He showed me photographs from his excavations at Dorstone Hill. The preservation of the timber was really extraordinary. Within the mass of burnt daub and clay were sizeable pieces of charred timber – you could see the grain of the wood, and even some examples of carpentry. Julian pointed out a forked piece of timber with a peg through it. 'We've got mortices, pegs – this was sophisticated carpentry and timber architecture,' he said.

Aside from those charred timbers, I was astonished by the size of the postholes they'd found. There were four huge holes, two of them slightly smaller (but still massive) and closer together, and a pair of larger ones, together forming a trapezoid. Such huge wooden posts – the size of whole tree trunks – could have easily supported a two-storey structure. The hall would have been large – 8 metres wide, judging by those postholes – and could well have extended to be almost as long as the mounds them-selves – 30 and 70 metres long, respectively. Charred, angled roof timbers – probably oak – suggested the roof may have been cruck-framed, similar to much later medieval barns and halls. It would have been a really substantial timber building, presumably with a thatched roof. It's quite incredible to think that this style of architecture has such ancient roots, stretching back thousands of years into the Neolithic.

Other halls like this – though none concealed underneath long barrows – are known from Britain. They date to the very earliest centuries of the Neolithic – so they seem to have arrived with the first farmers and before causewayed enclosures began to be built. But Julian and his team were the first to find one under a long barrow.

They soon discovered that the second mound at Dorstone Hill had also contained a timber hall – and both buildings had been similarly burned down before being 'interred' under mounds. The date of the burning of the timber hall places it right at the beginning of the British Neolithic, in the early centuries of the fourth millennium BCE. It seems that the conflagrations were far from accidental; Julian believed the burning to be an impor-tant part of the ritual process that transformed the hall from a functioning space for the living into a monument in the landscape. The burnt remains of each building were shovelled in and piled up, then covered with earth, retained by a timber palisade.

Much later, the archaeology showed how the mounds had been remodelled – covered over with stone to become cairns, with passages and stone-lined cists dug into them – probably around 3500 BCE. No human remains had survived, but both mounds contained features that Julian interpreted as mortuary chambers. But that was very much a later adaptation of an existing monument in the landscape.

This discovery at Dorstone Hill was clearly important, but there was always the possibility that these burned and buried timber halls were something quirky and local, rather than part of a more widespread ritual practice.

Then, in 2017, Jim Leary and his team started digging their site in the Vale of Pewsey, halfway between the iconic sites of Stonehenge and Avebury. The location was a place with a curious name: Cat's Brain. This is generally accepted as having nothing to do with cats at all, but instead refers to the type of soil: *cattes brazen* meaning 'stony, clay soil'.

(I was somewhat doubtful about this and checked it with my friend, Dr Janina Ramirez, an afficonado of Old English and its hidden meanings. And she thought there may be something feline about the name after all. *Cattes brazen* means a brassy (ginger) cat. Ginger toms are known for their stubbornness – and of course we still use the word 'brazen' in that way. So 'ginger cat' land could be a good description for stubborn soil, thick with yellow clay and stones. Catching at the plough – but, once ploughed, leaving a hillside looking like the back of a ginger tomcat.)

The potential of the site – and an intimation of what lay beneath that stony clay – had first been recognised from an aerial survey, using a drone. The archaeologists followed up with geophysical scans of the ground, which revealed what appeared to be a previously unrecognised long barrow, ploughed almost flat over the centuries. It was at least fifty years since any long barrow had been excavated in Wiltshire. Jim realised the site represented a very precious chance to carefully excavate an archaeologically untouched long barrow, using modern archaeological techniques – if anything of the barrow survived beyond that ghost they'd picked up on the geophysics, that was.

Jim Leary embarked on his dig, accompanied by a horde of university students – on what must have been one of the most exciting training digs in the country. And as soon as they started to excavate, removing the overlying topsoil, their hopes were fulfilled. There were clear features to be seen, starkly standing out in brown earth against the chalk bedrock.

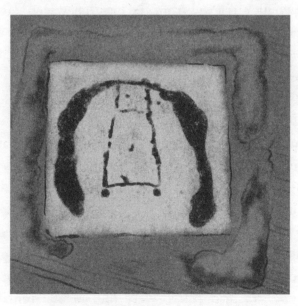

'Did you have any idea you were going to find that level of preservation when you took that top layer of soil off?' I asked Jim.

'No, none at all,' he replied. 'To find anything was extraordinary.' The plough soil was incredibly shallow in the field – the features lay just a foot below the surface. The most prominent was a horseshoe-shaped ditch – outlining the perimeter of the barrow – and inside it, a long, trapezoidal shape. They'd got another one – another building sealed under a barrow. 'The hairs on the back of my neck stood up,' said Jim. 'I knew at once we'd found a building – a large, early Neolithic timber hall. Not some kind of replica – but an actual building.'

Jim and his team went on to investigate the features, systematically excavating the soil from ditches and pits. The finds were coming out thick and fast: pottery, animal bone – and very typical Neolithic flint arrowheads, dating to around 3500 BCE. Jim showed me some particularly intriguing finds – large blocks of chalk retrieved from the pits. They were covered in grooves; I held one in my hand.

'This looks very deliberately made,' I remarked. 'And it looks like a rune. It looks like writing?'

'Well, the surface has been smoothed and then they've inscribed it with the markings,' said Jim, 'and these clearly had some symbolic importance to the community. That was deposited in one of those postholes. The whole building is imbued with that symbolism.'

Once again – as so often in prehistoric archaeology – the meaning of those symbols may be lost, but they were clearly significant to the person who made them.

But there were no burials in this long barrow – not a single human bone; instead, there were the skeletal remains of a timber hall in the form of postholes and beam-slots. Cat's Brain was an odd site, not at all what you'd expect from a Neolithic long barrow – had it not been, of course, for that earlier discovery at Dorstone Hill.

'We have this idea that long mounds are just cemeteries, just where people buried their dead,' said Julian. 'But each of the mounds at Dorstone Hill – and at Cat's Brain – was constructed over the remains of a building. It's not just that we're dealing with a tomb of the people; it's the tomb of the house. A transformation of a "building for the living" into a House for the Dead.'

These new discoveries suggested that the concept and use of the long barrow as a funerary monument may have been a later add-on. With these early barrows at least, the idea wasn't just to echo the form of a house in the construction of a tomb – the monument had actually started off as a timber hall, with the later mound being thrown up over the burnt remains of the building. It's a completely new perspective on the original function and meaning of these mounds. It may well be that other early Neolithic long barrows had similar origins – it's just that they have never been investigated as carefully or thoroughly.

The timber halls under the mounds were clearly once huge buildings, even by modern standards. 'Do you think it's significant that this was a time when people were becoming more settled in the landscape?' I asked him.

'Yes, I do,' he replied. 'And society is changing – they're forming larger, more complex communities, and one of the ways in which they could draw these communities together would be through a collective act of building something – which then serves as a symbol of the community. That's what these huge halls are.'

I always find this a really interesting perspective on the

purpose of ancient monuments – that the meaning of them doesn't just lie in their function once they are made, but also in their *making*. Similar arguments are put forward for the creation of megalithic monuments such as Stonehenge and Avebury. Building those huge timber halls, and those iconic stone circles, would have been a communal effort, bringing people together. (It makes you think differently, perhaps, about some of the big collaborative projects we have going right now. Archaeologists and anthropologists in the future may consider that the primary function, the real importance, of something like CERN was not actually to produce discoveries in nuclear physics, but to bring lots of people together, to create a scientific community.)

It's interesting to think about how our ancestors' relationship with the land, with territory, must have changed when that transition to a farming way of life took place. There are signs that Mesolithic hunter-gatherers were a little more settled in the landscape than their Palaeolithic predecessors, returning to places on such a regular basis that it was worth building permanent houses, rather than just more ephemeral shelters. But it's still likely that they occupied those dwellings in a seasonal way, moving from winter to summer camps, following the migrations of herds of animals. Their Neolithic, farming successors, on the other hand, were putting down roots – settling in the landscape, staying put in a place where they could tend their fields, their flocks and their herds. Perhaps the timber halls at the inception of the Neolithic helped to create a sense of community as well as a sense of belonging – within a particular landscape. And perhaps that spirit of collaboration was important for defusing the kind of tensions that could too easily spiral into conflict, ending with massacres like those we see in the LBK mass grave sites.

'I think the house symbolises something very important,' said Jim. 'It's more than just the household – it's a wider community. These are the pioneers. These are our country's first farmers, with the first domesticated species here. Out of this landscape, they're hewing out their society and identity – and all of that is represented in the building.'

'Do you think they're somehow commemorating that change in lifestyle, too?' I suggested.

Julian agreed. 'Yes – it's this moment of change that people surely remember, for many, many generations afterwards. So first of all, you build the halls, then you burn those halls down. You transform them into long mounds, then those long mounds attract further activity. People come and dig pits into the mounds and place objects like beautiful polished axes into them. And then there are more cremation burials, in pits in the long mounds.'

It's possible that the long barrow even represented a family or lineage – in the way that we sometimes still use the word 'House' today. 'To throw in a *Game of Thrones* reference,' said Jim, with a glint in his eye, 'think about House Tyrell or House Lannister, for example – or, historically, the House of York.' If that was true, then these monuments could have represented some sort of ancestral connection and claim to the land. And then it's easy to see how the function of the barrows – as funerary monuments – could have developed out of that idea. Placing the remains of the dead in the barrows may have symbolised that connection to ancestors, to the 'founding farmers' of the Neolithic, to the landscape – perhaps, even, a sense of territory.

Historically, some archaeologists have interpreted long barrows as principally religious sites – 'tomb-shrines' that could act as repositories for the dead and a focus for rituals. Others have seen them in more starkly economic terms, demonstrating an ancestral claim to territory – farmers carving up the landscape between them. In reality, it may be impossible to separate those ritual and economic imperatives. But with these new insights from Dorstone Hill and Cat's Brain, we can at least say that the function of long barrows as tombs came later. The origins of those early barrows suggests they started as a very visible way of venerating the house or hall itself – as a representation of the first farmers.

Julian summed it up. 'Everything that happens on this hilltop is venerating, remembering, thinking back to that moment of inception.'

Arrivals

But who *were* those early farmers in Britain? Were they the descendants of Mesolithic hunter-gatherers who cottoned on to a new idea from continental Europe? We know that those Mesolithic people had seafaring capabilities, so the North Sea, Channel and Irish Sea were never a barrier to the flow of movement, materials and people. Or was there a large-scale migration into Britain and Ireland – and a more wholesale population replacement?

In 1954, Stuart Piggott published his seminal *Neolithic Cultures of the British Isles*, in which he collected together all the evidence then available – albeit in the absence of the firm dates that would very soon be supplied by radiocarbon dating – to suggest how the Neolithic transition had come about in Britain. He imagined that the transition had begun with a large influx of colonisers, bringing their domestic species with them. Once those primary Neolithic cultures were established, indigenous hunter-gatherers then started to adopt the new lifestyle.

But in reality, questions about the nature of the transition have been impossible to answer, when all we could draw on were bones, artefacts and architecture.

Early archaeologists like Pitt Rivers tried to tackle such questions by comparing the shape of skulls through time. But in the twentieth century, craniometry became disastrously mired in racism and fascism. The bones were deemed untrustworthy; too difficult to interpret and too easy to misinterpret. Stuart Piggott thought that biological anthropology had nothing to offer regarding insights into the origin of the Neolithic, certainly. He looked at changing burial practices – but not the bones themselves. By the 1970s, though, biological anthropology had moved on, developing a more scientific basis. Forensic techniques were applied to the analysis of archaeological human remains. Anthropologists like the pioneering Don Brothwell began to shift their focus from individual case studies to whole populations. But efforts to understand what was happening with British populations during the Neolithic were hampered by the fact that detailed records were lacking for many of the long barrows that had been investigated by early antiquarians and early archaeologists.

So – what can we tell from artefacts and architecture? A profound and widespread culture change could suggest the arrival of a new population in an area – and that idea, the old culture-history paradigm, held sway in archaeology for many decades. But culture isn't tied to people like that. Ideas can pass horizontally between populations. Your biological ancestry doesn't determine what stone tools you make, what pottery styles you create, or whether you're a hunter or a farmer. But it does determine your genetic make-up. With the advent of ancient DNA technology, we are now able to probe these questions about cultural change and population movements in a way that's never been possible before. Sequencing ancient genomes allows us to test our ideas about the past, to understand what was really going on when we see a cultural change like the Neolithic rippling out across the landscape. Was it a movement of people or ideas? Does Stuart Piggot's model stand up to scrutiny, more than seventy years on? With advances in genetics – and particularly in ancient genomics – we're finally finding ourselves in a position to answer these questions.

Early genetic studies drew on variation in mitochondrial DNA and in sections of the Y chromosome. These relatively short stretches of DNA were small samples – but still thought to contain useful clues. Looking at variation in these samples of DNA across Europe today, geneticists suggested that the spread of Neolithic culture from the Near East was driven by a population expansion that saw the original hunter-gatherer population of the region largely replaced.

Ten years ago, Pontus Skoglund was working in a Department of Evolutionary Biology in his Swedish homeland. Rather than looking at variation in small pieces of modern DNA, from living people, Pontus wanted to approach the question more directly – using DNA from ancient remains. The archaeological record of the Neolithic in Scandinavia is similar to that in Britain: farming arrives some 6,000 years ago, and then there's at least a millennium where farming communities and hunter-gatherer groups are co-existing in the broad landscape. Pontus and his colleagues managed to extract and sequence DNA from four individuals who had lived and died 5,000 years ago in Scandinavia. Three had been interred in typical hunter-gatherer graves on the island of Gotland, while the farmer's remains were from a megalithic tomb. They analysed key points in the genome that are known to vary, and compared the ancient DNA in their samples with a database of modern DNA. Pontus and his co-authors published their results in *Science* in 2012. They had discovered that the Scandinavian hunter-gatherers they sampled shared a majority of genetic variants with northern Europeans today, whereas the farmer possessed more variants found in the eastern Mediterranean, in Greece and Cyprus. It seemed there really had been a migration – and that farmers and hunter-gatherers had stayed largely separate in northwest Europe, isolated from each other, for a thousand years. A few years later, another group published ancient genome data for five Neolithic individuals from Greece and Turkey – strengthening the link between those early farmers in the eastern Mediterranean with the spread of farming communities westwards, across Europe. It's now clear that migration played an important role in the Neolithic transition – that this was a movement of people, with ideas. Genetics has allowed us to map out that migration, providing us with an unbroken trail from the Aegean to the shores of the Atlantic Ocean.

But how did the Neolithic transition play out in Britain? What was the role of migration here – and how quickly did Mesolithic hunter-gatherers start to mix with the incomers, with their weird, new ways and their weird, new animals? The only way to resolve those questions is with local DNA samples – and over the past few years, several studies have begun to provide us with insights.

One research group surveyed genome-wide data from sixty-seven British Neolithic individuals, and – for the first time – also gave us a glimpse of the genetic landscape of the Mesolithic, with the sequencing of six hunter-gatherer genomes. The Mesolithic genomes were interesting in their own right, as the hunter-gatherers of Scandinavia and Western Europe were already known to be quite distinct genetically – but no one knew whether Britons would share more ancestry with one of these groups over the other. The six hunter-gatherer genomes in that sample included our old friend Cheddar Man (this being the self-same analysis that allowed the prediction of his skin, eye and hair colour), and they all turned out to be most closely related to the western European group. The results from the Neolithic individuals were fascinating – there clearly had been some mixing with local hunter-gatherers as the first farmers arrived, but a whopping 75 per cent of their ancestry was derived ultimately from Anatolian Neolithic farmers. This was the same pattern that had already been demonstrated in early Neolithic populations in central Europe and Iberia.

The Anatolian farmer ancestry in British genomes doesn't mean that farmers travelled all the way from the eastern Mediterranean to western Europe and Britain in a lifetime or two. This is where I think our language fails us. When we talk about ancient migrations, we're often speaking of people moving significant distances in a lifetime. The diaspora that underpins the spread of the Neolithic was much slower – a population expansion that extended over many generations, and thousands of years. And there are two main routes for this slow expansion and colonisation: along the Mediterranean coasts; and through central Europe, along the Danube corridor. Careful comparison of genomes suggests that most of the ancestry of the first farmers arriving in Britain – perhaps two thirds – maps onto that Mediterranean route, reaching

Iberia in the far west, before spreading northwards. In a very satisfying way, this echoes the origin and spread of megalithic tombs – with striking similarities in the dolmens and passage graves all the way from Iberia through France, Britain, Ireland and Scandinavia.

In the north of France, farmers with Mediterranean ancestry would have mixed with farmers of central European descent. The first farmers would have crossed the water to reach Britain from northern France, Belgium and the Netherlands, bringing that mixed ancestry with them.

Genome studies showed that early Neolithic Iberians had already mixed with local hunter-gatherers – so it may be that most of the Mesolithic ancestry detected in British Neolithic genomes came in with the first farmers themselves, with actually very little mixing happening in Britain. But this is very broad brush. With a large sample of Neolithic farmers from across Britain, the geneticists could see that there was geographic variation. In the west, Welsh famers had relatively little hunter-gatherer ancestry – and what was present could have already been there, in the genomes of the first farmers arriving to settle in Britain. Neolithic people in the southeast of England and Scotland had higher proportions of Mesolithic ancestry – so there might have been a little more mixing with local hunter-gatherers in the north and east. There seems to be an exception in western Scotland, though, where geneticists have found evidence of Neolithic individuals whose genomes suggest they had 'Mesolithic' ancestry within the last three generations – perhaps some of their great-grandparents were hunter-gatherers – probably within Britain. That might reflect different densities of populations across Britain – there may have been more hunter-gatherers living in western Scotland when the first farmers arrived there. Across the rest of Britain, there's less evidence of mixing. Preliminary results from Banks Tomb (the 'Tomb of the Otters') on Orkney suggest that those farmers fit into this pattern – their ancestry contains links connecting them back to those very early farmers in the eastern Mediterranean.

So, it seems that Stuart Piggott was right in one respect: the Neolithic transition in Britain was overwhelmingly mediated by immigration. As for that later adoption of agriculture by British hunter-gatherers, and the merging of the two groups – there's precious little evidence for that in the ancient DNA. Quite importantly, there's no evidence for increased hunter-gatherer ancestry in Neolithic Britain over time. This is different from the picture in continental Europe, where early farming communities and hunter-gatherers seem to stay genetically isolated for up to a couple of millennia – then hunter-gatherer populations become slowly mixed in. There's little evidence for that happening in Britain, where the Neolithic transition seems to have involved an almost complete population replacement. And indeed, this fits with what we find archaeologically. In Scotland, there's evidence for hunter-fisher-gatherers co-existing with farmers for a few centuries – before disappearing from the archaeological record. But in most places, the arrival of farming – of farmers themselves – means the end of a way of life that had sustained humans for hundreds of thousands of years. The future was: farming.

6.

AT SALISBURY MUSEUM, 8 JULY 2019

Bristol Temple Meads to Salisbury – just over an hour on a three-carriage train. Through Bath, that Georgian gem of the Avon Valley, with its Victorian railway station that tempts you to step off and spend some time among the ancient stones of the baths – reimagined in the modern spa delights of Thermae Bath Spa with its rooftop pool – and all those knowingly expensive shops selling all sorts of things you probably never needed. Through the Box tunnel – announcing itself so impressively with its castle-like portals, said to be aligned with the rising sun on Brunel's birthday. (It is, unfortunately, just a delightful rumour.) And over so quickly. It was the longest railway tunnel ever created when it opened in 1841. But now it's just a brief distraction from the sun-drenched landscape. Less than 2 miles long; less than two minutes of being plunged into the dark recesses of Box Hill. Then out – and onwards.

Sooner than I always expect, I'm stepping off the train onto the platform at Salisbury. Then I navigate my way down to the riverbank and meander towards the museum. I stop to snap two swans on my phone – arranging themselves perfectly symmetrically, framed by two arches of Crane Bridge. I'm so pleased with the image, I share it on Instagram immediately: 'Cygnine symmetry in Salisbury'. Some kind of bridge has existed here since at least 1300; its latest stone setting dates back to the end of the nineteenth century.

Salisbury Museum is easy to find, as someone has very helpfully placed an enormous stone spire close to it as a signpost. Walking across the grass of Choristers Green, I spot a skeleton, standing in a jaunty position, one arm leaning on the rail at the top of the steps. This, though, is not the museum. It's an art studio and gallery, trying to entice me with the promise of more bones inside. I resist and press on to my destination, arriving just as the bells of the cathedral ring out eleven times: right on time.

Tom Booth is already here, and the director of the museum, Adrian Green, comes down to meet us, then we follow him up the spiralling staircase to his office, where the floor-to-ceiling windows provide a fantastic view of the cathedral. Before long, Pooja and another archaeologist-geneticist friend, Turi King, arrive and join us. Adrian knows why we're here. His museum holds an extremely special collection of skulls and long bones, all excavated from a very tight location in Dorset: the Rushmore Estate on Cranborne Chase.

Augustus Henry Lane Fox Pitt Rivers is surely one of the most famous pioneers of archaeology. He was very firmly a member of the landed gentry, born in 1827, the son of an aristocratic army man, William Augustus Lane Fox, and Lady Caroline Douglas. Augustus followed his father into the British Army and took part in the Battle of the Alma in September 1854, during the Crimean War. But just a month later, a medical examination found him unfit for active service, and he returned to England. He still worked for the army, in training and logistical roles, but his health continued to deteriorate. By

1877, his active service had largely drawn to an end, and he officially retired, aged fifty-five, in 1882.

He had married Alice Margaret Stanley the year before he set off for the Crimean. They had nine children, and stayed together until Augustus' death in 1900. Alice's family had initially been less than happy with the match – indeed, her parents rejected Augustus' first proposal of marriage in 1849, only acquiescing four years later, after his older brother had died – boosting Augustus' potential share of inheritance. Although Augustus Lane Fox came from an extremely well-to-do family and, even as a younger son, would have expected to be comfortably well-off throughout his life, the Stanleys could not have predicted just *how* well-off he would become. The year 1880 was a life-changing one for him. Augustus received an unexpected windfall in the form of a large fortune, a new town house in London, and an absolutely enormous country estate. This estate – Rushmore, in Dorset – had belonged to his deceased great-uncle, the politician George Pitt, 2nd Baron Rivers. A condition of the inheritance was that the heir should assume the name of Pitt Rivers, 'either alone or in addition to his or their surname', which Augustus Fox duly did.

The Rushmore Estate, to the southwest of Salisbury, straddles the county line between Dorset and Wiltshire. It occupies more than 25,000 acres within the ancient royal forest of Cranborne Chase. Suddenly, Lane Fox – now Lane Fox Pitt Rivers – had become a major landowner. He had always been a passionate collector – of anything and everything, from fine art to ethnographic artefacts to guns. He was also a keen archaeologist. It seems he started excavating in Cork, in Ireland, when he was based there with the army in the 1860s. In London, he got involved with what we'd now describe as salvage or 'pre-construction' archaeology – visiting building sites and rescuing animal bones, human skulls and Roman artefacts, including pottery, coins and well-preserved leather shoes. He'd learnt excavation methods from the pioneering archaeologist Canon William Greenwell, in Yorkshire – who warned against the 'mere curiosity hunting' still typical of many antiquarians at the time. For Greenwell, and then for Pitt Rivers as well, the context in which artefacts were discovered was crucial. Endowed with their archaeological contexts, finds became much more than simply interesting curiosities, providing far-reaching insights into ancient cultures. Once he'd inherited his own estate, Pitt Rivers had the opportunity to focus his archaeological attention on Cranborne Chase. He wrote:

> Having retired from active service on account of ill-health, and being incapable of strong physical exercise, I determined to devote the remaining portion of my life chiefly to an examination of the antiquities on my own property.

Over the winter months of the 1880s and '90s, the agricultural labourers at Rushmore found themselves tasked with carrying out a different sort of fieldwork. Completely unskilled in archaeology at first, they were supervised by Pitt Rivers, aided by a small team of specialist assistants. These assistants also recorded the digs – surveying, creating illustrations and models of the landscape. Pitt Rivers wrote up the digs and published his analyses in four weighty volumes. Adrian had dug out one of these beautiful books for us to look at, down in the museum stores – but that wasn't all he had to show us.

We left Adrian's office and filed down the spiral staircase and out into the public galleries. Then we passed through a side door, just to the side of the entrance of the museum's main archaeological gallery, and we were back in the nether world, with that behind-the-scenes frisson of excitement I always get in these spaces. I've spent so much of my professional life in places like this, passing through doors the public visitors don't even notice, into stores and labs where treasures from centuries past are kept safely for generations to come. But that passage — from public to private space, from open to secret — never fails to excite me.

This store was an old gallery, repurposed. The corridor we entered through was painted verdigris green, with small landscape murals floating on the wall, missing the displays of artefacts that they were originally designed to contextualise. Around a corner, Adrian had assembled a few objects on a large table: one of the Cranborne Chase excavation volumes and two boxes. He opened the excavation volume to a page he'd bookmarked, then invited us to lift the lid on one of the boxes — and Turi did the honours. Inside the box was an exquisite scale model of an excavated grave: a skeleton buried in a cylindrical pit, dug down into the chalk. Then Adrian handed round a box of gloves — he only had small ones to hand — and we all squeezed our hands into them. Now we could open the second box. From its size and shape, I already knew what we'd find inside: a skull. Its fragments had been carefully assembled, glued together. The jaw was attached to the skull by monofilament fishing line, passing through a tiny hole drilled into the condyle of the mandible, and through the earhole — the external auditory meatus — of the cranium. Adrian had cross-referenced this small collection: the skull belonged to the burial illustrated in the model, and the page of Pitt Rivers' report bore a photograph of it.

We passed the skull round. Tom and I were particularly interested in the earholes. Was there any sediment still inside them? If so, the tiny ear bones or ossicles might well be in there – and very recent studies had suggested that it might be possible to obtain well-preserved DNA from these minute bones – saving us from having to drill samples out of the base of the skull itself. So it was worth a look – but in this skull, the meatus on both sides appeared to have been completely cleaned out, perhaps when the monofilament was passed through to attach the jaw. Never mind. The skull inside looked very well preserved. And from work that Turi had already done here, in a pilot study we'd carried out three years ago, we knew that there was plenty of DNA in at least six of the skulls from Pitt Rivers' Cranborne Chase excavations.

I first became interested in these skulls five years ago, when I was filming in Salisbury Museum for an archaeology series on BBC Four. We were upstairs in the stores that time, lifting down boxes of artefacts from Durrington Walls – the Bronze Age settlement site close to Stonehenge. As we chose artefacts to film – an antler pick, a thick pot sherd, a stone cobble – the curator, Jane Ellis-Schon, was telling me about how she's embarked on a huge project to re-catalogue the finds in the museum. Collections tend to grow in a somewhat haphazard way: archaeological digs turn up new material; private collections are bequeathed; museums close – or open – split and fuse. There's a need to keep track of everything, to match paper or electronic records with the physical artefacts themselves. A process of remembering. Jane was embarking on this task with a small army of local volunteers, and they were painstakingly combing their way through shelves, boxes, drawers – checking their contents and drawing up a new catalogue.

'We've a lot of material from Pitt Rivers' excavations on Cranborne Chase,' Jane told me. I was surprised at this. 'Really? I thought all the Pitt Rivers material ended up in his museum in Oxford?'

'Well, yes, most of his collection is there, of course – particularly the ethnographic material. But the material from his own Rushmore Estate on Cranborne Chase – that's here. Or at least, we knew the excavation volumes were here, and the wooden models of the landscapes – and even some of the archaeological artefacts. But what we didn't know – until we started this re-cataloguing – was that he'd kept hold of skeletons from the digs – and they're still here.'

'Really – whole skeletons?'

'No – it seems he just kept the skulls, and occasionally a few long bones as well, and got rid of the rest. Presumably he thought he was keeping the most interesting bits.'

'When do they date to?'

'Well, the whole time-depth of Cranborne Chase, so the earliest ones are probably pre-Neolithic, through to post-Roman – what Pitt Rivers called "Saxon".'

'How many do you think there are?'

'Well, we're still looking through the collection, but I'd say at least a hundred.'

The remains of over 100 individuals, spanning a time frame ranging over several thousand years – all in one locality. This was more than intriguing. I wanted to know more.

'Has anyone looked at them recently – done any analysis on them?' I asked Jane.

'No – we didn't even realise we had them. So as far as I know, no one's looked at them since the nineteenth century.'

'Are they well preserved?'

'Yes, they're really good. You'll have to come back and have a proper look,' she replied.

So I did. A few months later, I was due to be back at Salisbury Museum on a Sunday to talk at their Festival of Archaeology, and I arranged to stay down and catch up with Jane on the Monday.

I stayed near the museum, in central Salisbury, in a hotel with an arch that made it feel as though you should be arriving and departing by horse-drawn carriage. I walked into the museum, keen to start looking through the archive. Jane had pulled together a few items for me to look at. I sat down with one of the hefty Pitt Rivers Cranborne Chase excavation volumes. It was meticulously laid out – describing the excavations, trench by trench, with accompanying plan views of sites and section drawings. One of the sites, in particular, caught my eye – Woodcuts Common. Pitt Rivers defined it as a 'Romano-British' site – but it looked like an Iron Age village, with plenty of pits and what were surely the ghosts of roundhouses – ring-like features on the ground. There were more detailed illustrations of some of the pits, which contained human skeletons.

The really weird thing about this was that I had just seen something very similar – from a different site, excavated much more recently – in a talk that Miles Russell had given at the Festival of Archaeology – at Salisbury Museum. Miles had been talking about his late Iron Age/early Roman site near Bere Regis in Dorset. Miles argued that we'd been too focused on hillforts as sites of Iron Age activity in England – and they are certainly eye-catching features in the landscape. But his site near Bere Regis was a low-lying settlement under what are now wheat fields. He'd dug there for several years, researching the site as the same time as training archaeology students from Bournemouth University. It was a gift of a training dig, on a chalk substrate. Features – pits, postholes and the ring-ditches of roundhouses – stood out as dark marks on the white ground. Eventually, Miles and his team had unearthed the traces of nineteen roundhouses, with the wider geophysical survey suggesting there were at least a hundred more – a huge settlement by Iron Age standards. He needed to phase the site, to work out how long each roundhouse has been in use and how many roundhouses had been present there at the same time. But it was clearly a large, long-lived settlement. It was impressive enough to get into the newspapers; a large settlement, in the territory of the Iron Age Durotriges tribe – it was soon dubbed 'Duropolis'. But Pitt Rivers, it seemed, had discovered something very similar at Woodcuts. I wondered if Miles knew about it.

Jane brought out a cardboard box and set it on the table in front of me. From its size and shape, I knew what it contained before I opened it. I carefully lifted the lid and extracted the skull, resting it down on a sheet of foam on the table. Leafing through the pages of the excavation record, I found a very carefully drawn illustration of the very skull I was looking at. In the preceding pages, the precise context of this burial was laid out – one among many from Rotherley, another 'Romano-British' village.

I was already sure about two things: the skeletal material was very well preserved – certainly intact enough to take measurements from and assess for any pathological changes; and it was possible to cross-reference the physical archive with the excavation record. Each skull could – crucially – be tied down to a particular burial, a particular site. The very least we could do with this material would be to obtain some radiocarbon dates on the bones – pinning down the chronology of these sites on Cranborne Chase in a way that Pitt Rivers would not have been able to dream of. He dated his sites by the style of them – what archaeologists call 'relative dating'. That can work reasonably well – and to be fair, it was all he *could* do at the time – but it makes it very different to track cultural changes through time. He could use other aspects of material culture – pottery styles, metalwork – to provide a counterpoint, but it was all *relative*. Radiocarbon dating – which is possible with organic remains such as wood, charcoal or bones – provides an 'absolute' date: a stand-alone point in time, independent of other aspects of culture.

But I felt that this collection had more potential than simply providing us with an accurate chronology of those Cranborne Chase excavations, even though that in itself would be inter-esting. We learn so much by comparing sites – and with Pitt Rivers' meticulous recording of his excavations and finds, there was clearly the possibility of making comparisons with modern digs – like Miles Russell's 'Duropolis'. There was a fascinating historical dimension to this, too – comparing the way that the Cranborne Chase excavations were carried out and recorded – by this famous pioneer of archaeology – with today's methods.

Pitt Rivers had also drawn some conclusions – or at least made some suggestions – about population history, based on his measurements of the skulls. In particular, he believed he could detect an important change in skull shape between the Neolithic and the Bronze Age. And he interpreted this shape change as indicating the arrival of a new group of people into Britain. As the timing of the skull shape change seemed to coincide with the appearance of a new culture in Britain – the

Bell Beaker culture of the Bronze Age – Pitt Rivers suggested the two phenomena were linked. The new people, with their characteristic skull shape, had migrated to Britain from the continent, he suggested, bringing their tradition of burying the dead with beautiful pots or beakers with them.

This matching-up of cultures with particular populations makes archaeologists furrow their brows today, if not groan under their breath. It's a theory that was once pervasive – in early twentieth-century archaeology – and led to a characterisation of the past as a sequence of populations, each with its own distinctive culture, expanding and replacing earlier people and their cultures. It may be a caricature of the theory to say that the relevance of culture went no further than being a convenient label for a particular group of people – as though past populations were football teams with characteristic strips. But it did have an extreme focus on pigeon-holing, categorising. This approach is called the 'culture-history' theory, and it enjoyed its zenith in the 1930s, when this archaeological paradigm provided fascists with an argument for ranking populations and their cultures, and a justification for wiping out other ethnic groups. It's no wonder today's archaeologists are so nervous about the resurgence of anything that looks a bit like the culture-history model.

The culture-historical way of approaching archaeology was largely overturned in the 1960s, when a new theoretical approach came to the fore – focusing on the processes underlying changes that could be found in the archaeological record. The exciting term for this new philosophy is the New Archaeology. A more turgid description has it as 'processual archaeology', a phrase that makes me yawn just looking at it. Anyway, it was a return to a more anthropological approach – where the real interest lay in applying scientific methods to studying past lives, and placing those lives in context. It was more holistic than culture-history, ranging across human interaction with the landscape and natural world, technological and cultural development, and social structure. And it explicitly rejected the colonial packaging-together of ethnic identity and culture: pots, as the saying goes, are pots – not people.

In fact, Pitt Rivers' approach was much more akin to processual archaeology than to the intervening culture-history approach of the early twentieth century. He was ahead of his time in this, too. He tackled his own, rather expansive ethnographic collection as far more than just an assemblage of intriguing *objets d'art* from around the world – and more as a problem to be solved. He wanted to understand how culture had developed over time, and he believed that an evolutionary approach – having transformed biology in the nineteenth century – could be applied to human culture.

In the introduction to his 1874 book, *The Evolution of Culture*, he wrote:

> The collection . . . has been collected during upwards of twenty years, not for the purpose of surprising anyone, either by the beauty or value of the objects exhibited, but solely with a view to instruction. For this purpose ordinary and typical specimens, rather than rare objects, have been selected and arranged in sequence, so as to trace, as far as is practicable, the succession of ideas by which the minds of men in a primitive condition of culture have progressed from the simple to the complex, and from the homogeneous to the heterogenous.

His fascination with tracing the development and elaboration of technology through time seems to have been inspired by his military experience, during which he'd devoted quite a bit of time to investigating and improving the rifle. He'd delved into the way that these firearms had already been modified, bit by bit, over time. Henry Balfour – who was curator of the eponymous museum in Oxford where most of Pitt Rivers' collection ended up – wrote a preface to a posthumous edition of the *Evolution of Culture* book, in which he reflected:

> During his investigations conducted with a view to ascertaining the best methods whereby the service firearms might be improved . . . [Pitt Rivers] was forcibly struck by the extremely gradual changes whereby improvements were effected. He observed that every noteworthy advancement in the efficiency, not only of the whole weapon, but also of every individual detail of its structure, was arrived at as a cumulative result of a succession of very slight modifications, each of which was but a trifling improvement upon the one immediately preceding it. Through noticing the unfailing regularity of this process of gradual evolution in the case of firearms, he was led to believe that the same principles must probably govern the development of the other arts, appliances, and ideas of [hu]mankind.

But alongside these innovative, progressive and quite modern-sounding ideas about cultural evolution, Pitt Rivers was inextricably mired in the imperialist, colonialist, racist philosophy of his own era. Both biology and anthropology were being transformed by evolutionary theory, and yet this was a hugely value-laden idea of evolution – which worked to transform the 'lower' life form into the 'higher', the primitive into the sophisticated, the Savage into the Civilised Man.

For Pitt Rivers, looking at the stark variation in cultural achievements and technological sophistication around the globe, there was a clear and explicable pattern. Progress was not equal across all human populations. Some people had it in them to advance – others didn't. The Caucasian race was obviously superior, having achieved the technological mastery demonstrated by the artistic and engineering prowess of Victorian Britain. But among other populations, technological development appeared to have stalled – fossilised in a more primitive phase. The current state of technology around the world in the nineteenth century, then, provided insights into the historical process.

This is such a tricky concept to pull apart. We still fall into the trap today. We can quite reasonably identify progress – I don't think many people would argue that an increasing degree of sophistication in tool design and manufacture and an improvement in human health and longevity is anything other than progress. But the conditions that have led to that advancement, historically, are much more difficult to grasp. We seem to have a fundamental problem with accepting that progress can involve any element of randomness. We look for causes inside people – some are born great. Or we look for external causes – greatness is thrust upon 'em, by the environment – by having to survive in a harsh climate, as nineteenth-century analysers suggested – or it comes about through happening to live in places with readily available fossil fuels, as more recent commentators such as Jared Diamond have postulated. What these narratives miss, or downplay, is the role of chance in determining outcomes. This happens so often, so widely – through historical and contemporary analyses – that I wonder if it's something intrinsic to the way our brains work and try to make sense of the world around us. We love to find a *reason* for something. We hate it when we can't.

In biology, that tendency to overemphasise the role of causal factors over chance can lead to 'hyperadaptionism', where every facet of the structure and function of an organism is interpreted as an adaptation with a particular function that has been evolutionarily selected for. We know this is foolish, as we have plenty of examples of whole suites of character-istics that tend to be inherited together for no reason other than being influenced by genes that are physically close – on a chromosome – to a gene that is being selected for. Genes can also have widespread effects throughout the body, so while one of the characteristics influenced by a particular gene may be advantageous in some way, others just come along for the ride. A good example of this is the size of our big toes and thumbs. Researchers have argued, fairly convincingly, that the relatively large size of the first digit on the human foot, more familiarly known as the big toe, is an adaptation to bipedalism – our tendency to habitually walk around on two legs, rather than all fours, like other apes. Then there's the case for the chunky human thumb also having been positively selected for, during human evolution, as big thumbs make us more efficient stone tool-makers and tool-users. But toes and fingers share very sim-ilar developmental pathways in the embryo – genes operating on fingers as they form will also be operating on toes. Careful analysis suggests it was the big toes that were being selected for – because of the advantages they provided to an ape walk-ing on two feet. Big thumbs would then be just a side effect of having big toes. This isn't to say that large thumbs – once they appear – don't have their uses when it comes to making stone tools, but that this utility is 'discovered' later.

This evidence of coevolution prompts us to be careful about looking at every aspect of an organism as an adaptation – something emerging through the operation of natural selection. Another reason to be cautious is that natural selection is not the only process underlying biological changes over time. If most of the individuals in a population are wiped out in some sort of catastrophe, the lucky survivors are highly unlikely to represent an even-handed sample of all the variation present in the original population. The small sample will be skewed – and that skew will change how natural selection operates on the population, affecting the frequencies of particular genetic variants over generations to come.

Natural selection is also not the only process influencing how frequencies of genetic variants vary over time. There's a really important, practically random element that plays out too – especially in small populations – and that's called genetic drift. By chance alone, some individuals in a population will have more offspring than others, so frequencies of genetic variants will change over time – without selection being involved. Quite a bit of the variation we see among modern humans is probably down to genetic drift and chance – rather than to adaptations to different environments.

We're still struggling to work out how much of the variation in the shape of our skulls, for instance, is down to adaptation – perhaps to the wildly different environments that humans have ended up in across the globe – and how much is just genetic drift.

Going back to Pitt Rivers and his collection of skulls, there were two questions that had hooked themselves into my brain since that first meeting with Jane and the revelation that this skeletal material existed in the Salisbury Museum archive: might Pitt Rivers have been right about the changing shape of skulls at the dawn of the Bronze Age – was a population of long-headed people replaced by round-headed people? And if we had the craniometric and genomic data to answer that first question, would we also have in our hands the information we'd need to work out what – in our genome – produced differences in skull shape?

This second question seemed like a really knotty problem. But by comparing genomic variation and physical cranial variation, we might be able to identify areas of the genome that are linked to skull shape. Because natural selection leaves its mark on DNA, we should also be able to deduce whether particular variants linked to aspects of skull shape had been selected for – which would mean they're likely to be adaptations – and which were not, and so more likely to represent a history of genetic drift. Was a particular anatomical variant there because it had been advantageous in the past, or just because that's the way things had happened to turn out? Of course, not all of the variation in skull shape would be down to genetic factors. By doing this analysis, we might even be able to estimate how much of that physical variation was down to non-genetic factors, sometimes called environmental factors.

These questions intrigue me, but I'm also aware that the study of human variation can be highly politically charged. In the nineteenth century, phrenologists thought that they could measure people's skulls and estimate degrees of criminality, for instance. And anthropologists measured skulls not just to track changes in populations over time, as Pitt Rivers had attempted, but to rank races – though of course they always started with the presupposition that the White Man represented the absolute best that *Homo sapiens* could be. Pitt Rivers himself was very clear on this, from a cultural perspective – whereas other races had stumbled and fallen on the path to progress, white Europeans had forged ahead.

Pitt Rivers' theories and the language he used seem wildly out of date now. Although his approach to cultural evolution prefigures the process-oriented, scientific approach of the New Archaeology of the 1960s, his interpretations are infused with the value-laden perspective that infused culture-history. (And archaeological theory moved on again, in the 1980s, when a more subjective focus re-emerged – with 'post-processualism'. That's now been superseded by an approach that strives for objectivity while recognising the impossibility of escaping our own subjectivity even when we really want to . . . Phew!) We can recognise – today – that Pitt Rivers' views were shaped by the culture around him, and we see them as imperialist, colonialist and racist. But, with that on board, we don't need to throw out all of his data and interpretations *because* of that imperialist, colonialist and racist infusion. We should be open to the idea that some of his observations – despite that history – may be true today.

And what we need to be very careful about indeed is imagining that we are so advanced in our thinking now that we can successfully extricate ourselves from our *own* cultural milieu, and our *own* subjective lens. We can strive for objectivity, but need to be aware that this is an ideal that can never be fully realised. We are creatures of culture, after all; we can't escape it. We're also political creatures, and we need to recognise that our attempts to reconstruct how societies have operated in the past may be used by others to justify political actions today.

After looking at that one skull from the Cranborne Chase collection, I took the opportunity to explore the Wessex Gallery again, just round the corner, back on the public side of the museum – with Turi, Tom and Pooja. There were more of Pitt Rivers' incredible wooden models on display here, as well as more prehistoric archaeology from across Wiltshire – including Stonehenges of course. At one end of the gallery were two cases that particularly intrigued me. One contained huge red pots – Bronze Age funerary urns. Made before the potter's wheel was invented, they were fluted at the top, with patterns created by impressions on their surfaces. The other glass case was longer, lower and contained the skeleton of the famous 'Amesbury Archer', laid out just as he'd been discovered in the grave, with stone tools and curls of thin gold that must have been hair wraps. This was a burial; a person, with an incredible story to tell.

7.

THE AMESBURY ARCHER

Delusions of grandeur

Amesbury is a town in southern Wiltshire, 7 miles north of Salisbury and 1.5 miles from Stonehenge. It's famous for a rather odd, headline-grabbing claim that emerged in 2014, when archaeologists were digging a Mesolithic site at Blick Mead, on the banks of the River Avon, next to the Amesbury bypass. Mesolithic people had been in the area nearly 11,000 years ago; Amesbury was the oldest settlement in Britain (said the headlines). I don't believe it and I'm not even sure it's meaningful in any real way. There's plenty of evidence for human activity near or even under other sites that have developed into towns and cities. The caves at Cheddar contain even earlier Mesolithic material, if not a settlement as such. Star Carr, in North Yorkshire – with lots of very good evidence for actual settlement, including what are widely accepted to be the traces of Britain's earliest (discovered) houses – has dates going back as early as 9300 BCE.

Blick Mead, on the other hand, is late Mesolithic, with radiocarbon dates ranging from 7800 BCE to 4150 BCE. But the claim that it was continually occupied for the whole of the Mesolithic cannot be supported on the basis of the seventeen radiocarbon dates from the site, with a particularly stark gap in these between 7550 and 6700 BCE, for instance. The gap doesn't mean people weren't there – it just means that we don't have enough evidence to detect whether the site was continuously occupied, or, indeed, periodically abandoned. There's simply not enough data to draw on.

If Blick Mead doesn't quite stack up as a continuously occupied settlement, what about its other big claim to fame – that it's associated with Stonehenge? The archaeologists who dug the site acknowledged that it lay 'within what would have been excellent prehistoric hunting grounds'' – but they couldn't quite avoid leaping to the conclusion that it must have been more than just a hunting camp – that it must have been *really special* in some way. I mean – it's just so close to Stonehenge, isn't it?

The evidence from Blick Mead is in the form of thousands of pieces of flint together with thousands of pieces of animal bone. Although poorly preserved, it's been possible to identify many species, and the archaeologists describe an unusually high proportion of aurochs (ancient cattle) bones. They argued that this meant the site was less likely to represent a hunting camp, and more likely to be a home base – though with no evidence for structures such as those seen at Star Carr, this conclusion is extremely conjectural; one might even call it wishful thinking.

The idea that Blick Mead is *special*, linked to Stonehenge and perhaps even – as the archaeologists who dug it asserted – a *sacred* site, seems to represent a headlong fall into a very familiar archaeological trap. This trap is so pervasive, and so pernicious, that it needs a name, and I'm going to call it the SSSD.

This acronym is similar to the SSSI – Site of Special Scientific Interest, which is used for the appropriate recognition of sites which deserve conservation because they contain geological treasures or are habitats for rare butterflies or ancient trees. But my archaeological SSSD is much less deserving. It is the Special Sacred Site Delusion.

Imagine finding this site. It's exciting! You dig down and discover a rich seam of flints, as well as thousands of bone fragments – including species like aurochsen and wild pig – and even the tooth of a domesticated dog. It's clearly a Mesolithic site – and these are few and far between. It's on the banks of the Avon . . . Stonehenge is just over a mile away . . . your imagination starts to run wild!

When your radiocarbon dates come back from the lab, you have dates that match up with some of the earliest activity on Stonehenge Down, when people were up there digging some pits in the eighth millennium BCE.

Some other archaeologists visit your site and encourage you – saying things like 'You've found the people who started to build Stonehenge!' You laugh, but then start to take that too seriously. You decide this one site is unique, sacred and the home to the originators of Stonehenge. But in reality, you have no idea how many other Mesolithic camps there were along the banks of the Avon around here – where the floodplain opens up and where there were clearly plenty of animals to hunt. Probability would suggest that you've been lucky, certainly – lucky to find one of several such camps, rather than so incredibly fortunate that you've stumbled on *the one*, the unique, special and sacred site in the area. (And in fact, there is another known Mesolithic site, just downriver a bit, in West Amesbury.)

But there was a *lot* of flint at Blick Mead, compared with

other sites, including Star Carr – really impressive quantities of the stuff. Archaeologist Mike Pitts has compared the two sites, and the statistics work out like this: there's an average of 1,600 pieces of struck flint per square metre at Blick Mead; 250 per square metre on the dry-land areas of Star Carr.

That seemingly extraordinary density needs – as Mike Pitts has cautioned – to be sifted through and looked at in context. Because at Blick Mead, some 4,000 years of activity are compressed into a layer just 20cm thick. At Star Carr, the time-depth is a mere eight centuries. Taking that into account, the density of struck flint at Blick Mead works out as forty flints per century per square metre, and thirty-one flints per century per square metre at Star Carr. It's a crude way of trying to understand the data, but useful nonetheless – and shows Blick Mead to be less surprising or impressive than initial perusal of the figures might suggest.

Blick Mead is – like Star Carr – a waterside site. The mapping of finds across large trenches at Star Carr shows that flints are concentrated in areas that would have been dry land – and can be associated with activities like knapping (making stone tools) and butchery. Flints are often found near hearths, too – so we can imagine people sitting around fires and carrying out various tasks with flints – cutting up meat, carving antler, perhaps a bit of whittling. In the wetter areas at Star Carr, where Mesolithic people were laying down timber to make platforms or walkways, there are far fewer lithics. Although Blick Mead is waterlogged today, it's not clear that it was wet during the Mesolithic. It's close to water, certainly, but may not have been all that damp – corresponding more with the dry-land areas at Star Carr. Much has been made of the watery nature of Blick Mead – even going as far as to mention phrases such as 'sacred spring' – but there's no good environmental evidence – at least, not yet – to show that it was watery in the Mesolithic. And even if it was – that doesn't necessarily mean, of course, that it was sacred.

But Blick Mead is so close to Stonehenge – I hear you cry – they must surely be linked! Well, there are pits and pieces of charcoal up on Stonehenge Down that date to 9,000 to 10,000 years ago – which brackets the earliest date from Blick Mead. But those pits are nothing to do with the monument we're all so familiar with. The last radiocarbon dates from Blick Mead come in at 4250 BCE. The earliest ditch at Stonehenge dates to just after 3000 BCE, more than a millennium later, well into the Neolithic. While Stonehenge is that rare beast – a site that we can be more than reasonably sure is primarily about ritual and tradition – there's no indication of traditions stretching back through thousands of years into the Mesolithic. And in fact, I can't help thinking it would be more surprising if there were absolutely *no* signs of any earlier human activity in this landscape.

The archaeologists digging the site and analysing the thousands of pieces of stone and bones they discovered have argued that people had travelled a long way to get there, and that this was significant. There were types of stone in the haul that were 'exotic' – not local to the area – such as slate. Some of the styles of flint tools also seemed unusual. The archaeologists write that these out-of-place finds support 'the idea of long-distance travel and exchange'.

The single dog's tooth found at Blick Mead is a premolar from an upper jaw. The length of the crown, at just under 2cm, means it probably came from a domestic dog; wolf premolars are usually around 2.5cm long. Oxygen isotope analysis on this tooth came back with a low ratio, which could be read to suggest that the dog originated from somewhere a few hundred miles to the east or north of Blick Mead. The oxygen isotope ratios of aurochs teeth from Blick Mead were also low – again suggesting the animals had also started off somewhere more northerly when young, and migrated south. But in both the dog and the aurochsen teeth, analysis of another isotope – strontium – supported a local origin. Perhaps the oxygen isotope values in the spring water, or in rainwater, had changed over time, the researchers suggested. If the climate at the time the dog was alive was much colder, that could explain the discrepancy.

It seems we can't be sure, then, about the dog – or the aurochsen – starting off their lives hundreds of miles from Blick Mead. But even if they had – would that be particularly unusual or remarkable? Herds of animals migrate, sometimes over vast distances. Mesolithic people (and their dogs) may have followed those herds to some extent. So we could be looking at quite ordinary migrations, perhaps on an annual cycle. Or a response to changing climate and ecology.

The archaeologists were really cautious when they presented this evidence in the academic literature, acknowledging that it was 'difficult to reach firm conclusions about the dog's origin', while still putting it out there that it was 'hinting at an origin to the north or east'.

Writing about the site in a popular archaeology magazine, though, they were much less circumspect. Nuance had given way to certainty, and now the oxygen isotope results were described as 'tangible evidence of a long journey to the Stonehenge area' – in which the dog had accompanied its human owner. Going further – much further – the archaeologists argued that this small scrap of evidence (itself far from conclusive) suggested that this particular landscape was already seen as special – and would have been a gathering place, drawing people in across vast distances to 'hunt, feast, and exchange ideas, objects, and maybe even genes'.

The archaeologists have bewitched themselves with their own story. It's impossible for them to see Blick Mead as anything other than special, anything less than hugely significant. The site has evolved into a monstrous example of SSSD.

For what it's worth, I think Blick Mead is interesting and important as a Mesolithic site in its own right, and deserves to be the subject of further research. But I also think it's much more likely to be an ordinary camp, rather than a place of pilgrimage and reverence.

And Amesbury does not deserve the (meaningless) title of the earliest settlement in Britain.

But it does deserve to be famous for another reason. And that reason is, this time, a – *genuinely* remarkable – Bronze Age burial.

Discovery of the Archer

In the spring of 2002, archaeologists were carrying out a low-key excavation of a site to the southeast of Amesbury where a new school was going to be built. This is standard practice in the UK – developers have to build in archaeological assessment of sites when they're applying for planning permission. The professional archaeological unit, Wessex Archaeology – based in nearby Salisbury – had already carried out a 'desk-based assessment' – looking over old maps and reports to see if anything interesting had already turned up in the vicinity. They'd also carried out an aerial survey and scanned the ground using geophysical methods to check for buried archaeology. And in fact the proposed school site was just one part of a huge development. The archaeologists had worked with the design team to preserve some of the archaeology intact – without excavating it – under open spaces such as parks. Elsewhere, they recommended a 'strip, map and record' approach, where they would excavate a large area and record any archaeology that turned up.

Very quickly, they started to find features that had been completely invisible on the maps, aerial photos and geophysical surveys – two cemeteries full of burials. The graves – dug into the chalk, and then back-filled with chalk – simply hadn't shown up. They excavated one of the cemeteries, amounting to thirty-two graves, of a late Romano-British date. The other cemetery was left mostly unexcavated: the archaeologists could identify graves cut into the ground, but they didn't dig into them and exhume the skeletons. Instead, they advised changing the proposed site for the school itself so that these burials could be left undisturbed – they covered the area with a protective membrane, leaving it safely covered up under the school playing field. This meant that most of the graves in that second cemetery could be preserved *in situ*. But there were two unusual features – what looked like large, round, filled-in pits – at the northern end, lying right where a new road was planned. The road couldn't be re-routed – so the archaeologists had no choice but to excavate the two pits.

Right from the start, those features stood out. Their size and shape was completely different from that of the Romano-British graves. They looked more like the sort of trace that's left when a tree falls over, pulling its roots out of the ground, leaving a roundish pit that fills with a different type of soil over time. The archaeologists got on with digging the pits, carefully trowelling back and taking out the fill. It soon became apparent that these pits weren't tree-throws after all – they contained human bones. But these graves weren't Romano-British. They were much older than that.

When the archaeologists found pieces of a characteristic pot in the larger grave, they knew at once that they must be dealing with a Bronze Age burial – this grave was around two thousand years older than those in the Roman-British cemetery.

This was all happening on a Friday. The archaeologists thought they could work hard and get the skeletons fully excavated, photographed and lifted before the end of the day. They didn't want to start digging a grave and then leave it half-excavated over the weekend – that's just not the done thing. Not only that – this was a Bank Holiday weekend; the archaeologists certainly didn't want to go home and leave the grave for three days.

They managed to complete the excavation of one grave, but the other was proving more complicated. That afternoon, something appeared in the deeper of the two pits that made the archaeologists realise they'd found something very special: the gleam of gold.

Gold is the least reactive of all metals. If it's relatively pure, it does not rust; it does not tarnish. Silver combines with oxygen, sulphide or chloride – turning its surface a dull black, grey or white respectively. Copper loses its pink-orange lustre as it becomes coated with oxide, turning dark brown or, with carbonates, turning that beautiful sea-green shade known as verdigris. But gold – gold can be buried in the ground for thousands of years, and then, when an archaeologist's trowel reveals it, it shines again, bright and yellow, like a beacon from the past.

Site director Niels Daglass was on a training day in the office. The team rang him to tell him they'd found 'something shiny'. Project Manager Andrew Fitzpatrick thought he should probably go and take a look, too.

It was a small object they'd found in the grave on that Friday afternoon. A curl of thin, beaten gold, as long as the end of your thumb. A narrower strip peeled away and wrapped itself around the cylinder. Up until this point, the archaeologists had been taking selected soil samples from the grave to ensure all small bones were collected up, but now they realised that they had to be even more thorough. They would need to check all the soil that had already been removed from the grave – they bagged it up so that they could later carefully sieve it to make sure nothing had been overlooked.

More and more finds were appearing, alongside a single skeleton, and it was clear that they wouldn't finish before nightfall. Dramatic reconstructions of excavations on television often show archaeologists – and sometimes palaeontologists too – working away at night, under floodlights. That might look exciting and artistic, but digging is always best done in daylight. Having passed the point of no return, though, the team from Wessex Archaeology eventually realised they would have to carry on in the dark. Word of the gold object had already got out – the site would not be safe over the long weekend. So – illuminated by torches and car headlights – they worked on until late in the night. They knew how important the grave was, and they dug extremely carefully, recording the 3D position of every object before lifting it out of the grave, packing up each artefact and bone and labelling them all.

By the time they finished, they knew they'd just found something exceptional. At home that Saturday morning, Andrew Fitzpatrick searched through the literature. And then he knew: this was the most richly furnished Bronze Age grave that had ever been discovered in Britain.

Excavation – that prising of objects out of the ground – is only ever the very start of the process of pulling the past out into the light. A huge team, with experts from many different disciplines, would pore over these remains dug up on the outskirts of Avebury. Analysis of the skeleton itself, and of the many objects placed in the grave, provides us with an incredible picture of this man (for he *was* a man) and his culture.

Looking at clues from the grave, the archaeologists believed that the body had originally been interred in a wooden mortuary chamber. The wood had long since rotted away – but they found compacted chalk around the edges of the grave, which they interpreted as material that had been packed around the sides of a wooden box, inside the pit that had been dug for it. The rest of the chalk that must have been dug out to create the pit itself was 'missing' – it could have been piled on top of the grave to form a small mound, which had long since disappeared. The way that the man's hand bones were scattered within the grave looked as though his body had lain in a cavity for a while – rather than being immediately surrounded by earth – and that perhaps rats had got in and moved things around a bit. His chest had slumped too – something that could only really happen if there was once space around his decaying body. There was what looked like a stake-hole in the bottom of the grave – maybe something to do with the construction of the wooden chamber. A thin layer of fine silt covered the base of the grave; it could have been sediment that had dropped down into the chamber – or perhaps even the remains of a bed of rushes or other plants.

His skeleton was quite well preserved. The skull had warped a bit and the surface texture of some of the other bones had been changed by processes of leaching and decay – 'taphonomic changes' as we call them in the business.

He was middle-aged when he died. Precise estimates of age at death are tricky in adults, so biological anthropologists use wide ranges, and the Archer fits into a 35–45-year range. The man was buried lying on his left side in a flexed position, knees drawn up almost level with his hips, as though he was asleep. His right arm was flexed at the elbow, the hand resting up by his left shoulder. His left arm appeared in an odd position – and looking all the more odd because of the way his chest had slumped forward – but it seems his arm may have been arranged out to the side, his elbow bent and his hand pointing down, lying close to his right elbow.

The grave was *full* of objects – made of bone, stone, copper and gold. He must have been fully clothed when he was laid in the ground, but the organic material has long since rotted away. Objects made from more resilient materials remain as clues.

A long, rectangular piece of stone lay along the bones of his left forearm. It's been interpreted as a wristguard or bracer – to protect him from the recoil of the bow. Some archaeologists think this object could have been more symbolic than functional, though. I'm not sure why – it seems like such an obviously functional object, even if it also conferred status on the wearer. Lying on and along the wristguard was an antler pin, which probably fastened clothing. And, tucked up under

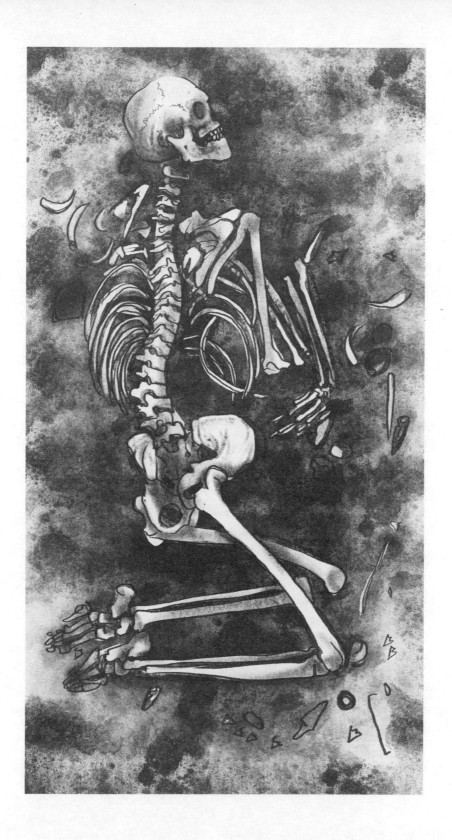

his right shoulder, a small, tanged copper blade – a knife he may have been wearing close to his chest.

Just in front of his forearms lay a concentrated scatter of objects. They may well have been collected together in a bag when placed in the grave: some flints, an antler tool, two boar's tusks, another copper knife, a piece of iron pyrites (probably used for fire-lighting), two pieces of worked antler and a pierced oyster shell. Some of the flints were scrapers or blade-like knives; others looked like they were rough-outs for arrowheads. There were more flints behind his back, together with two more boar's tusks and a cushion stone, used for metalworking. There were also eighteen – beautiful, tanged – flint arrowheads around the body: four near the pelvis, one among the pelvic bones, one at his waist, one at his feet, one close to his right shoulder. Then there were four in front of his knees, and another four towards the foot of the grave – all at slightly different levels in the earth – suggesting they had been attached to shafts, perhaps thrown into the grave after the body had been lain on the base of the chamber. A further two arrowheads were recovered from soil samples taken from the grave fill.

Further from the body, level with his knees, the archaeologists found another wristguard, made of reddish stone, together with a shale ring and yet another copper knife, and another antler strip. And, in front of his knees, not just one, but two gold objects – decorated, delicate curls of gold.

Arranged around the body – two up in front of his head, one behind it, one just below his hips and another at his feet – were the smashed-up remains of *five* pottery beakers. All of those pots – though fragmentary when found – had clearly been tipped onto their sides, before breaking. Again, this is consistent with the grave having contained a chamber – the pots could have toppled over when the roof of the wooden chamber collapsed in.

The style of the grave goods dates it to around 2400–2100 BCE – to the early Bronze Age. And it fits a pattern of graves known – from the inclusion of those characteristic pots – as Beaker burials.

When Andrew Fitzpatrick, who led the excavation, described it in his report, he emphasised just how richly furnished this grave was. 'Previously,' he wrote, 'burials had been considered "rich" if they contained more than a handful of objects, one of which was of copper/bronze or gold.'

But here was a grave containing nearly a hundred objects. The gold ornaments – perhaps earrings, perhaps hair-wraps – were *very* rare in Britain. Finding three copper knives in one grave – that was unparalleled. And the arrowheads and wrist-guard represented the largest collection of Bronze Age archery equipment ever found. After they had completed the excavation of the cemetery, the archaeologists made their discovery public. An outside-broadcast van turned up to report on the extraordinary find. On the BBC evening news, the reporter referred to the individual, which the archaeologists simply called Burial 1291, as the Amesbury Archer. And the name stuck.

The sumptuousness of the grave caught everyone by surprise – because, up to this point, it had been assumed that early Bronze Age societies were not all that hierarchical. There wasn't much evidence – before the Amesbury Archer was discovered – of widely varying status or rank being expressed in the way people were buried. But here, as Andrew Fitzpatrick put it, was an individual 'of a wealth and status that was hitherto unimagined'.

And there was another burial nearby, which seemed to

further throw the Archer's status into relief. Another man, somewhat younger – perhaps in his late twenties – was buried with a pair of gold basket earrings and a single boar's tusk, and that was all.

Andrew Fitzpatrick finished off his initial report of the discovery with a question: 'What was the relationship between the two men, and, if they were of an elite, what was the basis of their authorities?'

Identity of the Archer

Who was this man? Well, an archer for sure – with all those beautiful flint arrowheads in his grave. And his bones corroborated the story. Jacqui McKinley, senior osteoarchaeologist at Wessex Archaeology, examined his bones and found that the bony prominence of his shoulder blades, arching over the head of the humerus, were separated from the rest of the bone – on both sides. This condition is known as *os acromiale*. The projection of the shoulder blade is known as the acromion – it is the high point of the scapula, just as the acropolis is the high city in Athens.

In most of us, the acromion is a separate bone while we are still growing, joined to the rest of the scapula by a thin seam of cartilage. But when we reach adulthood, the cartilage is transformed to bone and the acromion fuses to the spine of the scapula. You can feel these bony features easily on yourself. Reach up and over a shoulder with the opposite hand. Under your fingertips you should be able to feel a ridge of bone running almost horizontally. In fact, it is slanted upwards – walk your fingers along it, moving to the side, towards the outer edge of your body. It keeps going; as you move laterally, you will feel that bony ridge expanding into a broader projection – above your shoulder joint. If you're in the right place, on the acromion itself, you can move your arm around and the acromion itself does not move.

Whereas the acromion usually begins to form between the ages of fifteen and eighteen, and fuses by the time you're in your mid-twenties, it stays separate – on average – in about 7 per cent of cases. This condition of having a separate bone, or *os*, at the tip of your shoulder is an anatomical variant that you may not even know about if you had it, as it doesn't always cause problems – although sometimes it can be painful. The main clinical relevance of *os acromiale* is that – while it doesn't cause problems itself – it shouldn't be mistaken for a fracture on an x-ray.

Anatomical variants like this come about through a mix of genetic and environmental factors. Some variants are highly heritable, mostly decided by our genetic make-up. Others are more influenced by environmental factors – including the things we do with our bodies. Auditory ossicles – bony growths inside the ear canal – tend to form in people who regularly swim in very cold water, presumably irritating the delicate periosteum of the ear canal, which panics and pumps out new bone in response. The fact that rates of *os acromiale* vary so much between widely geographically separate populations – from less than 6 per cent in some to more than 18 per cent in others – suggests that there is quite a strong genetic component to developing the trait. But on the other hand, a study examining the frequency of *os acromiale* in a sample of hundreds of cadavers in South Africa found that it disproportionately affected the left side – supporting a mechanical explanation as well: the suggestion that activity-related stress on the developing acromion could also be important.

Two large muscles attach in part to the acromion and the spine of the scapula: deltoid and trapezius. Deltoid attaches from the scapular spine, acromion and – round the front – the clavicle, and its fibres sweep down and converge on the outer (lateral) surface of the humerus. It's like a large, wrapped-around triangle – which is why it's called 'deltoid' – it looks like an upside-down Greek capital delta: Δ. The upper attachments, on the scapula and clavicle, are the anchor – it's the lower attachment, or insertion, on the humerus that moves. When deltoid contracts as a whole, the humerus is moved out to the side – a movement called 'abduction'. But you don't have to employ all the muscle fibres at once – you can selectively recruit just the anterior part of the muscle, at the front, to swing the humerus up in front of your shoulder – as you would do if you were pointing at something in the distance, in front of you. And you can recruit just the posterior part of the muscle to swing the humerus in the opposite direction, up behind your shoulder. Trapezius muscle is also named after its shape – it is, roughly, a broad trapezoid. It attaches from the back of the skull and down the spine, then its fibres run out to the side and converge on the spine of the scapula, and round onto the upper surface of the clavicle. It has a free upper edge, running down from the skull to the lateral clavicle, and a free lower edge, between the spine and the scapula. Contracting the whole of trapezius pulls your scapula backwards on your ribcage, towards the spine. You do this automatically if you reach your arms behind your back. But once again, you can selectively mobilise just the upper part of trapezoid – to shrug your shoulders upwards – or the upper, outer fibres to elevate the lateral corner of the scapula, helping it rotate outwards and upwards as you raise your arm to the side – when deltoid and trapezius work in concert with each other.

That's quite a bit of anatomy. But it's important to look at bones in context. We can't understand changes in bone unless we know exactly what attaches to a particular piece of bone, or what lies close to that bone. Skeletons look like stand-alone structures when we dig them up in archaeological sites, but of course, in living bodies, they are components of the musculo-skeletal system. We can't begin to understand them if we don't think about them in the context of the muscles, tendons and ligaments that attach to them.

Heavy use of the shoulder, then, involving deltoid and trapezius tugging hard – exerting strong forces on the acromion – could theoretically deter the bone from fusing. Two studies of English medieval skeletons (including bones recovered from Henry VIII's famous warship, the *Mary Rose*) found unusually high rates of *os acromiale* in the shoulders of male skeletons – attributing this to strenuous training in a particular weapon: the longbow. Drawing a longbow requires a huge force. Both arms and shoulders – the one pushing the bow forwards *and* the one pulling back on the arrow – are placed under enormous stress. The draw weight of a medieval longbow is predicted to have been at least 100 pounds – or 45 kilograms. Modern composite bows are lighter, with a draw weight of around 45 pounds or 20 kilograms – and prehistoric bows are thought to have been somewhat similar to these modern versions.

All of this brings us back to the Amesbury Archer, or skeleton 1291, as he is technically referred to in the Wessex Archaeology report. The bones of his right arm were slightly larger than the left, suggesting he was right-handed. His arms were not massively robust, though the deltoid tuberosity – the raised bump of bone where deltoid inserts on the humerus – was fairly well developed. (In some humeri, it's almost impossible to see, it's so slight.) He had marked muscle attachments for a square muscle stretching between ulna and radius, pronator quadratus, which twists the forearm. Other than that, his skeleton didn't suggest that he had unusually prodigious upper-body strength. It's easy to leap to conclusions based on the presence of *os acromiale* in his shoulders – especially with this being one of the traits found at high rates among the skeletal longbowmen of the *Mary Rose*. But, writing the bone report, Jacqui McKinley was characteristically carefully cautious about over-interpreting this feature: while archery may well have been something he did regularly, it was unlikely to have been 1291's 'primary activity'. And indeed, the whole idea of a primary activity, occupation or specialism – which seems so much part of the way we structure our societies today – is not so relevant for these prehistoric societies.

The robust pronator quadratus attachments in the forearm speak not of archery, but of some other manual task requiring strong wrist control – we may never know what this was. The rest of his skeleton bears a range of interesting conditions, some of which were congenital, others acquired throughout life; some of which he may have been painfully aware of, while being completely oblivious to others. Two of the bones in his feet, on both sides, were fused together – probably with a fibrous joint – rather than possessing the usual mobile, fluid-filled joint between them. This rare variation, present in less than 3 per cent of the population, can produce a painful, flat foot – or may be completely asymptomatic. In his jaw, the Archer (if we can permit ourselves to call him that) had a hole level with the roots of his right lower first molar. He must have had a painful abscess there at some point – before it pointed and the pus escaped through the bone and gum. It had healed a long time before he died. There were more signs of what appeared to have been infection in his left knee, which was quite misshapen, especially at the front, where the patella, or kneecap, normally sits. And then there were all sorts of asymmetries and oddities in his spine – evidence of an unfused spinous process on the tenth and eleventh thoracic vertebrae; a twist in the lumbar spine reflected by misshapen individual vertebrae; the lowest lumbar vertebra was almost fused to the sacrum; the back of the sacrum had not closed – a condition known as spina bifida occulta – or 'hidden' spina bifida; the holes or foramina allowing spinal nerves out of the central canal of the sacrum are larger on the right than on the left. These peculiarities in the spine are reflected by an asymmetry in the Archer's legs. The bones of the left leg are thinner, slighter on the left – and the muscle attachments barely marked at all – compared with the right. The left patella or kneecap was completely missing from the grave. The odd shape of the lower or distal end of the left femur suggests that the bone wasn't somehow lost *post mortem* – it was never there to begin with.

A congenital absence of the patella is rare and, in 70 per cent of cases, affects both sides. One-sided, or unilateral, absence of a kneecap is even more unusual. Very often – quite remarkably – this condition is asymptomatic, and people with it can still flex their knees normally and have perfectly strong quadriceps muscles. But sometimes an absent patella is accompanied by a deformed, bent knee – and significantly affects mobility, making it difficult to run or even to stand up straight. It's not so much the missing patella that causes all these problems, but the concomitant muscle defects that go along with it.

In the clinical literature on the subject, missing patellae are usually just one of the features of wider syndromes affecting other parts of the skeleton too. But the Archer doesn't seem to have had one of these syndromes. There's another possibility though: that the Archer had not been born without a patella; he'd lost it later in life. This sounds quite careless. But the clues are there in the misshapen end of his left thigh-bone, which has the hallmarks of having been ravaged by bone infection, or osteomyelitis. We could well be looking at the long-term effects of a nasty, penetrating injury to the patella, perhaps even shattering it and causing infection of the underlying joint. In an era well before surgery, the patella has no chance of reuniting, healing – and is eventually completely eaten up by inflammation. The infected knee remains painful and the bones of the leg start to change shape, to deform, in response to changed patterns of weight-bearing. If this was indeed the Archer's history, he suffered a horrendously traumatic injury to the knee, followed by what must have been a long convalescence, during which he could easily have died of sepsis if the infection had spread. But he survived it all and carried on – though he'd never be able to straighten his left knee again, and his left leg would wither. But – at the top of that left femur – pronounced gluteal muscle attachments show that he was still using, still moving that leg, at the hip. Try walking while keeping your knee slightly bent, around thirty degrees, and you'll realise how much work your muscles are doing around your hip, as you limp on the affected leg. His right leg remained strong.

So this is a man who lived with a disability. This tells us something not only about him – about the pain he suffered and his resilience – but about his society. We can presume he was looked after when the knee infection laid him low. We can also see that his disability did not detract from his status in society, as he was buried in the most lavish grave ever discovered from the British Bronze Age. Perhaps his disability was even bound up with his status — like a battle scar, or something marking him out as a survivor against the odds; someone seemingly supernaturally untouchable — until the very end.

He's emerging now, as an individual. Someone with a life history that we can pick up the threads of, so many millennia on. But there's more. More clues hidden — in all those wonderful objects that accompanied him to the grave, and preserved deep within the substance of his bones — and his teeth.

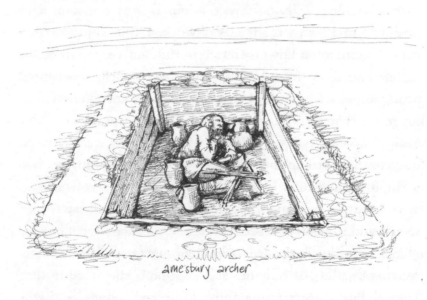

amesbury archer

Grave goods

My old *Time Team* mate — archaeologist extraordinaire and flint afficionado — Phil Harding (he of the khaki felt hat with feather — yes, him), inspected the collection of flints from the Archer's grave and described them in detail in the report. Flint artefacts are the most common grave good found in Beaker burials, and this one was absolutely replete with them. It's interesting to contrast this huge haul of flints with what you might reasonably expect a man to have carried with him on a daily basis. A glimpse of that comes from another body – found high in the Alps – now know known as Otzi. Dying alone on a mountain, Otzi shows us what at least one late-third-millennium BCE man carried around with him – rather than revealing, as the Archer does, what people thought was important to include in a grave. Otzi had just six flint objects with him: a knife, a scraper, a pointed drill, a flake and two arrowheads. And in fact, most Beaker burials only contain a small number of flints, three or four being the norm. The Archer's grave, with 122 pieces of worked flint, is just exceptional. There are a few other rich burials across the country; Phil mentions one from Wellington Quarry in Herefordshire, which contained a range of flint arrowheads, knives and flakes but fewer than twenty pieces in total – still way short of the Archer's spoils. And of the flints with the Archer, *eighteen* were arrowheads – prompting the name we now know him by. The norm in these Beaker burials is just one or two arrowheads – there's only a very small handful of graves which have ever been found to contain more than ten. One exceptional burial, near Reading in Berkshire, contained eighteen – the same as the Archer. But the only other grave goods surviving in that Reading burial were a single flint knife and some pieces of a pottery beaker.

There must have been all sorts of organic materials in the Archer's grave that have rotted away without trace, from furs or leather, grasses, food and drink, to anything made of wood. We'll never know, unfortunately, whether or not he was buried with a bow. But the organisation of the persistent flints and other durable objects around the body hints that they were wrapped up or contained in something, perhaps within bags or baskets around the body. There's that group behind his back – a large cache of flints together with two boar's tusks and the cushion stone – and the collection just in front of his forearms – flints, antler artefacts, two more boar's tusks, a copper knife, that piece of iron pyrites and the oyster shell. Similar concentrations – perhaps all that's left of a whole bagful of offerings – have been discovered in other Beaker graves: in Irthlingborough in Northamptonshire, and Radley in Oxfordshire. Fire-making kits – flint strikers together with nodules of iron pyrites or marcasite – have also been found in other Beaker graves, associated with both inhumation and cremation. Where it's been possible to determine the sex of the deceased, they are most often male. Otzi had just such a little fire-kit, or 'strike-a-light', in a pouch at his waist. The lump of iron pyrites in the Archer's grave had been well-used, with grooves along its sides from all the times it had been struck with a flint to create a spark. A fire-making kit sounds like quite a mundane, practical set of objects to be carrying around – but Phil suggests it could also have been 'a symbol of power, espe-cially as it related to the newly discovered metal technologies'. And this man also had two small copper knives and one larger copper dagger buried with him, as well as his gold ornaments: he was a man of this new Age of Metal. Other archaeologists have suggested that the significance of the fire-kit placed in the grave is that it represents light and warmth, and could help the bearer on the journey into a cold, dark afterlife. Whatever these kits meant, it seems they were important during the late third millennium BCE – and then their significance somehow diminishes; we no longer find them in graves.

But what do all these objects tell us about the man himself? Well-furnished Beaker burials tend to fall into three broad categories – identified from the selection of grave goods. There are 'artisan burials' with flint axeheads or antler tools; 'arrowhead burials', relating to hunting or feuding; and then there are these rare, exceptionally high-status, VIP burials. As far as those go, the Archer was a Very, Very Important Person. But then he also has an antler tool – a spatula that could have been used for pressure-flaking flint, Phil thinks. If so, he's an artisan too – though Phil also says he reckons that most men at this time would have been capable knappers – and, you know, maybe even some women were as well. Anyway, the Archer may have been personally responsible for at least some of the lovely, tanged and barbed arrowheads that were in his grave. He also had that cushion stone – a polished, fine-grained stone that's interpreted as a surface for metalworking – for beating copper or gold sheet. His grave has it all – it looks like a VIP/artisan/arrowhead extravaganza.

Another way to interpret the grave goods is to try to separate them into personal objects and offerings placed into the grave by others. The flint knives and fire-making kit, scrapers and some of the arrowheads were probably personal possessions, Phil argues. But the scatters of arrowheads around his feet and knees were most likely from arrows ceremonially placed in the grave, on the body. Some of the other flints might have been used in mortuary rituals, then interred in the grave. The shale ring found some distance from the body may originally have been closer, used to secure a belt. The position of such rings in other graves suggests that they are just that: the fixings on a ring belt. One end of the belt is secured onto the ring, which forms a sort of tongueless buckle. Wrapping the belt around the waist, the free end passes through the ring and is then tied off with a simple half-knot. (It's difficult to explain in words, so I have drawn it.)

The two stone bracers – one dark grey, one wine-red, both with holes at each end for fixing in place – are beautifully made objects. One was lying adjacent to the Archer's left forearm, so he was probably fully clothed and wearing the bracer in the grave. The other could have been on him originally – or perhaps added to the grave as an offering. The bracers join a collection of 109 found across Britain and Ireland. Similar examples are found across continental Europe too, often from Bell Beaker burials inserted into pre-existing megalithic, Neolithic tombs. (Sites of this age – with this diagnostic pottery – are usually called 'Bell Beaker' in Europe; in Britain we're lazy and just go with 'Beaker' – the pots are still *bell-shaped* beakers, though.) The Irish and British Beaker burials are different though, found in much more modest, purpose-built tombs. They have more in common perhaps with the Bell Beaker culture as it appears in Germany and the Netherlands.

And there's another link here – in the style of the pottery placed in graves. British beakers from this period are covered in patterns created by pressing cord into the surface of the clay – and they're very similar (in decoration but also shape) to beakers from the Rhineland, and beyond. Copper knives and daggers just like those found with the Amesbury Archer are also spread widely across western Europe. Analysis of impurities in the copper suggests that the raw material for these knives came from at least two different sources – two may have been made from Iberian copper, and one from western French copper. I wonder if the Archer knew about the provenance of that copper – and whether there were stories attached to those special knives he had.

And now – what about those gold ornaments? What do they tell us, glittering through the centuries down to us in the twenty-first century? They are described as 'basket-shaped' – and they are like tiny garden trugs. Each one is made from a flat oval of gold sheet, with a tang protruding from one of the long sides, and each is curled around – one with its long tang wrapping around the outside; the tang of the other has broken off. Again – perhaps difficult to imagine from words, so here is a picture.

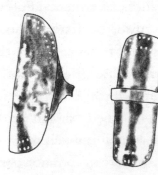

Each of the gold ovals is decorated with a double row of impressed dots around the outside. A very similar pair of gold ornaments was found in the nearby grave of the 'Archer's Companion'. This young man, who died in his twenties, had the same rare fusion in his foot bones as the Archer. It's not definitive, but certainly suggests there may have been a genetic link – that the Archer and his Companion may have been related. And a bit of the Archer's high status seems to have rubbed off on his kinsman, too. They may well have been alive at the same time. The radiocarbon date range for the Archer's grave is 2380–2290 BCE, and his Companion's 2350–2260 BCE.

The gold ornaments are rare – we can safely presume you had to be pretty special to possess such bling – but they're not unique. There are some twenty-four now known from Britain – from Moray in the north to Hampshire in the south; some discovered as pairs, in burials, others turning up as single finds, some found by metal detectorists. Three such ornaments – one pair and one single find – have been discovered in Ireland. Then – elsewhere – there's just a fragment from Brittany, three examples from Portugal, plus another possible fragment, and two from Spain. And, as Andrew Fitzpatrick has just let me know, another pair recently discovered in Belgium.

In northern Spain, during the latter half of the third millennium BCE, there was a vogue for reusing Neolithic megalithic tombs for Bell Beaker burials. There's a lot of variation as to where those burials are placed: some in the overlying mound, some tucked between stones in the passages. There are new mounds built in northern Spain as well, and in one of these – El Virgazal, at Tablada del Rudrón – archaeologists found a pair of beautiful, cylindrical gold ornaments, associated with an adult man's burial, at the centre of the mound. The golden cylinders were originally thought to be finger-rings, but they're so thin and frail – in that respect, just like those from the graves of the Amesbury Archer and his Companion. They also have tangs, but they are much larger than the Amesbury ornaments.

These finds are so obviously related to one another – part of a consistent tradition or fashion – but it's very hard to know where this trend originated. There are other types of coiled or spiral ornaments from central Europe, but the British type seems quite distinct, even within the western European tradition. They seem to fall into the same broad, European category of ornament – but with a local flavour. It also seems most likely that the Archer's ornaments were made in Britain, rather than being imported from elsewhere – even though they have those generic connections with continental jewellery.

But what exactly are they? How were they worn? Often found in pairs, sometimes near the head of a skeleton in a Beaker grave, they've traditionally been described as earrings – but the shape seems a little odd for that. In the 1980s, anthropologist Andrew Sherratt suggested instead that they were hair-wraps – decorating plaits or dreads, perhaps.

But Stuart Needham – who curated the European Bronze Age collections in the British Museum for thirty years – argued that the delicate nature of these ornaments in the Amesbury graves made them very unlikely to have been *either* hair ornaments or earrings:

Firstly, it may be questioned whether their very thin, ribbon-like tangs are well suited to penetrating through (already) pierced flesh . . . On the contrary, the tangs give the impression of having been curled into place just once, and then remaining *in situ*. If fixed permanently on the body it is hard to see these delicate ornaments surviving so well; there would be particular risk of crushing during sleep. These difficulties would apply equally to the hair tress and earring interpretations.

In some of the graves where similar ornaments have been found, they were close to the head. But it's not consistent – and the Archer's gold ornaments were down by his knees. Stuart Needham suggests they may nonetheless have been part of a special garment – a headdress or collar perhaps – that for some reason was placed lower in the grave in this instance.

What type of headdress could such ornaments have formed part of? Examining them carefully, Stuart Needham was sure they had been wrapped around *something*. He doesn't take that thought much further, but there is a possibility that's extremely enticing – if ultimately untestable – and it's that those golden wraps could have been decorations wound around the shafts of large feathers – eagles' feathers, perhaps.

How wonderful – to think of the Amesbury Archer placed in his grave with a magnificent, eagle feather headdress laid at his knees!

Now, this may seem like clutching at straws, or feathers, but there are of course many, many ethnographic examples of people wearing feathers on their heads, tucked into hair or headbands, or attached to hats. Native Americans spring quickly to mind – that lingering objectionable stereotype from a century of cowboy films – the 'Red Indian' chieftain in his white headdress. However appropriated and denigrated that image has become, through being pressed into service for sports team mascots and mangled into chicken-feather pastiches for fancy-dress parties and festivals, there's a real tradition lying under it all. For the Lakota Sioux, eagle feathers were sacred and could be earned for acts of bravery – until a warrior collected enough to make into a headdress. In the eighteenth century, Hungarian foot soldiers were recorded as adding a feather to their caps every time they dispatched an enemy. During the seventeenth century – perhaps influenced by images of Native Americans – soldiers from the Scottish Highlands began to decorate their knitted bonnets with ostrich feathers; those fluffy feather bonnets are still worn by some modern pipers and drummers. And there are images of people wearing feathers on their heads back in the Bronze Age: Libyans often appear in Ancient Egyptian art with such adornments. In a painting from the Tomb of Seti, dating to around 1300 BCE, four Libyan princes process, each with tattooed arms and legs, long, resplendent robes and a neat goatee beard, and each wearing two ostrich feathers sticking out atop his immaculately coiffured, shoulder-length black hair. Later Bronze Age depictions of the warlike Sea Peoples, who seem to have habitually made a nuisance of themselves marauding around the eastern Mediterranean, show warriors wearing feathered caps or helmets. A pair of late Bronze Age helmets from a bog west of Copenhagen are decorated with pierced studs – which analysis has revealed were mounts for feathers. And recently discovered figurines from a burial site in Novosibirsk, Siberia, dated even earlier, to the third millennium BCE, include one wearing a feather headdress.

No feathers have been found in any other Beaker burials – they're organic after all, and would be part of that vast missing catalogue of ancient culture that rots away as surely as all the soft tissue from the bare bones of our ancestors.

But some Beaker burials in continental Europe have been found with what appear to be other parts of headdresses. At Szigetszentmiklós near Budapest in Hungary, a collection of plate ornaments, made of silver-gold alloy, found with the central burial in a Beaker cemetery have been interpreted as decorations on a headdress. Similar plates have been found in graves in the Czech Republic. At Fuente Olmedo, in Valladolid in Spain, a young man was buried with a locally characteristic triad of beaker, serving dish and bowls, together with eleven copper spearheads and one copper knife, a sandstone wrist-guard and an arrowhead. He also wore what has been called a gold 'diadem' on his head – a flat strip of gold with a series of pierced holes at each end, and a couple along its length. It could have been part of a composite headdress – at the very least, it must have been laced together to form a closed loop.

So perhaps those basket ornaments from the Archer's grave, and that of his Companion, were parts of headdresses – and, specifically, wrapped around feathers. We can entertain that as a hypothesis certainly, even while we must admit to ourselves that we will never truly know their nature, their function. Andrew Fitzpatrick is still more of a fan of the hair-wrap idea, and he may be right. Hair decorations or headdresses or some-thing else entirely that we haven't thought of yet – they remain, quite deliciously in a way, wreathed in mystery. What we can say for certain about them, though, is that they represent some of the earliest gold work anywhere in northwest Europe, from the glimmering dawn of the new, metal age.

The Boscombe Bowmen

A year after the Archer and his Companion were discovered on the outskirts of Avebury, more building work was being carried out – about half a kilometre north of those graves, where the ground rises towards Boscombe Down. On the morning of 22 April 2003, archaeologist Colin Kirby, working with the developers, was carefully watching a small digger excavate a trench for a water pipe. Suddenly, he saw that the digger's bucket had cut through a patch of dark earth. He quickly looked through the earth that had been scooped out – and sure enough, there were pieces of human bone and pottery in it: another Beaker burial. He called up his colleagues at Wessex Archaeology – the team that had excavated the Archer and his Companion – to come in and help.

This grave turned out to be complex. A pit around 1 metre wide and 2.5 metres long had been cut right down into the chalk bedrock. Once again, it looked like this grave had once contained a wooden chamber, packed around with rubble. And that chamber contained the remains of at least nine individuals – one relatively intact, articulated skeleton among a jumble of disarticulated bones, and the cremated remains of an infant. Along with the human remains, there were sherds from eight beakers, an antler pendant, a boar's tusk and flints including arrowheads. Part of the grave had been damaged previously by a trench for an electricity cable, so there must have been even more artefacts accompanying the original burials – and perhaps more individuals, too.

In very general terms, the Bronze Age in western Europe was marked by a change of burial practice – from the communal, collective approach of the Neolithic, to individual burials, often under tumuli, often with grave goods, including weapons. But the Boscombe Bowmen were all buried together, in a communal grave – this looks like a continuation of Neolithic practices. Opening up a tomb – moving around earlier interments and placing new bodies in it – clearly echoes the burial practices in early Neolithic chambered tombs, over a thousand years earlier. There are other burials similar to this – around seventy examples – from Wessex and also further north, in the Yorkshire Wolds. They have been interpreted – just as chambered tombs have been – as 'family vaults'. There's a wide range of ages represented in this grave – from the cremated infant to several juveniles, whose bones were still growing, to five adults. The adults all appear to be male. Now – it could be that there were females in the grave too – remember part of the grave had been damaged previously, and it wasn't possible to assign a sex to all the disarticulated remains. But on the other hand, this seems to be a pattern that's repeated in other graves in the area of a similar date – altogether, a minimum number of forty individuals have been discovered, half of whom were immature, and of those twenty adults, seventeen were male. It's certainly suggestive of a very gendered approach to death and burial. It seems that adult women must either have been buried elsewhere, in separate graves – or perhaps they even had a completely different sort of mortuary ritual – something that means their remains are archaeologically invisible, such as cremation and scattering.

Although some other collective graves are known from the Bronze Age, the Boscombe Bowmen's tomb does seem unusual, particularly in combining what seems like a focus on the individual – with grave goods being included – in what, over time, becomes a multiple grave.

The objects interred with the Boscombe Bowmen are similar to the spread of finds with the Amesbury Archer (though no gold, this time), and include five barbed and tanged arrowheads – enough to give them their name. And then pieces of eight beakers – some squatter, some more slender – but all of them with that lovely, characteristic upside-down bell shape. I love this pottery – the shape of the beakers is so elegant and somehow satisfying. They're amazingly regular and symmetrical – especially when you consider that these are not wheel-thrown. The pottery wheel is a much later innovation, which comes along in the Iron Age. I find myself being surprised at the skill of those ceramicists – and then have to ask myself why I'm so surprised. A sense of the aesthetic and the ability to master a skill, to take pride in craftsmanship – humans have possessed these capacities and capabilities for thousands and thousands of years, as archaeology so graphically attests. But could *I* make such perfect pots, pinched into existence, so expertly formed, from a lump of clay? I'm not sure. And perhaps that's where my admiration comes from – my own naivety!

The variation among the beakers in the Bowmen's grave suggests that they were made by several different potters. And it seems that some may have been in regular use before being selected for inclusion in the grave – one has a bit of telltale wear on it. (Another, though, shows evidence of having cracked pre-firing – which probably means it wouldn't have been serviceable, and may have been made specifically for a funerary purpose.) Analysis of residue from the inner surface of the sherds of the used pot turned up traces of animal fats and plant oils. What we can't possibly tell is whether those traces relate to food eaten during prior domestic use, or at a funeral feast – or whether the food was placed in those beakers as provisions for the deceased in their afterlife.

All of the Boscombe Bowmen's beakers were covered in decoration on the outside. The styles fall into several categories of well-known pottery patterns. Seven beakers belong in the generic 'All-Over-Cord' (AOC) group, and one to the 'Cord-Zoned-Maritime' (CZM) category. Putting things in categories like these – AOC and CZM – seems a bit . . . OCD, perhaps. But the real value of these careful diagnoses emerges when you look at the bigger picture – and see how styles vary over time and across landscapes. The categories allow you to find connections that reveal how ideas were spreading and taking hold. But hold that thought for a second, because those patterns on the surface of the beakers are worth a more detailed, intimate look.

I remember very well excavating a small Bronze Age grave in Leven, Fife for a *Time Team* programme in 2001. We were investigating the site before work started on a new housing estate – and uncovered a cemetery. The sides of the graves were lined with slabs of reddish and yellowish sandstone, and many contained the bones of children – including the one I excavated. Most of the skeleton had disintegrated in the free-drawing soil, but there was enough there – unfused bones of the pelvis, and a scatter of teeth – to estimate the age of the child, who had been around twelve years old. That small body was placed tenderly in the stone-lined pit, lying on its right side, with knees drawn up – as though sleeping. And next to where the head must have been, there was a beautiful – completely intact, unbroken – pot. I prised the soil away from it very carefully. I used a wooden pottery-modelling tool – often my weapon of choice for delicate bones, as well – to flick away flakes of soil without touching the bowl itself. Eventually, the pot lay on just a small pedestal of earth, and having got ready a box with tissue paper to receive it, I could lift the bowl out of the grave. I held it in my hands and peered at it close up. It was a gorgeous object – covered with a pattern of stripes that, when I looked carefully, I could see had been created by pressing string into the damp clay when the pot was made. Over and over again – a small section of string had been gripped and impressed into the surface, making a regular, repeating pattern. The bowl looked as though it had never been used – as though it was a brand new object when it was buried: it was *made for* the grave.

Looking at those string impressions on it, I was struck by such a sense of those moments in time. Not the whole time it takes to make such a bowl, or to prepare such a grave, but those *moments* – when the string is pressed into the clay. Human experience is built of moments – and here were two, linked together across millennia. The moment I lifted the bowl out of the grave, my hands earthy from digging; the moment the potter (the mourner, the parent?) held the bowl in their hands, making that corded pattern, their hands covered in clay.

The Bowmen's beakers contained many of those moments, their surfaces amply covered in cord impressions. Look carefully and it's clear that some patterns were formed using plaited cord. Two of the beakers from the Amesbury Archer's grave were decorated in a similar way. The Cord-Zoned-Maritime pot from the Bowmen's grave has a characteristic banded pattern, with sets of stipples made by pressing a comb diagonally into the clay, separated by lines of twisted-string marks.

Radiocarbon dating places the earliest burial in the grave of the Boscombe Bowmen at 2500–2340 BCE – potentially quite a bit earlier than the Amesbury Archer. The later burials could have been contemporary with, or even slightly later than, the

Archer; the last of them dates to 2330–2200 BCE. The widest range possible here, for all of the Bowmen, looks like 2500BCE to 2200 BCE, spanning three centuries. But this is an artefact of the wide ranges on the individual radiocarbon dates. The archaeologists believe the grave was in use over a much shorter span, perhaps between twenty-five and fifty years.

The Cord-Zoned-Maritime beaker may have belonged to the earlier burials, but it seems that both styles also existed alongside each other – both in Britain and in France. Careful analysis of styles, along with radiocarbon dates, can suggest where these fashions originated – and how they spread. Both the All-Over-Cord and Cord-Zoned-Maritime types are linked to pottery styles in western Germany and the Netherlands, but they also appear in France, and this may be the proximate source for the Wessex beaker styles. The mix of pottery forms and decoration in both the graves of the Boscombe Bowmen and the Archer shows just how complex cultural evolution is – pointing to a wide range of influences and geographic connections. Cord-Zoned-Maritime beakers are quite rare, and often coastal – found at Bridgewater and Brean Down on the Somerset coast, for instance. And the one from the Bowmen's grave is quite similar to one found hundreds of miles away, at Upper Largie in Kilmartin Glen, in southwest Scotland, showing just how mobile people and ideas were in the early Bronze Age.

The pots and their patterns are fascinating – as pieces of material culture. Not all inhumations from this period contain beakers, so those that do are saying something quite definite – demonstrating affinity with a particular culture, a certain belief system, a specific identity. Where we find beakers in graves, they clearly stand for something: they are more than just containers or vessels. They are symbols – even if the meaning of those symbols has faded away through time. As an embodied element within that culture, the beaker clearly worked well. It was a successful, physical meme that spread and took hold.

Let's give the Boscombe Bowmen and the Amesbury Archer (and his mate) a bit more context, then. They're Beaker graves – part of a wider Bell Beaker culture that extends across Europe in the third millennium BCE. It lasts from around 2750 BCE to 2100 BCE – so it spans the end of the Neolithic, and in Britain seems to keep going longer, well into the Bronze Age.

In the old, three-age system of dividing up prehistoric archaeology – Stone, Bronze and Iron Ages – we'd find ourselves slotting these Beaker burials into the early Bronze Age. But archaeologists are increasingly advocating for a new Age to kick off the dawn of metalworking, separated out from the preceding Neolithic and the succeeding Bronze Age – before people start to blend tin and copper to make bronze. This new inbetweener era is called the 'Chalcolithic' – literally 'copper-stone' – or more simply, the 'Copper Age'. Copper – and gold – are worked before bronze technology takes off. The dates of the Amesbury Archer *et al.*, who died between 2500 BCE and 2200 BCE, fit into the Copper Age – as do their grave goods: copper, gold – but no bronze.

Back to the Bell Beaker culture. This is a European-wide phenomenon, with key features appearing across a great geographic spread, including: bell-shaped beakers (of course), wrist guards, copper knives (and in Iberia and France, copper spear points too), and bone or jet buttons with V-shaped holes. Anthropomorphic grave markers are also part of the Bell Beaker trend on the continent (sadly, not in Britain). But despite all the similarities that clearly bind groups of people together, or at least represent a culture with some kind of shared history, there are plenty of local variations. In western Europe, there are some collective tombs (like the Bowmen), including the reuse of Neolithic tombs; further east, away from the Atlantic coasts, it's all about individual burials. Houses vary in shape and construction – some are round, some rectangular; some timber, some dry stone. And while swathes of Europe are united by making those characteristic bell-shaped beakers, they're creating very different sorts of pottery for regular use – what archaeologists would slightly disparagingly call 'common ware'. Jugs with handles are one popular form that appears first in the Hungarian Neolithic and continues into Bell Beaker sites around 2700 BCE, then spreading south and west, reaching France by 2300 BCE. Another type of pot that follows a similar trajectory is the 'polypod cup' – more of a bowl, really – with poly pods: many feet. Pots with a line of holes near the top (for a laced decoration? To secure a lid?) emerge in the late Neolithic in northern Italy and spread north during the third millennium BCE. These trends hit at cultural *ideas* moving east to west in Europe, and south to north. But what were *people* doing?

Moving around

For decades – centuries, even – archaeologists have tried to understand the movement of people and the evolution of culture and technology by examining changing styles of objects in different places, over time. Accurate dating methods contributed enormously to the challenge – breaking the circular argument based on changing styles alone. (An object's style is identified as early in a certain context, a certain site; another site is interpreted as early based on an object's style. You could tie yourself up in knots quite easily.) With dates and careful analysis of the types of materials used, form and style – cultural evolution could be tracked and understood. That is interesting in itself. But what we really want to know, surely, is not just *how* particular ways of making flint arrowheads, specific pottery styles and new technologies like metalworking got going and spread – but *who* was doing, making, moving. We examine the objects in such detail because we want to see our ancestors, to understand them, more clearly.

Anthropologists have long sought to answer questions about migration and mobility in the past by looking at variation in bones and teeth from inhumation burials – like Pitt Rivers with his mildly obsessive skull measuring. The skulls of the Boscombe Bowmen were too fragmented to do any robust measurements, but – superficially – the shape of the skulls was short and broad. They fitted with that brachycephalic form that seems typical of Bell Beaker populations.

But now we have other ways of interrogating those human remains – to find out where their owners lived and how much they moved around during their lifetimes. Oxygen and strontium isotopes in teeth can provide clues as to where someone grew up. When your teeth are forming, they capture the chemical signature of the drinking water you imbibe and the plant food you eat – and fix it in the mineral in enamel, which stays in those teeth for life, and death. Ultimately these isotopic signatures tie you to a particular geology. Your teeth grow to match the rocks through which your water has percolated, on which your food grows.

These analyses have been applied to the remains from Amesbury – with intriguing results. The oxygen isotope results for the Archer were way too low for Amesbury. Too low for Britain, in fact. He was an isotopic alien. Instead, his isotope values match up to a geological stripe across Europe, from the Alps in the south, through central Europe, up to Scandinavia. The date of the burial, and the style of his grave goods, suggest links with the southern end of that band — around the Alps.

His Companion had different results for teeth that form at different times — suggesting that he may have started life living on the chalk downs, but moved to spend his teenage years somewhere eastwards, perhaps around the Alps again. The radiocarbon dates for the Archer and the Companion mean that the two of them may have been alive at the same time, and with those rare, fused foot bones, they were most likely related. They may have made that journey, from the Alps to southern Britain, together.

The results for the Bowmen were less clear. Many of them seemed to have started life somewhere that wasn't Wessex — but that could have been either elsewhere in Britain, in Ireland, or continental Europe. The individuals who were first buried in that multiple grave seem to have moved from one area to another during their childhoods, before ending up on Boscombe Down. Perhaps the most likely origin in Britain, based on the isotope results, is somewhere in Wales or Cumbria. Wales — now this starts to get interesting.

The first monument at Stonehenge was constructed in the late Neolithic, around 3000 BCE — a circular ditch, flanked by banks, which circumscribed a cremation cemetery. Then, around 2500 BCE, the famous standing stones were set in place: the huge sarsen stones — probably relatively local sandstone from the Marlborough Downs, 20 miles away; and the smaller — but more enigmatic — bluestones. Analysis of these dolerite stones suggest they originate from west Wales – the Preseli Hills in Pembrokeshire. Some commentators still believe that these stones could have been carried to Stonehenge, or at least to some-where nearish, by the action of glaciers during the Ice Age. But most archaeologists see little evidence for that mode of transport. And if natural forces were not to blame, human agency must have been responsible: it was not Pleistocene ice but Neolithic humans that moved the stones – more than 250 kilometres, from Pembrokeshire to Salisbury Plain. The clincher for this hypothesis is the astonishing recent discovery by Professor Mike Parker Pearson and his team of the traces of what was once a stone circle at Waun Mawn in the Preseli Hills. It appears to be the original setting of the bluestones, arranged in a stone circle matching the diameter of Stonehenge – that was then dismantled and moved, wholesale, to Wiltshire. Over the ensuing centuries, those bluestones were rearranged, and it may be that the process of remodelling Stonehenge was still going on when at least the earliest of the Bowmen was buried.

So is it possible the Bowmen came from the same place as the bluestones? Is it possible they even accompanied the stones on their journey to Salisbury Plain?

Possible – certainly. Definitely? Not at all. And we *must not* fall into that old familiar trap, so graphically demonstrated by Blick Mead. Sure, Stonehenge is nearby, but let's not get our knickers in a twist about that. Stay calm, and beware the SSSD. You may *entertain* the hypothesis that the Bowmen are associated with the bluestones, but you mustn't get too excited, and you must remain aware that this enthralling possibility is one among many. And it's important to note that archaeology suggests that there's a distinct cut-off between late Neolithic culture and Bell Beaker culture.

Now go and have a cold shower. Or a cup of tea. Whatever it takes to calm you down.

It is important to look at the wider archaeological context for these intriguing isotope results. But let's forget about Stonehenge for a while, and instead look at what the objects in the grave might tell us about connections with other places in Britain, and Europe more broadly. Unfortunately, it turns out there are loads of links, and so the origin of the Bowmen and their culture is difficult to resolve beyond 'not Boscombe'. Nevertheless, taking all the evidence in hand, Andrew Fitzpatrick believes that a continental European origin is most likely. This is what he concluded about the journeys of the Boscombe Bowmen:

> The international nature of the finds in the grave, with wide-ranging connections evident in the pottery, arrowheads and antler pendant, make it difficult to rank one region above another as a possible source. The collective burial rite is characteristic of much of western Europe . . .
>
> The evidence further emphasises the extensive mobility of the period and the suggestion that the Boscombe Bowmen came from beyond Britain is consistent with their position as one of the earliest Bell Beaker graves in Britain, and with the practice of collective burial . . . the physical similarities between the Boscombe Bowmen . . . and the fact that the adults made very similar journeys at the same ages and possibly at the same time, indicates that they belonged to a close-knit group.

There's a longstanding theory that the Beaker culture spread to Britain from the Rhineland – based on the similarity of styles of All-Over-Cord beakers from each of these areas. (There was an earlier link postulated too – with pieces of lava from the Rhineland turning up in a few Neolithic sites in southern Britain. I thought this was completely fascinating until Andrew Fitzpatrick told me these lumps of lava are now thought to be Roman. Just a few thousand years out, then!) But the source of the Beaker culture in Britain more generally may actually have been much wider – stretching across northern France – bringing together influences from both western and central Europe. This debate taps into a more general argument that has rumbled on about where the whole Bell Beaker thing started in the first place. Some argued for the Rhineland – believing that Beaker burials evolved out of an earlier fashion for graves with smaller pots, in the Netherlands. Others suggest Portugal – suggesting that Bell Beakers develop from earlier 'copos' (cups) found around the Tagus estuary. Portugal now seems to be winning, as their beakers, of the striped Maritime type, are dated earlier than anyone else's – to around 2750 BCE. The addition of weapons to the set of grave goods looks like an idea that comes in from the east – where nomadic herders originating on the Pontic steppe constructed elaborate pit burials. This culture is called Yamnaya (from the Russian for pits: *yama*) and has long been recognised to have connections with the Bell Beaker phenomenon in western Europe. Yamnaya migrations are also thought to be linked to the spread of Indo-European language – including the 'ancestors' of most of the modern languages we speak across Europe and South Asia. Yamnaya culture ripples out from the steppe, evolving as it spreads. By 2500 BCE, the Beaker package, or complex, had spread across central and western Europe, and northwest Africa too.

If the Amesbury Archer grew up in the Alps, he may have travelled north along the Rhine Valley and over the Channel to Britain, or – more likely – west, across France, to the Atlantic coast, and perhaps even to Ireland, before ending up in southern England. Ultimately, we can be reasonably sure he started his life living near the Alps, and we can be absolutely sure that he ended up at Amesbury. But the route he travelled, the details of his journey – those are secrets that he took with him to the grave.

And that grave remains the richest Beaker burial, not just in Britain, but in Europe. While none of the objects in his grave are particularly rare on their own, it's this rich mass of them that's unique. That set of bow and arrow, bracer and dagger is familiar from a few Beaker graves – we can see it as representing warrior status in an archetypal way. At this time, bows and arrows were the most common weapons – used not only for hunting animals but for bringing down humans. A burial discovered at Stonehenge, in the ditch, demonstrates this graphically: a young man, an archer himself, judging by the bracer in his grave, whose ribs had been grazed by arrowheads, with one lodged in his breastbone. Objects like flint knives, bone belt-rings, antler spatulae and fire-making kits are also exclusive to male graves. This looks like a society with very clearly defined, visibly demonstrated, binary gender roles. But the association of particular objects with genders does vary geographically. In some graves from central Europe, there are females buried with bracers and copper knives, for instance.

Was status inherited or acquired? The discovery of some Beaker graves of children with high-status objects suggests that family ties were important. A 10-year-old in Moravia was buried with a copper knife, gold hair ornaments and five pots. In Bohemia, a child's cremation burial was accompanied with a bracer, antler pendant and arrowheads.

The cushion stone in the Archer's grave is particularly interesting. Does it mark him out as a craftsman, a master metallurgist? The tradition of including metalworking tools and moulds in burials seems to come from far away – eastern Europe into western Asia, beyond the Black Sea, in those *Yamnaya* burials again. In Copper Age burials in Ukraine, some individuals are buried with a range of metalworking paraphernalia, from clay crucibles to tuyères (furnace pipes) and moulds. In the west, the tools seem to relate more to the finishing of metal objects – the cushion stone was most likely used for beating copper and gold sheet.

We are so used to metal objects today. They are part of our lives. The laptop I'm writing this on contains all sorts of metal components, from its aluminium case to its LCD screen, which contains tin as well as the much rarer indium, to the printed circuit boards with copper and iron. There's a metal cup on my desk, holding a motley collection of pens – many of which have metal nibs and clips – and another pot with paintbrushes, their bristles held in place by metal ferrules. (The etymology of ferrule is fascinating. I'd always assumed it came straight from Latin, as *ferrum* is iron. But its origin is actually *viria* – the Latin for a bracelet worn by men, from a Proto-Celtic word, *weros*, which means turned or twisted. But *ferrum* seems to have influenced its evolution over time into ferrule. Anyway, the ferrules on my paintbrushes look more like brass – an alloy of copper and zinc.) The anglepoise lamp on the corner of my writing desk is mostly aluminium, with less malleable, steel fixings, I think.

The Amesbury Archer lived in a time when metal was brand new in northwest Europe. His copper knives and gold ornaments are the earliest known pieces of metal in Britain. The first metal to be used may have been gold – as natural nuggets of pure metal can be found. Later, people worked out how to obtain metal from ores. This development emerged after pottery became widespread, in the Neolithic. The ability to control fire within a kiln, to get the temperature just right for firing pottery – that lays the foundation for creating a furnace. And I imagine it was probably noticing an accident during firing of pottery that unleashed the metalworking revolution. Copper could be freed from its ore and worked into jewellery and tools – though it was much too soft to challenge flint as the material of choice for axes and arrowheads. The Amesbury Archer's copper daggers may have *looked* good – but they weren't as useful as his flint knives. It wouldn't be long, however, before experiments (or more likely, happy accidents – perhaps somewhere like Cornwall, where both ores can be found) proved that mixing tin with copper could make a metal strong enough for serious tools and weapons: bronze.

The journeys of the Archer and his Companion, and indeed those of the Boscombe Bowmen, taking place when they did, seem to be part of the story of the arrival of the Beaker culture in Britain. And that may be linked to the spread of the new technology – metallurgy – though there's not a hard and fast link between the two. In fact, most Beaker sites in Britain and Ireland are metal-free.

Their individual journeys seem to be links in a wide network, through which sources of metal, skills and stories were shared. And if knowledge and stories were being shared, that might explain how a language family takes root and flourishes: as a *lingua franca* across that widely stretched network.

But how did the majority of people engage with that network? Was it hung on the long-distance journeys of just a few, elite individuals who took their skills and status with them when they travelled? Or were there larger-scale migrations driving the change?

The 'Beaker Folk' were once seen as invaders – a warrior culture sweeping in to replace the indigenous population of Britain, to take control of the precious sources of metal. Other explanations for the sudden appearance of beakers in Britain were that they were prestigious, prized objects, exchanged through trade networks, or indeed, sacred vessels associated with a new religious cult. The break between the late Neolithic and the Copper Age certainly looks abrupt. In the late Neolithic, the predominant funerary rite (at least, that which actually leaves a trace) is cremation – then the 'Bell Beaker Set' appears. Beaker burials, with their typical grave goods, spread extremely rapidly across Britain and Ireland in the twenty-fourth century BCE.

In the 1960s, when the culture-history paradigm went out of vogue, and models of cultural diffusion – ideas moving *through* populations – came to the fore, British scholars still tended to make an exception for the Beaker phenomenon. The arrival of that culture in Britain was still thought to have been borne on a wave of invasion. The Amesbury Archer himself demonstrates that some individuals really did travel great distances. So just how much of this change – the spread of the Beaker culture and metallurgy – is linked to mobility of people?

Archaeologists studying the Beaker phenomenon across Europe in the past two decades have placed emphasis once again on population movement. New measurements of old skulls and isotope studies of teeth in continental Europe have strengthened the case for a significant role played by migration. But did that wave of migration wash further west? And if it did, are we talking about just a few, influential immigrants arriving in Britain, or a bigger influx? How typical is the Amesbury Archer?

This is a hard – well, impossible – question to answer looking at just the material culture and a handful of isotope studies. A bigger net is needed – and that has emerged recently in the form of a huge isotope study called the Beaker People Project. An international team headed up by Mike Parker Pearson investigated around 300 skeletons – sampling their teeth for isotope analysis, and obtaining 150 new radiocarbon dates as well, together with some genetic data. The team was also keen to test that old idea that the appearance of beakers in the archaeological record coincided with a change in head shape, from long-headed to round-headed people.

The new radiocarbon dates were important – they allowed the archaeologists to see how Beaker burials spread across Britain. They first appear in Wessex, by 2400 BCE – then the Peak District, then Scotland, and finally Yorkshire, by around 2300 BCE. In each place, they appear suddenly; they don't seem to evolve out of an existing burial practice. Beakers continue to be used in British graves for five or six centuries, finally disappearing between 1900 BCE and 1800 BCE. There are changes in style over the time – of the beakers themselves, and the grave goods buried alongside them. The earliest ones are classic Bell Beakers, with low, rounded or keeled bellies, similar to those on the continent – and are found with the sorts of grave goods familiar from the Amesbury Archer's grave, from stone wristguards and arrowheads to flint tools, boar's tusks, copper knives and gold ornaments. After 2300 BCE, the style of beakers changes and becomes more diverse – they don't really look like upside-down bells any more. Archaeologists have suggested that Beaker culture changed from being a select, discrete identity to becoming much more mainstream at this time – that the diversity represents a reduction of a need to stick to a more narrowly defined Beaker identity. The following century, bronze starts to appear. The last phase of Beaker burials, after 2000 BCE – when we are out of the Copper Age, into the early Bronze Age – sees huge pottery urns joining funeral ware, accompanying both inhumation and cremation burials.

Across their sample of hundreds of burials, the Beaker People Project team found evidence for a lot of moving around. Based on strontium isotope analyses, nearly 30 per cent had moved from one geologically distinct area to another during their lives. Isotope studies are always a little tricky to get your head around as they only provide that measure of geological difference between the places where you lived out your childhood and later life. That geological difference doesn't translate into miles. You could have moved from living in Yorkshire to living in Kent, and the strontium isotopes in your bones and teeth wouldn't notice the difference. You could move from the Midlands to Wales – and there would be a strong signal of mobility. This means that some journeys over a lifetime – even over large distances – will be 'missed' by stable isotope analyses, whereas other, quite short translocations, will show up in the data. So, that 30 per cent of movers in the Beaker People Project could relate to individuals who moved within Britain, as well as journeys between Britain and Ireland and continental Europe. And the 70 per cent who don't appear to have moved will include people who lived in the same village all their life, but also some who travelled vast distances but happened to end up living on the same sort of rock.

A third of people moving from the place in which they grew

up seems high. Something that could explain such a high level of moving around, over those centuries, could be the exchange of marriage partners – and, in that way, communities forging and maintaining links, sharing cultural know-how and practices, across wide expanses. Interestingly, there's not much difference between men and women in these results – both sexes were moving around equally.

If this pattern can be explained by migration and inter-marrying, this suggests the 'Beaker Folk' were not 'invaders', but people whose individual journeys – some from the continent into Britain (and presumably, some in the other direction as well), others within Britain – added up to something significant, helping to spread a consistent culture across Europe, including Britain. It also perhaps explains why, within that theme of common culture – within the 'Beaker package' – there's plenty of local variation.

There must have been something about the Beaker way of life that made it attractive, too – and it certainly was successful, if we can judge success based on the growth of Copper Age communities.

And now here we are, at the dawn of the Age of Archaeogenomics, where geneticists can suddenly make a massive and meaningful contribution to these debates about ancient migrations, evolving cultures and that enduring question – who *were* the Beaker People? Across several separate studies, the genomes of individuals buried in Beaker graves in Germany and the Czech Republic were shown to blend inheritance from local Neolithic farmers and incomers whose ancestry hailed from the Eurasian steppe. That link with the Yamnaya culture – and Proto-Indo-European languages – was written into their DNA. Indeed, the title of one of the publications of genomic research was 'Massive migration from the steppe was a source for Indo-European languages in Europe'.

A massive study of 400 ancient Europeans – published in 2018 – looking at genome-wide patterns of variation and comparing Neolithic with Copper Age and Bronze Age genomes, has provided the most complete picture to date. The picture for Britain was particularly arresting. Genomes are very different after 2500 BCE; Neolithic ancestry is almost completely replaced, in the Copper Age, by genomes that share ancestry with central Europeans associated with the Beaker complex (and they in turn possess a high level of steppe ancestry). The level of population turnover over the second half of the third millennium BCE was about 90 per cent, judging by genome-wide changes. A similar degree of replacement is seen in Y chromosomes, where a new type, or haplogroup, arrives in the Copper Age – and this 'family' of related Y chromosomes quickly spreads, to be found in 90 per cent of the population. But it wasn't just new male lineages arriving – mitochondrial DNA (inherited down the maternal line) changes, too. It seems all too easy to slip into another trap here – that of gender stereotypes. It's interesting to think about the roles of men and women – and children – in past societies, but important not to jump to conclusions or make assumptions. I think we should be cautious – suspicious even – about tales of heroic men: those smiths and warriors on their epic quests. When it comes to women, the story is usually considerably less epic – more passive, even: they move to get married. But the genetic data provides us with a disinterested, objective picture: men and women were *both* travelling, moving around an increasingly Beaker-dominated Europe, at this time. And the people arriving in Britain would have looked different from the existing

Neolithic population. The geneticists were able to look at specific gene variants, revealing that the incomers possessed genes
associated with lighter skin tone and eye colour.

The genomic data also reveals astonishing insights into familial relationships among these people. Tom Booth, together
with Jo Bruck from University College Dublin, have been
poring over the data, pulling out these connections into plain
view. Of twenty-one early Bronze Age individuals sampled
from Wiltshire, for instance, twelve were close relatives –
ranging from parent–child or siblings to first cousins. Eight of
the eleven people sampled from around Amesbury were also
closely related. Two of these related individuals were within
the Boscombe Bowmen's grave: an articulated male skeleton
turned out to be a second- to third-degree relative of an individual represented by a disarticulated skull, found at his feet.
The isotope results from those two individuals suggested that
they were not local – and that they had grown up in the same
area in childhood – although whether that childhood home
was Wales, the Midlands, Cumbria or Scotland, or indeed
Brittany, it's impossible to know. (The articulated male was
also interesting as his burial is classically 'Beaker' but he has
a high level of indigenous ancestry, suggesting that one of his
parents was descended from Neolithic ancestors – in Britain
or perhaps Brittany.) So, just as we have seen with the genetic
revelations from Neolithic tombs, there seems to have been a
very clear awareness of family ties and lineages in the Copper
Age and early Bronze Age. While people were moving around,
then, they were maintaining those family connections.

At first glance, the genetic data seems inconsistent with
the isotope studies – which showed that, while some people
moved to these islands from the continent, most of the mobility

written into Copper and Bronze Age teeth happened *within* Britain. In other words, while there is evidence for longer journeys, we're seeing much *more* evidence for *short* journeys. Those could have included seasonal movements – following herds, or meeting up for ceremonies and festivals, places were marriages might have been forged. But isotopes and genes are measuring different things, each telling us different stories. The strontium in your teeth records where *you* grew up. It doesn't tell us where your parents, grandparents – or indeed, any of your ancestors – came from. So, if we're trying to track migrations, it's only going to reveal first-generation migrants. An added complication is that – according to the isotope signature in your teeth – you could have grown up anywhere with a matching geology. In terms of where the migrants into Britain are coming from, that's somewhat tricky to pin down at the moment. There's a suggestion of a genetic link with the Netherlands, though this is based on genomes dating to the early Bronze Age – too late to be sure that this is where the British Beaker folk really came from. And it's not a connection we can test with isotope studies of teeth – even if we catch the actual migrants – either: the geology is too similar on either side of the North Sea.

Andrew Fitzpatrick urges caution about making sweeping statements about the demographic changes in Britain, too, as the data is still quite patchy. Only a handful of British Beaker individuals were analysed in that big 2018 study, and most were from around Amesbury (the Archer himself wasn't included, but his Companion was – and he had a high degree of steppe ancestry). On the near continent, slightly later early Bronze Age burials from the Netherlands were sampled, but it would have been great to have some French and Belgian Copper Age

Beaker samples too. Although each genome effectively provides a sample of all the ancestors of that particular individual, we're still missing detail – and looking at a very geographically limited region of Britain – and indeed the near continent. We're at the point where some real revelations are emerging, but it leaves us hungry for more. (This is why I'm so excited about Pontus' new study – when all those new samples are sequenced.)

What we can say, though, is that it seems the archaeologists of the nineteenth and early twentieth century – like Pitt Rivers – really were on to something when they identified those burials-with-beakers with a particular group of *people*. But, as we've seen, that type of explanation for cultural change in archaeology became deeply unpopular after the 1960s – viewed with extreme suspicion, linked as it was to ideas of racial supremacy, even eugenics and the worst atrocities of fascism.

The latest generation of geneticists, though, are very careful to emphasise that the spread of the Beaker complex cannot be simply mapped onto the expansion of a genetically homogeneous population. On the one hand, the role of migration in establishing Beaker culture across Europe was clearly profound. But on the other, cultural transmission clearly played a role as well. And the relative importance of migration and cultural diffusion varied *a lot* from place to place. For Andrew Fitzpatrick, this was one of the important insights provided by that large ancient DNA study. In central Europe there's a very strong signal of steppe-related ancestry – linked back through the generations to the Yamnaya of the Great Eurasian Steppe – sweeping through populations and coinciding with the spread of Beaker culture. That result has been seized upon by the popular media, spawning stories and headlines about war-bands of horsemen marauding across Europe. Now, the change of ancestry may be abrupt, but we simply don't know how dramatic or violent the transition was. What we can say with some certainty is that it's likely to have varied a lot from place to place. And there's also a vast region where the arrival of Beaker culture was *not* linked to a genetic turnover. In Iberia, the people who made the Beaker complex were genetically most similar to the people who had lived in Iberia during the Neolithic: there was very little population turnover. But there's no hard and fast divide – a few Bronze Age Iberians do have steppe ancestry. Ancient genomics provides us with this amazing power to look at how migrations and mobility influence culture changes over time – but at no point should we find ourselves falling back under the spell of the old culture-history paradigm. What the Iberian results show us is that the Bell Beaker network, as Andrew Fitzpatrick has put it, 'was connected as much by ideas and beliefs as it was by migration'.

Genetic identity and social or cultural identity are two separate things: sometimes they happen to coincide; sometimes they don't. The picture is complex and complicated – and nowhere can we point to a circumscribed Beaker 'race'. (Well, of course not – because the fundamental idea of 'race' is flawed. It makes no sense biologically or historically. In fact, it doesn't make any sense to anyone apart from people who are determined to ignore complex reality in order to persist in being racist.) The spread of the Bell Beaker culture was mediated by migration, but the culture has a life of its own as well – as a network of ideas.

In Britain, the arrival of that steppe ancestry in the third millennium BCE is part of a massive population turnover. Remarkably, despite all the comings and goings that have happened in these islands over subsequent centuries – all those historically attested invasions of Romans, Anglo-Saxons, Vikings and Normans – the genetic background of Britain is still predominantly that of the Bronze Age. (Tom Booth has told me there's evidence emerging of another population turn-over, though not so profound, in the middle Bronze Age as well – which could be when Celtic languages spread through Britain – and then genetic continuity through the subsequent Iron Age – in stark contrast to the old, traditional theory that the first millennium BCE saw major 'Celtic' migrations into Britain.)

What do these revelations from ancient DNA, from all those thousands of years ago, mean for you? Well, no matter how far back your roots go in Britain, this does not mean that *you* have Bronze Age DNA. You have twentieth- or 21st-century DNA, and hidden away among its billions of letters are fragments from some (but not all) of your ancient ancestors. The value we may attach to decoding ancient DNA lies in understanding the past better. And although it feels personal, it doesn't confer any rights or privileges – or indeed, any stigmata or stain. You don't need any genetic connection to feel part of a place, part of a community. And the past – well, the past belongs to everyone.

In terms of what ancient DNA can reveal about the past, it is: a lot. But there are plenty of things it cannot tell us.

There's an internet phenomenon called 'unboxing' where people receive a parcel and film themselves opening it. It's something I find very hard to get my head around. Why would anyone want to watch someone else opening a parcel? Many people, it turns out. So much so, that companies now pay even more attention to the design of their boxes, and either make their own unboxing videos or send complimentary products to famous Unboxers in the hope that they will play along and deliver a free advert. There are children doing it too. A kid called Ryan is already making a handsome living by unboxing toys on Youtube. His channel has – wait for it – 24.6 MILLION subscribers. The world has gone mad. Imagine what the Amesbury Archer would make of it all. Anyway, I digress. There is a point to Unboxing (at least, there is in the world of metaphors; I'm still not sure there is in Real Life). Science, you see, is the ultimate Unboxer. What it unboxes, though, are not *things* – but knowledge. Inside every box is the solution to a scientific question. But science takes unboxing to an absolute extreme. Because every package contains another. Every answer to a question opens up another question; often, a whole load – a panoply even – of questions.

Some of those boxes are, in theory at least, openable. Others – we must admit to ourselves – are not. Sometimes the evidence is long lost. Sometimes the questions we're asking are ones that science simply cannot answer (and there are plenty of those). Some may be answerable in the future, but not yet.

Ancient DNA can provide insights at different scales. It can give us a bird's-eye view of population movements and migrations across vast landscapes. We can zoom in and look at individuals, finding relatives interred in the same tomb; even beginning to be able to reconstruct appearances. We'll see how diseases have ravaged and shaped human history – Pooja's particular fascination. The DNA is part of the story, but not all of it, by any stretch of the imagination. And we still need archaeology to explore past human experience more fully – to look at what happened when different communities came together, how individuals made a place for themselves in the world, how identities were expressed in different societies, through culture. But the power of ancient DNA to settle some very longstanding debates is profound.

Archaeologists have been asking the question about ancient migrations and culture for so long, with no real means of answering it, that the question seemed to have elevated itself to some metaphysical level – where the only means of approaching it was through theory. As one suggestion fell out of favour, another would emerge to take its place, and all of them were ultimately untestable. The debate becomes quasi-theological. How many angels could possibly dance on the head of a pin?

Then a new branch of science comes along, with some seriously disruptive technology, and says: we may be able to provide an Answer to this Question. The priests of Archaeology stroke their beards (some of them really do have beards, even quite long ones – while many don't) and express doubts as to whether a geneticist could even begin to understand the Question. But the geneticists go ahead and drill the bones, extract the ancient DNA, retreat to their labs, do some fancy statistics, and – like some kind of alchemist cooking up a dull lump of lead into gold – they come up with an Answer. They present it to the priests: 'We think this is what you've been looking for.' But the priests narrow their eyes, sigh and fold their hands in their laps. 'It's just Fool's Gold,' they say. 'Iron pyrites. You can make fire with it. But it is not the Answer. It isn't the Answer because it doesn't agree with the sacred texts of Post-Processualism.'

The geneticists are not at all helped by the media, who so often take an Answer and run with it, coming up with a great variety of interpretations that are neither suggested by the data, nor indeed within the power of science to offer up (though some archaeologists think certain geneticists have also not helped themselves – setting out to tackle big archaeological questions while seeking very little engagement with their archaeological colleagues). When the big Beaker paper on the 'genomic transformation of northwest Europe' came out in 2018 – authored by Iñigo Olalde, David Reich and – if my count is correct – 142 others, the headlines were particularly florid. One proclaimed, 'Ancient-genome study finds Bronze Age "Beaker culture" invaded Britain', and another asked, 'Did Dutch hordes kill off the early Britons who started Stonehenge?' (Remind you of Blick Mead, anyone?)

The data supported a population replacement, but that's not at all the same thing as an invasion – which surely implies a violent seizing of territory. There's no evidence for increased violence in this period – and as the DNA shows, both men and women were migrating into Britain. As for the question asked in the second headline, the answer is: we don't know, we can't know – and anyway, 'Dutch hordes' is extremely questionable.

From what we can tell of demographics, it looks like there was a rapid increase in population during the first few centuries of the Neolithic, in the early fourth millennium BCE – largely driven by migration. Radiocarbon dates on preserved grains show that crops spread rapidly across the British Isles. But then, in the later fourth millennium BCE, it seems that cereal cultivation was abandoned and there was a switch to more nomadic pastoralism – with plenty of wild foods being eaten alongside domesticated livestock. It's likely that the change in farming practice was linked to a deterioration in climate. And along with that, there was a population collapse. Long barrows fell out of use. Causewayed enclosures fell into ruin. Fields were abandoned. (And in fact, we don't see a resurgence of cereal farming until even later – around 1500 BCE – with a second agricultural revolution coming along in the middle

Bronze Age.) So this is the background to the arrival of the Beaker complex in Britain – it follows that Neolithic population collapse.

The genomic transformation paper certainly set the cat among the pigeons. But this was not a clear case of geneticists versus archaeologists. In fact, there were plenty of eminent Bronze Age archaeologists among the authors on the paper. But there was much consternation in the archaeological community more widely. They'd spent years avoiding imperial, colonial, nationalist reconstructions of the deep past. The culture-history paradigm had been consigned to the dustbin of history, together with all its nasty, divisive and even dangerous associations – and here it was, raising its ugly head again. And it was all too easy for such results to be picked up and either over-simplified or knowingly framed to suit a particular political end.

And there was an important finding from the archaeological record that needed to be accommodated – and that was the persistence of Neolithic culture into the Bronze Age. The incomers didn't completely wipe out what went before, starting out afresh. The Bronze Age people also seemed to respect their Neolithic antecedents as well – in some places, inserting burials into already-ancient tombs. The Beaker complex is a 'new thing', but there's cultural continuity too. There could be some bias in the genetic data, simply because it is based on bones from inhumation burials – which are part of the Beaker complex. If indigenous people were practising other mortuary rites, they become genetically invisible. This is particularly pertinent at this point in time, as cremation – which completely destroys DNA – was the most widespread mortuary rite before the appearance of the Beaker complex. But the original authors of the paper countered that criticism: steppe ancestry persists through time in the British population – although there is an increase in old, Neolithic-related ancestry after 2000 BCE. That could come from communities who had persisted in Britain, perhaps remaining quite separate from those Beaker people for a while, at least – or from other places, where Neolithic ancestry persisted.

Some archaeologists have strongly resisted the ancient DNA story. Neil Carling, at University College Dublin, called the proposed link between demographic and cultural changes in the third millennium BCE a 'curious assumption'. He and others see it as regressive – and they are of course right to be wary about the misappropriation of history for political ends. History involving migrations is particularly incendiary – having been variously used to fan the fires of anti-immigration rhetoric; to justify imperialism and colonialism; to support theories of racial supremacy. It's hugely important to be conscious of the malevolent ends to which impartial facts can be turned.

And yet, that's not a reason to deny the facts. And if we do, dark forces will enjoy that even more. We need to be as objective as possible in our approach to history and archaeology, while recognising that our interpretations will *always* be coloured by our own political and cultural perspectives. There's a formidable culture clash playing out right now in the territory that genetics and archaeology are fighting over. A couple of years ago, the German prehistorian Philipp Stockhammer – whose work focuses on linking up these disciplines – summed it up: 'Half the archaeologists think ancient DNA can solve everything. The other half think ancient DNA is the devil's work.' Archaeology has been rattled by technological innovation before. Archaeologists like Pitt Rivers had only the relative positions of objects and features in the ground, and comparisons with other sites, to help them work out sequences of events in prehistory. Then, in the mid-twentieth century, radiocarbon dating came along and offered the potential for pinning actual, 'absolute' dates on discoveries. That was another cat-among-the-pigeons moment. Suddenly, some questions became easy to answer. It caused a philosophical shift in archaeology – once archaeologists had dependable dates and sequences, they could shift more of their focus to the interesting questions – about what those sequences *meant*.

The new technology was tricky, though. Radiocarbon dating, it's fair to say, was somewhat dodgy at first. It got much more reliable over time. We've seen the same thing with genetics – with tantalising but fragmented and sketchy data emerging first, from very small samples. In fact, the very first ancient DNA paper ever published, back in 1985, presented genetic sequences from an Egyptian mummy that are now thought to be rogue DNA in what must have been a contaminated sample. Geneticists have got much better at eliminating contamination, and the speed of reading the DNA code has massively accelerated. In 2010, the first complete ancient genome – from a 4,000-year-old Greenlander – was sequenced. Just ten years on, we're in the era of 'big data', with the potential for sampling and fully sequencing thousands of ancient genomes. It's now hard to imagine archaeology without techniques like radiocarbon dating being available – and perhaps, very soon, we'll think about ancient genomics in the same way. And just as the radiocarbon revolution caused a shift in the kinds of questions archaeologists were able to pursue, genomics is likely to create a philosophical ripple, too.

The fusion of genomics and archaeology that is happening right now is fascinating – two disciplines with two very different approaches, speaking quite different languages, are coming together. The union will be tricky, especially as ancient genomics pays little heed to archaeological theory – to culture-history, to processualism, to post-processualism. In some ways, geneticists may be able to help unpick longstanding archaeological debates, not only because of the data they offer, but perhaps precisely because they come unburdened by that theoretical baggage. Archaeologists are probably right to be wary about overly simplistic interpretations, driven by shiny new technology. There's a balance to be struck. A blending of two ores that will, I am optimistic, make archaeology stronger. That's Pontus' aim, certainly – and his Thousand Ancient Genomes project has been collaborative from the very start. And Tom Booth represents the fusion of the two disciplines in a single person, being that curious hybrid: both an archaeologist *and* a geneticist.

But the Unboxed answer will still always lead to a plethora of new, boxed-up questions. What motivates migrations? If there was this profound population turnover in Britain that coincides with the Beaker complex, how did that play out over the centuries? There would already have been connections between populations either side of the Channel and the North Sea. Did a few Beaker farmers come over and set up enclaves, inviting more cousins from across the sea to join them, generation by generation? Did itinerant metal prospectors journey here – did the exchange of raw materials and technological ideas promote mobility and migration? Were there clashes between Beaker warriors and Neolithic farmers? How did those two communities interact? How can the genetic signal of population turnover be squared with evidence for cultural continuity? Some of these questions are answerable; some more difficult. At the moment, we can tell the 'bigger picture' story with increasing accuracy – we can see that large-scale population replacement happened in Britain during the Copper and Bronze Ages. But what we really want to know is what that looked like on a local level. (That's one reason I'm so excited by the chance to unlock the ancient genomes from Cranborne Chase, as they represent a deep slice through time, in one place.) Inevitably, the answer will never be a one-size-fits-all, but a varied pattern – the details of which may never be uncovered, though glimpses may appear here and there. The Amesbury Archer is one of those 'glimpses' – a man whose burial tells us so much about his culture, and about how his community respected his status. There's so much we know about him, with the powerful scientific tools we can now employ to mine secrets from bone and teeth. But, on the other hand, there's so much that we will never know, and can only guess at.

Many archaeologists have suggested that Bronze Age smiths were high-status individuals – able to harness that fiery magic, and – alchemist-like – transform material reality, pull metal from stone. Some have even put forward the idea that the status of metalworker could have been so high that a 'smith' would also, automatically, have been a 'chief'. Now, this is where we leave the science behind and wander off into the realm of speculation. But it's interesting to speculate.

In the Copper Age, metal was still very rare – being a smith, a metalworker, must have been far from a full-time job. Instead, it may have been a special, rarely used ability. It could have been linked to privileged access to both knowledge and raw materials – and perhaps it's relevant that the Archer was buried a long way from any sources of metal.

Metallurgy, then, would have been a kind of superpower.

Not something you did all day, every day. The metalworker status embodied in some graves seems tied up with warrior status too. And that's certainly the case with the Amesbury Archer, with his arrows and his daggers.

If you go on a pilgrimage to Salisbury Museum, then, you can see him – laid out just as he was in his tomb, with all those astonishing grave goods arrayed around him. There he lies: the warrior-smith from the dawn of the Copper Age, forty-three centuries ago.

A metal-bending, bow-wielding, time-travelling magician.

8.

THE CHARIOTEERS

The Romans did many things for us. They built aqueducts, sewers, roads. They brought irrigation, medicine, education, wine. They created public baths, law and order. But they also left us with a portrait of the ancient Britons – before Roman invasion and colonisation – that has coloured our perceptions of the British Iron Age for far too long.

The classical caricature of the Iron Age people of northwest Europe, often known as the 'Celts', is that they were a fairly uncivilised lot. They may have been good fighters, but they had no real knowledge, science or art. They were warlike and hard-drinking. They even drank undiluted wine! They wore barbaric clothes – trousers! And that was when they were wearing clothes, I mean; they went practically *naked* into battle, just wearing gold torcs round their necks! And they went in for headhunting and human sacrifice. And they even – perhaps worst of all – had *women leaders*. Utterly, utterly barbaric.

We don't know what the Iron Age Britons thought of those stereotypes – because they didn't leave a written record. The Greeks and the Romans got in there with their new-fangled literacy and could peddle their propaganda to us without contention. But there is another way for us to uncover a – perhaps more accurate – portrait of the ancient Britons. And that is through burial archaeology.

So, what do our Iron Age ancestors tell us about themselves?

Pocklington

Across much of Britain, there's not much trace of the dead of the Iron Age. They are missing from vast swathes of the countryside. And then there are 'islands' where they're suddenly very visible and – occasionally – nothing short of spectacular, with burials packed full of grave goods. Inhumation cemeteries are known from Dorset and further southwest, and then up in Yorkshire, with a scatter elsewhere that have perhaps been overlooked or wrongly dated until quite recently. Of course, this doesn't mean that people weren't practising funeral rites elsewhere, but that whatever they were doing – cremations, excarnations, the odd pit burial – left less of a lasting archaeological impression.

Yorkshire seems to have been a focus for a very specific and elaborate funerary rite: chariot burials. Twenty-five examples have been discovered in Britain – and all but three of them are from east Yorkshire. It looks like the signature of a group of people with a distinct identity. Although the word has some problematic connotations, some would venture to call them a 'tribe'. Their archaeological signature is named after the farm in whose fields it was first recognised – 'Arras' culture.

In 2014, archaeologists were busy working on the edge of the Yorkshire Wolds, readying a site to the southeast of the village of Pocklington for a new housing development. The area was known to be rich in Iron Age archaeology, and aerial photographs taken in 1973 had shown plenty of cropmarks in the fields around Burnby Lane – the site of the intended development. So the team from Malton Archaeological Practice (MAP) decided to carry out a geophysical survey before breaking ground. On their scans, they saw clear traces of around ten barrows. Not Neolithic long barrows or Bronze Age round barrows this time – but square barrows, typical for the Iron Age in this area. So when the archaeologists started digging, they'd anticipated uncovering a small cemetery. As soon as they stripped the top-soil away, they found dark features: rectangular ditches, with central pits. But as they continued to dig, the scale of the ceme-tery exceeded all their expectations. They ended up extending their archaeological interrogation over 4.4 hectares. More and more barrows appeared, each containing several burials. Over the next three years, they would uncover a total of eighty-three square barrows and come across the skeletal remains of a 172 Iron Age individuals interred within them. Overlying red Mercian mudstone, the soil was quite acidic and the bones had not fared well – they were extremely fragile.

Most of the graves were very simple – only twenty-seven contained anything in the way of grave goods. Among them, there were a few beads and copper-alloy brooches and bracelets. Some individuals were accompanied by iron objects – perhaps studs of some kind. A couple of graves contained bone or antler toggles; one had a pottery vessel. The bones of a juvenile pig accompanied one burial in the centre of a square barrow – this being the only grave containing any sort of identifiable food offering. There were just two accompanied by weapons: one of a young male with an iron sword and five spearheads, and another individual buried in a crouched position on top of a large, rectangular shield, only the harder edge of which had survived. There was one other cart or chariot burial – in Barrow 85. It was plough-damaged – one of the wheels and half of the skeleton had been destroyed, but the remaining wheel was quite extraordinary. Laid flat in the grave, the iron tyre survived, but here the ghost of the wood in the soil was easier to pick out. The archaeologists could carefully trowel around the outline until the whole shape of the twelve-spoked wheel was revealed. This grave also contained the skeletons of a pair of ponies – but these two had been laid in the grave on their sides, their hooves interlaced above the head of the grave's human occupant. Aside from the human burials at Burnby Lane, there were two complete cows, buried in their own rectangular graves – one old, one young.

The vast majority of those 172 burials at Burnby Lane were adults. There were just four children under the age of twelve and three older juveniles, in their teens when they died. There was a fairly standard, familiar roll-call of injury and disease among the skeletons – fractures, joint disease and signs of vitamin deficiency. But against that background, there were some more remarkable pathologies: a young man with severe infectious lesions in his bones; a young woman who had suffered a terrible blow to her left thigh; and an older man who had broken his left forearm, and the bones had failed to fuse.

In 2016, the Maldon archaeologists uncovered another Iron Age cemetery in the southern Yorkshire Wolds – seventeen barrows, and among them, once again – a chariot burial. Just like the one at Burnby Lane, that chariot had been dismantled and its components laid flat, before the body was placed in the grave. Radiocarbon dating of the bones yielded a date of 328–204 BCE.

And then, in the spring of 2018, the team made a sensational discovery. A mile away from the original site, they found the unmistakeable traces of another, very large square barrow.

Archaeologist Mark Stephens was leading the excavation and quickly realised he was dealing with something quite exceptional. As his team dug down within the rectangular ditch that marked the periphery of the barrow, they found two curved, heavily corroded iron objects. Mark knew immediately what they were: the tops of the rims of two wheels, standing upright in the ground. Mark expected those iron rims to reach down some 90cm below the surface. Wheels like that – inside an Iron Age barrow: Mark knew what this meant. He'd discovered a chariot burial – and right from the start, it looked special.

The chariot

The Pocklington chariot burial clearly belonged to that well-known Arras culture. But there was something different about it. Most chariot burials – including the two that MAP had uncovered in those previous excavations – involve a vehicle that has been completely dismantled, taken apart, with the wheels laid flat in the grave. Only a handful of others like this – one from Newbridge near Edinburgh – had ever been recorded: containing an intact chariot – 'up and ready to go', as Mark Stephens put it.

His team of archaeologists continued digging, under a small tent to protect the remains, as they were exposed for the first time in over two millennia. Behind the iron-rimmed wheels, they found a rectangular stain of darker soil – all that was left of the wooden or wicker carriage of the chariot. And within the carriage, the skeletal remains of the driver, his body tucked into a crouched position to fit him in. In front of the chariot, the archaeologists began to uncover even more bones. Not human this time – but a pair of skeletal ponies. A chariot *with* horses – this was very unusual indeed. Then, as the archaeologists carefully revealed the skeletons of the two ponies, they discovered something striking about the animals. Rather than having been laid down in the bottom of the grave – those dead horses were standing upright in it.

Iron Age expert Dr Melanie Giles, from Manchester University, couldn't wait to get a glimpse of the excavation. 'It's a once-in-a-lifetime opportunity,' she said, visiting the site. 'This is one of the most dramatic burials we know of, from this area, in the Iron Age.' Paula Ware, the director of MAP, had seen chariot burials before – but nothing quite like this. 'This is one of the most significant chariots that we've excavated,' she said. 'It's changing our outlook and perception of the Iron Age.' They both knew – before the excavation had even finished – that this was one of the most exciting Iron Age discoveries ever to be found in Britain.

When the dig was over and the team had had a chance to start the post-excavation work – commissioning tests and specialist reports, pulling all the evidence together and starting to make interpretations and draw conclusions – I met up with Melanie and Paula to pick their brains about this utterly extraordinary grave.

They showed me the photogrammetry of the grave – photos stitched together to create a 3D model – with the two pony skeletons fully excavated. It really was incredible – I'd certainly never seen or heard of anything quite like it.

'We were really surprised,' said Paula. 'Two upright ponies, the chariot, the skeleton – just amazing.'

We looked at the 3D model together, rotating it. Something was clearly missing from the horse skeletons – they had no skulls. But Melanie was sure that we weren't looking at evidence of a macabre ritual – instead, this was just the result of later damage to the grave.

'The poor ponies have lost their heads,' she said. 'But they would have once been up higher, in the barrow, but they've been sheared off by the plough – millennia ago, probably.'

'How do you think they got the ponies into that grave, in that upright position?' I asked her.

'Well, from what we can tell, they're an old pair of ponies,' she replied. 'So they're a tried and tested team. And maybe they trust their owners – enough to go down into the pit. I would guess they're encouraged to take that jump down into the grave pit, on their own, and then you get the chariot in, harness them up – and perhaps slit their throats as you back-fill rapidly around them.'

This did sound particularly macabre – though we should be careful not to impose our 21st-century sensibilities on the past, of course. Whatever the details, it seemed most likely the ponies had entered the grave alive – and had not been dispatched until the grave had been sufficiently filled in, to stop them falling over. Of course the other option is that they could have been buried alive. Consigning two, presumably valuable, animals to a grave like this – along with the chariot itself – must have represented a significant sacrifice for that community. A sacrifice that surely marked their respect for that man and his status.

The chariot's wooden structure had completely rotted away, although there were ghosts in the soil. Traces of the wheel – its wooden rim inside the iron tyre and, with the eye of faith, even the spokes – were appreciable through subtle changes in texture and colour – to an experienced archaeologist. The metal components had stood the test of time better. There were brass rings – bright green with verdigris – which would have capped the hubs; a rusted lump of iron was the linch pin that would have held the wheel in place on the axle.

But everything was very fragile. Once the circular iron tyres of each wheel had been fully excavated, the archaeologists encased them in plaster of Paris to provide support, before gently lifting them out of the grave. Each tyre had been forged as a continuous ring of iron – rather than a bent and welded strip – to avoid points of weakness; they had been made by highly skilled metalworkers.

In 2015, I was lucky enough to take a reconstruction of an Iron Age chariot, made by Robert Hurford, out for a spin, driving it along the flat sand of Burnham Beach in Somerset. The metalwork on it was functional but also beautiful – including decorative, glittering brass fixings. These chariots were lightly built, for speed and manoeuvrability, pulled by two ponies. We know (Julius Caesar tells us in quite a bit of detail) that these chariots were used for warfare. But it's very likely that they were much more widely used, for patrolling territory and for travel – and that the ability to roam in that way was inextricably connected with political power. Across Europe in the Iron Age, horses were both essential mechanisms and symbols of power.

And Yorkshire still bears the traces of horse-drawn travel and transport in the Iron Age.

Landscape archaeologist Peter Halkon, based at the University of Hull, has spent years scouring the Yorkshire Wolds for traces of Iron Age activity. Using aerial archaeology in particular – looking for traces of buried features in crop marks – he's detected previously unrecognised trackways. Excavating a portion of one such trackway, he uncovered ruts created by chariot or cart wheels. The spacing was right – exactly the same width as that between the wheels on their axle in the Pocklington burial.

We tend to think of the Romans building the first roads in Britain – but Peter had uncovered evidence that Iron Age Britons had roads centuries before the Romans arrived. Their trackways appeared to have been specially prepared, rather than simply forming through use; it looked like they had deliberately removed topsoil to expose the hard-wearing surface of the chalk. The network of trackways was extensive: hundreds of them, connecting communities across the Wolds. One of the ancient trackways runs very close to Pocklington – it may even be the road on which the chariot travelled, on its last journey, to the grave.

This landscape archaeology tells us something about the wider community that the Pocklington charioteer – or perhaps, chieftain – was part of. It was clearly a well-connected, organised society, and 'not a woodland full of wild people!', as Peter Halkon has put it. When the results of the isotope analysis of the charioteer's teeth came back from the lab, they showed that he had most likely been a local, born and bred on the chalk uplands of the Wolds. But he must have known the wider landscape well. The chariot in his grave is a symbol of status, even more potent than a Mercedes today, speaking not just of wealth, but of the ability of this man to travel, to control territory.

The skeleton

I looked at the skeleton of the charioteer with Paula and Melanie. The bones were relatively well preserved, compared with some of the other Pocklington burials.

'He looks old. These are not the bones of a young man,' I said, peering at the joint surfaces, and at the very few remaining teeth clinging on in his jaws.

'He's got a lot of wear and tear – and not many teeth left,' Melanie agreed.

All of his front teeth were long gone – he would have had a toothless smile.

It's hard to age adult skeletons accurately – we all age at slightly different rates, from a biological point of view. What we do with our bodies has an enormous effect. An active lifestyle is generally protective – keeping the heart healthy as well as maintaining strong muscles, protecting joints from premature degeneration. But on the other hand, overly strenuous activities can cause injuries. Careful assessment of the bones of this man suggested that he was at least forty-six years old at death, though I wouldn't be at all surprised if he'd been a decade (even two) older than that. There was plenty of evidence of degenerative joint disease in his skeleton. Along with dental disease, osteoarthritis is the most common pathological change seen in archaeological human remains. It's hard to draw robust conclusions from them on an individual basis; we end up with vague pronouncements such as 'he had a strenuously active lifestyle'. But as well as those fairly non-specific signs of joint disease, there was more particular evidence of stress on certain tendons and ligaments. Along the edge of each of his finger bones – or phalanges – was a prominent ridge of bone. This is where the tunnel-like ligaments that retain the long finger tendons are attached to the bones. It suggests that this man had a powerfully developed grip. It is very tempting of course to link this to his style of burial: here lay a charioteer, with the marks of rein-work wrought in his bones. But I have to be strict with myself about drawing such conclusions. Bones respond to a multitude of strains and stresses over a lifetime. If we'd found another skeleton with these signs, we wouldn't say: this was definitely a charioteer.

What was conspicuously absent from the bones was any sign of violent injury. But this fitted with wider assessments of Iron Age human remains from this area.

'Amongst these communities in Yorkshire, there are actually lower rates of sharp force – penetrating violence from blades like swords and axes – compared with many other regions in Britain,' said Melanie. 'To me, it's a bit of a puzzle, because on the surface of it, when you look at the chariots, the swords, the shields – they look like the most martially obsessed group in Britain. And yet – violence is lower. And I can't help but think that's because they're actually quite successful at doing a lot of posturing. All that swaggering, bravado – it's quite effective at keeping the actual bloodshed to a minimum.'

It is curious, because a lot of the graves from Iron Age Yorkshire certainly seem to *imply* the existence of some kind of 'warrior culture' – in well-furnished burials, men are buried with spears, swords and shields. It's all very macho.

The Shield

There were no swords or spears in the Pocklington chariot burial. But once the archaeologists from MAP had cleaned up and removed the bones of the charioteer from his grave, they came across something metal, lying in the base of the chariot – under the body. As they exposed the object, it appeared larger and larger – until it was clear that it was about 75cm in diameter. Green with verdigris, it was the bronze front of a shield. The wooden body of the shield was long gone, like every other scrap of timber in the grave. But the bronze looked well preserved. The shield was encased in plaster of Paris, lifted out of the grave, and sent off to the conservation labs to be expertly cleaned up.

Does the shield signify that this man was a warrior, or could it just be a symbol of power? Another common trap in archaeology is assuming that an artefact has a single, simple explanation: a spear is for hunting, or sticking into someone; a shield is for protection in battle. But often – usually – there are wider and deeper meanings contained in objects.

One of the most iconic Iron Age objects ever found in Britain is the stunning Battersea shield. Once again, the object itself is just the metal facade of the original shield, which would have been made of wood. The Battersea Shield is a rounded rectangle in shape but, like the round Pocklington shield, it also has an embossed La Tène pattern, with three circular panels filled with characteristic sinuous designs. Part of the design involves twenty-seven roundels, each decorated with red glass, pressed in around a swastika-like design in brass wire. Now, the glass is dull and opaque – but it would have been clear and ruby-like back in the day.

The shield was dredged up out of the Thames, near Battersea, in 1857. It was an object in isolation; the river was its only context. Archaeologists have speculated that this prestigious object, speaking so strongly of wealth and power, was ritually deposited in the water. Many pieces of Iron Age metalwork have been found in watery places like rivers, lakes and bogs. The practice (whatever it really was) extends back into the Bronze Age as well. The metal objects are often interpreted as votive offerings – gifts to sacred waters or the deities that dwell within them, perhaps. Water could represent life and death. Rivers and lakes may have been seen as liminal places, boundaries between worlds of the living and the dead.

But with so many 'missing dead', I have always wondered if something else is going on – if some of these metal objects might have effectively been grave goods. A mortuary ritual could have involved a scattering of cremated remains into a river, along with objects either belonging to the deceased or representing something about their status in the community. Or a whole body could have been placed on a raft, with clothing and pos-sessions – pushed out into the current to start their journey to the afterlife. The raft and the body would eventually break up and rot away; bones would be scattered, fragmented (and odd human bones, including skulls, are often dredged up from the Thames as well) – and any metal would sink to the bottom, divorced from its context as part of a funerary ritual that leaves no other traces.

Whether the Battersea Shield was associated with a dead body or not, it certainly represents a considerable chunk of material wealth. All that metal, all that skilled crafting. It says something about the wealth and power of the people or person who consigned it the river – their status was such that they could afford to give up such treasure. The Battersea Shield is thought to have been symbolic of power, without ever having actually been used in warfare. There are no traces of it ever having received a battering.

Once conservation on the Pocklington shield had been completed, its full glory was revealed. Like the Battersea Shield, it's decorated in that La Tène style of the late Iron Age. It's lozenge-shaped (though thought to have been attached to an almost rectangular wooden shield), and its pattern is more fluid, with flowing arcs connecting embossed three-legged triskeles and shell-like bumps. It is a stunningly beautiful object.

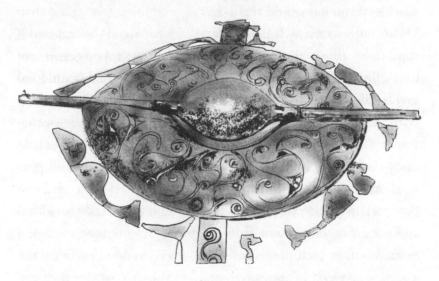

Like other La Tène objects from Britain and Ireland, it demonstrates a very clear cultural connection with the continent, where the style originates. But the British and Irish artisans certainly weren't just blindly copying designs – they were playing with the style, making it their own. We see the style reaching its apogee in metal objects – swords, scabbards, mirrors, brooches, torcs and shields. The combination of highly skilled metalworking and artistic flair represented in La Tène artefacts from Britain and Ireland is something we still marvel at, more than 2,000 years later. And the shield from the Pocklington chariot burial is one of the most exquisite examples we now have – with stylistic links to both the European continent and Ireland. Melanie Giles pulled no punches, describing the shield, dating to the second century BCE, as 'the most important British Celtic art object of the millennium'.

Unlike the Battersea shield, the Pocklington shield showed signs of use – and damage. This came as quite a surprise; it challenged the idea that Iron Age shields were always princi-pally ceremonial objects. This one was obviously more than just a status symbol. It had a history of its own. It bore a punc-ture hole, most likely from a sword, as well as evidence of having been repaired. Like the ponies, then, it had been tried and tested.

I asked Melanie if she thought this man had actually been a warrior, then – rather than his grave-goods simply representing an abstract expression of masculine identity. What could the chariot and the shield really mean?

'Well, I think the chariot is so much more than just a weapon,' she said. 'It *can* be a weapon, and particularly – as the Roman authors tell us – a weapon of intimidation. But it's also a stage for oration. It's a very dramatic way of arriving in a village if there's a dispute. To command people, or persuade them, perhaps, that they should resolve their differences. He might have been seen as quite a powerful peace-figure. Somebody who was able to mediate in disputes.'

The shield had seen action, but by the time the man was buried, it could have been a symbol of battles fought long ago – reminding people how he'd won his power and status, and that he was worthy of respect.

'The shield does speak of that martial culture,' said Melanie. 'But I think it's there to remind us that his time for being a warrior is over. He's still a defender of his community and, if need be, he can use all his power and his connections to protect them.'

There was more evidence in the grave of the esteem in which this old warrior was held – evidence that helps us recreate the scene of the funeral.

As well as the bones of the man himself, and the sacrificed ponies, the archaeologists found bones from joints of pork as well. As they lifted one set of pig ribs, they found an iron hook lying among them, passing between them. This meat hook would have been used to hang the meat to roast it over a fire – and it's a unique find in a British Iron Age grave. The bones were from young animals – suckling pigs. Killing and eating animals so young implies a wealth of resources.

Melanie showed me some of these animal bones from the grave, including that rack of ribs on its hook. The soil had been cleaned off enough – but not too much – so that the collection still held together. Finds like this are so evocative – letting us imagine what the funeral, and the scene at the graveside, would have been like.

'They've brought meat over to grave on the meat hook – this is hot from the feast,' she said. 'There's this moment of ceremony when someone brings that and places it beside the chariot in the grave – an offering to a man they respect and want to send off with this gift.'

The pig bones represented at least six different animals. This looked like it had been a big, lavish feast.

'We have a hog roast for a special occasion like a wedding,' she went on, 'and expect that to feed a large number of guests.

So to have sacrificed six pigs – that tells us this was a massive funeral ceremony.'

This extravagant show of wealth and generosity – this was about the people who survived, as much as it was about honouring the dead man. The funeral itself was a very visible demonstration of affluence and abundant resources. With the loss of this important member of the community, perhaps even its leader, there could have been the potential of a power vacuum. Whoever rose to succeed him would have needed to stake their claim, to demonstrate their worthiness. And the funeral could also have provided opportunities to cement alliances. What people brought to the grave, how they helped honour that man, that day – those gestures would have helped to make sense of loss and grief, but would also have been about individuals, and perhaps families, negotiating their status in the bereft community. And all of it focused on this event – the funeral and the feast that accompanied it.

There's a key set of Iron Age finds that suggest that feasting was very important during this period: cauldrons. There are more than seventy known, from Britain and Ireland – and they form part of a tradition that existed right across northwest Europe. Most cauldrons are single, isolated finds – but a couple of impressive collections have been discovered. One came to light in 2017, when archaeologists were carrying out a pre-construction dig on the outskirts of Leicester. Associated with evidence of a long-lived Iron Age settlement, each one of those massive cauldrons had a capacity of around fifty litres. Residue analysis on cauldrons has shown that they were used for a range of food and drink, from meat stew to mead. Eight of the Leicestershire cauldrons had been buried in close proximity, in a ditch around a building that had otherwise disappeared.

Perhaps they were buried or left there to mark the end of a tradition of feasting at that particular site. Another large assemblage, this time of a whopping seventeen cauldrons, was found near Chiseldon in Wiltshire, back in 2004. Iron Age people clearly loved a feast.

Those feasts could have been part of marriage or funeral ceremonies, or perhaps formed part of festivals held on a regular cycle – to bring people together, to create and cement connections between communities. Feasts could also have been about social obligations – creating them or fulfilling them. You could imagine someone might have provided a feast for a group of people who had come together to help build a new roundhouse perhaps – in the manner of a barn-raising in North America. Feasts have been described as the glue that held Iron Age society together.

The Pocklington grave took eleven weeks to excavate. And the end of digging is always only the start of the investigation – many more weeks of post-excavation analysis then take place. Some of the secrets from this burial are still being extracted, unravelled. While I was writing this book, Melanie emailed me a photograph of one of the objects that had been cleaned up and conserved – a gorgeous little bronze brooch with a coral bead decorating it.

'Sophie Adams, brooch specialist, reckons it is meant to conjure the figure of a dragonfly in people's minds,' she wrote, and went on, 'You find this creature on Samurai warrior armour: display, martial skill, patrolling its territory . . . so this tiniest object in the grave also alludes perhaps to the identity of the man.'

It's graves like these that offer us startling glimpses – detailed portraits – of Iron Age people and their culture.

The Pocklington grave represents a life and a death that took place probably in the penultimate century of the first millennium BCE.

The Iron Age is still prehistory from a British perspective – those Britons were not writing anything about themselves. History is starting to expand, though, and we do have those accounts of Iron Age Britain and its inhabitants written by outsiders – by the Greeks and Romans. But archaeology provides us with direct evidence that we can interpret and then compare with the written sources. The separation of archaeology and history – find and document – during the initial work on any site, is essential. We should not in the first instance make interpretations about the nature of the archaeology based on our reading of the histories. And neither should we interpret the history through the lens of archaeology. Each source of evidence should be carefully considered and interpreted in isolation before we bring those two sources together. The same principle should hold when we bring archaeology or history together with genetics. Otherwise, we simply use a new or different line of evidence to illustrate or flesh out what we already know. We'll get much further if we use it to *test* the hypotheses emerging from analysis of other sources.

Melanie summed up her thoughts about the information and understanding that we could draw out from that astonishing Pocklington chariot burial.

'It's valuable because these Iron Age people didn't write records. It's only in unpicking the bodies of the ponies, the bodies of the individual, the finds – the crafting behind them, and the drama, the spectacle of the burial – that we'll fully understand his story,' she said.

'So the way in which they're orchestrating this funeral – with the ponies pulling the chariot, the drama that happens around this, the placing of the body, the placing of the joints from the feast, the other grave goods, the degree of craftsmanship that's gone into the making of the things that go into that grave – the technology of the chariot – all of this enables us to tell a much richer story of these people than we could ever have gleaned from the classical authors' accounts.'

The Romans painted the ancient Britons as barbaric and warlike – in need of being conquered and civilised – but the archaeology provides us with a different view. We see a complexity and sophistication in the material culture that speaks of highly developed technological know-how and elaborate belief systems.

And yet, we still need to be careful not to impose our own prejudices, and our own ideas about social norms, on the past. There are other ways in which Iron Age burials have led us to challenge our preconceptions – and perhaps they might even teach us to view ourselves, our modern society and culture, differently, too.

Wetwang Slack

Of all the cities that suffered bombing during the Second World War, Hull experienced it worst. It was almost bombed out of existence.

Growing up on the junction of the rivers Hull and Humber, the town got rich from its wool exports in the Middle Ages. It became the principal port in northeast England. By the late seventeenth century, grain and wool was pouring out of Hull, while timber, tar, hemp and flax – for ships and their ropes and sails – poured in. The fishing fleet burgeoned too, and by the early twentieth century, Hull had become Britain's main fishing port. But it was oils that would really grease the wheels of Hull's industry – rapeseed oil, then whale oil, then petrol.

The Luftwaffe could drive a sword right into the heart of Britain's food, fuel and industry by bombing Hull. The bombers targeted the oil mills, grain mills, the gas works and the docks – but the city centre was also bombed. Ninety-five per cent of houses were damaged. The bombs killed 1,200 people, injuring a further 3,000. By the end of the war, around 150,000 people – nearly half the city's population – had lost their homes to the bombs.

In the 1960s, with many families still living in 'temporary' 1945 prefabs, Hull Corporation began work on what may have been the largest council estate in Europe at the time: Bransholme. In 1963, an old gravel pit in the valley between Garton-on-the-Wolds and Wetwang was reopened. It would become the source of thousands of tons of gravel, destined for the new estate. The pressing demand for construction material perhaps meant that the engineers missed a note on the Ordnance Survey map of the area, from 1850 – 'British urns, weapons and skeletons have been found here'. Or maybe they didn't exactly miss it, but chose to ignore it. (Today those sorts of clues are exactly what archaeologists look for when they do their initial, 'desktop assessment' of a site.)

So the diggers moved in, and pretty much straight away they started to turn up human bones. Local archaeologists became involved, and as the quarry grew larger, more and more ancient remains were uncovered. Between 1963 and 1990, a huge, broad swathe of the valley bottom, around 180 metres wide and 2 kilometres long, was stripped and quarried. It's hard to know how much was uncovered – and destroyed – as it was only from 1970 that decent records were kept. But that 17-hectare area in the dry valley, known as Wetwang Slack to the west and Garton Slack to the east, contained at least forty Neolithic or early Bronze Age barrows, and a profusion of Iron Age archaeology dating to around 300 BCE: a large settlement with more than a hundred roundhouses, three later farmsteads and some 540 burials. Among them at Wetwang Slack were three chariot burials, with another at Garton Slack – with a fifth found later at Wetwang Village.

The archaeology at Garton–Wetwang seemed to have the potential to solve, or at least feed into, an enduring 'invasion debate' about Iron Age people and cultures.

The distinct funerary tradition of the late Iron Age in East Yorkshire – including these remarkable chariot burials – turned up first at Arras Farm, near Market Weighton, when barrows were investigated by antiquarians in the early nineteenth century. The practice seemed to be restricted to East Yorkshire, within Britain, but bore striking similarities to middle Iron Age burial practices in northern France and Belgium – associated with a wider Iron Age culture known as 'La Tène'. Cue: a now very familiar debate about whether the appearance of a new culture (new artefacts, new practices) in Britain represents a spread of ideas or of people (or both). The Romans recorded a tribe called the *Parisii* living in the Seine basin – their chief city later becoming known as Paris. The similarity between their funerary rites and those of the Arras culture led to a suggestion that there had been a very focused migration from northern France to east Yorkshire. And in fact, there's a tantalising historical clue as well. Writing in the second century CE, the Greek mathematician and geographer Ptolemy notes the existence of a tribe called the *Parisi* in east Yorkshire. It's just a single reference – and must have come from other sources, as Ptolemy almost certainly never visited Britain – but it echoes that link seen in the material culture, and seems like more than a coincidence. But we shouldn't overlook the possibility that the classical writers might have conjured up this link themselves, having noticed a similar culture in the two areas.

In the 1970s, the 'invasion debate' was lively, and the discoveries at Garton–Wetwang provided the first decent opportunity to link up burial practices with the culture represented in a settlement. And here – while the burials were of that exotic, Arras-culture type – the roundhouses, weaving combs and ring-headed pins from the settlement looked thoroughly indigenous. So how did the burial tradition take root? It's certainly tempting to explain the disparity by the arrival of a foreign elite in Yorkshire, who may have adopted local styles of everyday living, while remembering their roots, emphasising their special status, in their burial practices. Ultimately, it should be possible to test such hypotheses using the insights we can glean from ancient genomics.

Arras Farm

The original Arras burials, giving their name to the culture that is enshrined in these elaborate, mounded graves, were dug by three local antiquarians, William Watson, Barnard Clarkson and the Reverend Edward William Stillingfleet, between 1815 and 1817. The cemetery contained more than 100 square barrows, and several stood out as representing extreme high status. One of these was the grave of a woman.

She'd been buried with a rich panoply of grave goods, indicating her high status in the community. Recording the find,

Reverend Stillingfleet described her as 'the chief female of the tribe' – and her grave was dubbed the 'Queen's Barrow'. Of course, that's entirely speculation – a standing and a title conferred on her more than 2,000 years after she lived and died. But it's interesting that this nineteenth-century man writes this about her, giving her high status in her own right, rather than simply connecting her with a powerful man. But how can we know if Iron Age British women could, independently, hold such high status?

The skeleton from that grave has disappeared, so we must trust the nineteenth-century antiquarians in their assessment of the bones – that she was indeed female. The grave goods were divided up among the three antiquarians who excavated the barrows, with some of them ending up in the Yorkshire Museum, some in the British Museum, and others sold off to dealers in antiquities.

In February 1847, a letter from the Rev. Edward William Stillingfleet, about the barrows 'at Arras and Hessleskew', was read at the monthly meeting of the Archaeological Institute in London. The vicar described the position of the monuments in the landscape:

> The ground is very elevated, on a kind of table land . . . above the vast plain, which stretches from the Humber to the Hamilton Hills, and across the Vale of York to the Highlands of the West Riding . . . Few situations could have been better chosen for observation.

He goes on to describe the careful opening of one of the barrows, 'dignified by the name of the Queen's barrow: the barrow of the chief female of the tribe.' Under the mound, which was about three feet high, they found 'a cist, which, on being excavated to the depth of about a foot, was found to contain the skeleton of a moderately tall female, lying with her head to the north, and her feet gathered up . . .'

> Her ornaments remained; and these were found near the head and the upper part of the body. They consisted of about one hundred beads of glass . . . generally opaque, and of three or four patterns. Two sorts had different shades of blue as their ground; these were spotted or zigzagged by white. A smaller number of transparent green glass beads had a serpentine line of opaque white entwined around them. Besides these beads, a ring of red amber was found near the neck or breast . . . a radiated brooch of curious workmanship; and a singular round ornament . . . two bracelets of inferior workmanship . . . a small ring . . . a pair of tweezers; and a pin of two inches in length, with a ring at its end, to fasten the robe of this British lady.

The 'radiated brooch' was particularly spectacular – a find that now resides in the Yorkshire Museum. It looks like it's made out of fat beads of something white, like chalk, attached to the shaft, and radiating out on pins from the ends of the brooch. But in fact that white stuff is bleached coral – back in the Iron Age, this coral brooch would have probably been a gorgeous bright pink. The pin is polished from wear, so this was an object that had been used – that had a history of its own – before it entered the grave.

The 'singular round ornament' is a kind of medallion, with a large, red-painted pottery button surrounded by three concentric rings of bleached coral. The tweezers are part of a toilet set, along with a small, forked nail cleaner. We might think of our prehistoric ancestors as looking a bit dirty and dishevelled – but here was a woman who took some care over her cleanliness and appearance.

The haul of beads from the 'Queen's Barrow' are now split between the collections of the British Museum and the Yorkshire Museum. I was lucky enough to see some of these beads, liberated from their case, on one visit to the latter. They are lampwork glass beads, made by heating and melting a rod of glass, and twisting it onto a thin metal rod called a mandrel. Dots or lines of contrasting coloured glass can then be added to the surface of the bead, while it's still hot. The beads are quite diverse – they don't look like they were created as a set. Instead, it's thought that they would have been collected together over time – perhaps inherited or gifted – and that these beads therefore represent connections between different communities or families. The blue beads decorated with white or yellow spirals are similar to ones found in southwest England. Varying patterns of wear on the beads suggested they'd been strung differently – some knocking up against each other on the thread, others separated by knots or perhaps wooden spacers – before coming into the possession of this woman.

Some of these beads – perhaps a third of them – are thought to have been lost. And there's another artefact that's not to be found in any of the museum collections, but which the Reverend Stillingfleet recorded in his report. 'At this barrow,' he continues, 'I received from the hand of my labourer, a ring of gold . . . clasped in a kind of rose, or quatrefoil; and it is an ornament by no means of despicable workmanship.' A similar ring was found in a much later Iron Age hoard, from Jersey – and these rings are thought to have come across from continental Europe.

A final object was placed on the grave of this woman as it was closed – becoming the first artefact that the excavators would find as they dug down through the barrow. It was a lump of iron pyrites. This could have been symbolic of the importance of iron itself – or it could have been a strike-a-light again, helping her light her way to the afterlife. We'll never know, but it's still wonderful to think that stories about the departed going into the darkness, bearing their own light, could have been told though the generations – from thc time of the Amesbury Archer all the way to the time of the Queen of Arras.

The variety and richness of the grave goods from the Queen's Barrow tell us something about concepts of material wealth and status in the Iron Age, but also reveal wide-ranging connections, both within and beyond Britain, in the case of the coral brooch and medallion, and that lost gold ring. Amber's more tricky – it could have come from the Baltic, but it is also found in glacial deposits, and on beaches in Norfolk. En masse, these artefacts surely represent an exceptional degree of personal wealth, high standing in the community, and the wherewithal to acquire exotic objects through the flourishing exchange networks of the Iron Age.

That equation – wealth = power – seems self-evident. It leaps out at us as the obvious meaning of high-value, beautiful objects. But archaeologists – like Rachel Pope, who always likes to challenge preconceptions – ask if we can really be *sure* that's what such artefacts mean. Objects that seem to be exotic, rare, precious or costly could represent the identity of a whole group, rather than just the person in the grave. Or the deceased could have belonged to a large extended family who all brought precious things to lay in the grave. The objects then would mark a different kind of status – not a high position in a hierarchy, but *a lot* of personal connections. They could mark out a different kind of social status – in terms of a person being well-connected and well-respected, not necessarily in terms of material wealth or more formal political power.

In 1877, another high-status female grave was discovered at Arras. This time it was found during chalk quarrying, and it became known as the Lady's Barrow. The woman buried in it was probably around her late thirties when she died. She was around 5ft tall, and her bones were robust – suggesting she was likely to have been fit and well-muscled. She was buried with a precious iron mirror with bronze handle decorations, as well as bronze horse-trappings. And she was laid to rest on a dismantled chariot.

Women and chariots

She's not alone: two of the chariot burials from Wetwang also contained female skeletal remains. And it may be that there were even more among the earlier sites excavated by antiquarians – as they had a tendency to ascribe sex on the basis of grave goods, rather than on the skeletons themselves. They may have assumed that a person buried with a chariot must have been male. But it's important that we don't jump to conclusions in this way, either. Firstly, just because someone was buried with a chariot, it doesn't necessarily mean that they were a charioteer. But if we *do* take it at face value – if they *were* a charioteer – why should we assume that they could not have been female? And indeed, there are examples of women driving chariots in the later literature. In the early medieval Irish stories – which may draw on Iron Age mythology – Deichtine, the mother of the hero Cú Chulainn, drives her father's chariot: 'Conchubur sat in his chariot together with his grown daughter Deichtine, for she was his charioteer.' And of course there's that iconic image of the Iceni Queen Boudicca driving her chariot, enshrined (in a clumsy, Victorian way) in the Thomas Thornycroft bronze sculpture on Westminster Bridge in London. It was inspired by a passage in Tacitus – which also tells us about the status of women in British Iron Age society.

> *Boudica, curru filias prae se vehens, ut quamque nationem accesserat, solitum quidem Britannis feminarum ductu bellare testabatur . . .*
>
> Boudica, driving her chariot with her daughters before her, approached each tribe, declaring that it was customary for Britons to be led in battle by a woman . . .

There are layers of intent, spin and bias in just this sentence. Some classicists have suggested that Tacitus is deliberately portraying Boudica as a domineering, bullying woman – and very un-Roman in this respect. She's the complete antithesis of the ideal – demure, restrained – Roman woman. And if the Britons really are accustomed to following female war-leaders – what does that say about them? Well, they are barbarians, after all. (The roots of the patriarchy run deep!)

We do have to look carefully at our sources. Tacitus didn't ever see Boudica driving up and down, addressing her troops. And yet it is a near-contemporary account, featuring in a book he wrote about the *Life and Death of Julius Agricola*, the Roman general who spent much of his military career in Britain, and who just happened to be Tacitus' father-in-law. And Agricola was in Britain, serving as a military tribune, at the time of the revolt in 60–61 CE. So although Tacitus is thought to have written the biography around 98 CE, almost forty years after the Boudican revolt took place, his father-in-law may well have been able to provide him with an eyewitness account. Even so, some modern authors have even suggested that Boudica herself was a fiction, a piece of propaganda, directed against the ineffectual Emperor Nero – his power and his provinces being symbolically threatened by this mere woman. But on the other hand, it's clear that Tacitus had access to good sources, and we would perhaps be excessively sceptical to suspect him of completely inventing historical characters. Most scholars trust him on this. It seems most likely that Boudica was real, and she really was a queen. (Although some male scholars seem a little unsettled by this, and have suggested her status was only ever symbolic.) But did she really drive a chariot? The answer to that has to be: probably. Tacitus didn't witness that – but Agricola may well have done.

With written accounts of women driving chariots, holding powerful positions in society, and with archaeological evidence of women being buried with chariots and other high-status grave goods, it would seem obtuse and contrary not to accept that Iron Age British women could have been both competent charioteers, and respected leaders. And there are even more clues from archaeology – a female skeleton from an Iron Age cemetery at Rudston in Yorskhire with healed cuts on her face: she may have been a warrior. More persuasively, there are plenty of images of female warriors on Gaulish coins from Iron Age France, holding swords and shields and sometimes riding horses too.

The iron mirror is a curious artefact, in the Lady's Barrow. It's easy to leap to conclusions about this too, and to see it as simply a personal object – mirrors are so easy to come by today. But

Iron Age mirrors are quite rare, and the workmanship that would have gone into making it – polishing and polishing it until it offers back a true reflection – must surely have made it as prestigious and precious an object as a high-end sword or scabbard. And perhaps, like those martial objects, a mirror also spoke of power. It could have been viewed as a magical object too. We know from later, written history that mirrors were sometimes seen as a means of supernatural communication – a way of looking into other realms, spying on enemies or divining the future. They might have had a sort of military connection in that way, too – later bronze mirrors have swirling decoration very similar to that seen on swords. But whether the mirror was about checking personal appearance or communicating with spirits – or indeed both – it does seem to be an object that was considered to be linked to female gender. The Wetwang female chariot burials also contained iron mirrors.

Mirror = Woman

Thinking about sex and gender in prehistory – this is very much an area where we need to proceed with utmost caution when it comes to imposing our own ideas on the past. We can never escape our own cultural lens – we can never be truly objective.

But we can at least ensure that we are aware of our subjectivity and how it might influence our interpretations.

It's easy to criticise Victorian antiquarians for assuming a grave belongs to a woman if it has beads or a mirror in it, and a man if it contains a sword or a shield. We think of ourselves as far more enlightened, because we now use very reliable osteological methods to 'sex' a skeleton. The accuracy of the methods – which focus on features in the skull and pelvis – have been tested out on collections of human skeletons from individuals who lived and died recently – for whom we have biographical information.

One study involved looking at 262 pelvic bones and 180 skulls of men buried in a mass grave in Serbia. An experienced anthropologist sexed the bones with 100 per cent accuracy, and a less experienced apprentice still managed to get it right 95 per cent of the time.

But in case that gives you the impression that every skeleton falls comfortably into a 'definite female' or 'definite male' category, let me reveal the existence of other categories commonly used by the modern osteoarchaeologist: 'probable female', 'probable male', and 'indeterminate' or 'ambiguous'. The reason we're so good at accurately sexing skeletons is that, when we can't be sure, we place them in the 'indeterminate' category. Every feature we look at in the skeleton when we're trying to determine sex varies on a continuous spectrum. At the extremes, a bony pelvis may have a very masculine, narrow, J-shaped greater sciatic notch around the back – all the way to a more feminine, wide-open, C-shaped version – and everything in between. A skull may have a jutting brow ridge over the eye sockets at one extreme, and a gently rounded forehead, merging smoothly with the bridge of the nose at the other – and everything in between. There are no natural cut-offs: we impose the categories on the bones. In any one skeleton, the various traits an anthropologist would look at might vary in whether they look more female, more male – or in between.

Even in that Serbian study, where all the skeletons were male, the experienced anthropologist classified plenty of individual traits in the bones as 'ambiguous' or 'female'. For instance, that ridge over the eye sockets was classified as 'female' in 19 per cent of the skulls, and as 'ambiguous' in 33 per cent. Even the greater sciatic notch looked 'ambiguous' in fifty-one out of 259 pelvic bones, or 20 per cent, and 'female' in three. Based on the skull alone, that experienced anthropologist would have classified 127 skeletons correctly, whilst interpreting twenty-six as female and twenty-seven as ambiguous. It was when the pelvic bones were added in that – even with individual features sometimes classified as 'female' or 'ambiguous' – the anthropologist's overall assessment was that all of the bones were all male – and they were right. What that study didn't reveal, with its all-male sample, of course, was how well the anthropologists would have done with female skeletons.

A further complication is that the spectrum of difference varies from population to population, and that the differences between male and female don't really start to develop until puberty – so determining sex in the skeletons of children is somewhere between difficult and impossible. But, lumping other studies together, the general accuracy of sex determination for adult skeletons, based on pelvic features, is still high – more than 80 per cent. That sounds great – but it does mean that the assigned sex could be wrong in up to one in five skeletons, which sounds . . . less great. There are cases when the skeleton of a man may appear female, and vice versa.

That's not too surprising; I think most of us notice that some men have quite feminine facial features, for instance, whereas some women can look quite masculine. This doesn't mean that we should give up on trying to determine biological sex from bones, but that we need to bear the level of accuracy in mind, especially if we only have fragmentary remains to go on, when we make wider interpretations about grave goods associated with each sex – and what that tells us about gender and society in the past.

It's also important to think carefully about how sex and gender relate to each other. Often, biological sex is talked about as a strict binary – where any one individual may fall into one of two categories, separated by a firm dividing line. The variation in skeletons – all those features that can exist in a range of forms on a spectrum of variation – shows us that the line between the categories can be very blurred. Defenders of the strict binary might say: yes, but bones can lie, chromosomes do not – everyone is either XX or XY. But while that might be true most of the time, it certainly isn't *all* of the time. Firstly, there are rare conditions where a person might have three sex chromosomes (XXY) or just one (XO). Then there are conditions where, despite having an XY genotype, a fetus develops female characteristics – or, despite having XX, becomes male. There are layers and layers of interpretation, involving chemical signals, such as hormones, between the chromosomes and the phenotype – the body that ends up being built. But even without considering any of the disorders or differences of sexual development, the way that male and female bodies develop can be quite variable. Genitalia – both inside and outside – are most constrained, for obvious biological reasons, into separate male and female versions. Skeletons – less so, with the pelvis

332

being the most 'sexually dimorphic' part (and therefore the most useful for determining sex in skeletons), precisely because of its close association with the reproductive organs – and the need to accommodate the birth canal in a woman.

Other organs of the body – kidneys, livers, even brains – are much less differentiated between the sexes, to the extent that it's nigh-on impossible to predict the sex of the owner by looking at isolated organs. The human body is very broadly dimorphic (two main forms), but with a whole load of variation both within and between those categories in many of its parts. Some people prefer to conceptualise that complexity as binary (even if they admit there are exceptions). Others – and I would venture, most human biologists – recognise a reality that is more complex than just two, clearly separated categories. Dr Anne Fausto-Sterling, Professor Emerita of Biology and Gender Studies at Brown University, caused a veritable firestorm of debate when she published a paper called 'The Five Sexes' in 1993. Since then, she's moved away from trying to come up with categories at all – she has written: 'sex and gender are best conceptualized as points in a multidimensional space.'

So – biological sex is complicated.

And then there's how it feels to be in that body – and how that person is seen within society. More layers of interpretation! That personal and social experience of biological sex is what we usually mean by 'gender'. And because humans are deeply cultural creatures, our ideas about our own identities will inevitably develop in a social and cultural context – you just can't extract yourself from it. In a society with a very strict binary approach to both sex and gender, an individual may feel that they fit very neatly into one category or the other. Or they might feel that their anatomical sex is at odds with the way they experience their own gender. And that's before we even consider sexuality!

Understanding the complexity of sex and gender is important in discussing human rights today, particularly in relation to women's right and trans rights. For some, conferring rights on trans people implies an erosion of women's rights, because it challenges a definition of 'woman' that depends on a strict, biologically-defined binary. But as we've seen, even biology is not that definite – and even if it were, this is a complex social and political question that requires us to have a much more holistic conception of personhood. You can't reduce 'woman' to 'someone who possesses XX chromosomes' or 'someone who produces ova' or 'someone who can become pregnant' – and indeed, many feminists have been very keen to challenge such narrow stereotypes over the decades. But the current debate seems in some ways to have promoted a stricter policing of strictly binary gender categories – with no exceptions – on both sides.

If we have such differing opinions being voiced about gender and identity today, we should surely be *very* careful about assuming particular attitudes towards gender and identity in the past. Tacitus certainly hints at a different concepts in the Roman world compared with the barbarian north – with Boudica brazenly blasting through any Roman ideal of who a woman should be, and how she should behave. That Roman ideal persisted long after the classical empire crumbled, in the religious empire and system of political control into which it developed: Roman Catholicism. In 2019, indeed, the Vatican found it necessary to issue specific guidance about gender, entitled 'Male and Female He Created Them'. The paper embraces a strict binary – no exceptions – and ascribes different aptitudes to each sex as well as different roles in society, appropriate to each gender. 'Women have a unique understanding of reality,' we are told, and 'are ever ready and willing to give themselves generously to others, especially in serving the weakest and most defenceless'.

Well, moving on – let's return to the archaeology, and ask what meaningful inferences we can make about Iron Age society by looking at skeletons and the objects buried with them. With all the caveats and complexity in mind, we can determine the sex of a skeleton with a reasonable level of accuracy. That means that, with large enough numbers, we should at least be able to detect patterns – of particular grave goods being associated with a particular sex – if there are any. And those objects may symbolise gender roles and attitudes in society. (Though of course, the link we don't have – and are left cautiously assuming it – is that between biological sex – or at least, the apparent sex of a skeleton – and gender for any individual. We may be sure that a skeleton is female, but we could be looking at the remains of someone whose body was anatomically female but who self-identified as male, and was seen by his community as male.)

In 1999, an intriguing Iron Age burial was discovered on Hillside Farm on the island of Bryher, one of the Isles of Scilly. And it was a real head-scratcher. It refused to be neatly categorised according to how we (or thought we) understood Iron Age burial archaeology at the time.

It was clear that Iron Age burial rites varied considerably across Britain. That even seemed to fit quite well with the picture of the political landscape that the Romans give us, both before and after much of Britain becomes subsumed into that huge, literate empire. They tell us that Britain was divided up into territories, a different tribe occupying each: the Dumnonii in the southwest of England, the Durotriges in the south, the Cantiaci in the east; the Iceni in north Norfolk; the Caledonii in Scotland. I love the fact that these names come down to us directly in the literature, but also travel through time and evolve into names we are more familiar with today: Dumnonii – Devon; Durotriges – Dorset; Cantiaci – Kent. How amazing, in many places, that the administrative framework of 21st-century Britain still cleaves to Iron Age political geography. The Romans didn't invent their own administrative structure – they superimposed their governance on the existing framework. In some places, they did this without a break, getting a buy-in from British leaders, who became client kings.

But the picture is too neat, too reassuring. Because we have those names, we feel that we have a sense of understanding, which the history does not in fact give us. What does 'Dumnonii' actually mean? Does it just refer principally to a geographic area? Or an ethnic group? Or simply a political grouping? (And we cannot escape the fact that such political organisation may even have emerged *in response* to the threat from Rome and interaction with the empire – forcing Iron Age polities to crystallise and coalesce.)

Archaeologists have had different perspectives on this – sometimes bundling up territory with ethnicity and material culture too – giving us a heavily culture-history-laden concept of Iron Age tribes. And tied with that, there was an expectation that burial practices would vary, region by region, tribe by tribe.

In the far southwest, people were buried in stone-lined casts. In Dorset, bodies were laid in a crouched position, in shallow oval graves. In East Yorkshire, people were buried under square barrows. Those are the burial rites the archaeologists can *detect*, but there must have been many others – the 'disappearing dead' of the Iron Age escaping detection by being cremated, excarnated or consigned to watery graves. Those 'invisible' mortuary rites were considered to have taken place right across Britain – a background, homogenous tradition. But the visible rites, in Yorkshire particularly, also suggested another consistent Iron Age concern: a focus on status and gender.

It was assumed that swords and mirrors – pieces of high-quality craft – reflected wealth and indicated the social status of an individual, as well as representing gender stereotypes: male strength and power; female beauty. Appearing at widely geographically separated sites, those swords and mirrors were thought to encode a consistent, very strictly binary idea about high-status, gendered identity. The British sword burials appeared to be a local variant of a continental tradition of Iron Age warrior burials – men buried with various sorts of weaponry. The mirror burials seem to be a peculiarly British tradition, though.

It's always annoying when such a lovely, neat theory is disrupted by evidence. But a recent, wide-ranging and in-depth (I know – impressive!) analysis of Iron Age burial practices across Britain has challenged lots of the assumptions that have become embedded in archaeology – particularly the idea of consistent rites within certain regions, but even the idea of a background of consistent 'invisible rites' right across the country. Instead, the survey showed a glorious diversity of practices. In light of all that diversity, the idea that a sword or a mirror in a burial might have a consistent meaning – right across Britain, and over hundreds of years – seems questionable.

The degree of diversity also warns against over-generalising.

On the one hand, a well-furnished burial presents us with a kind of microcosm of a culture and a society, in one neat package. But on the other – it's just one grave, in one place. It can't 'stand for' a homogenous culture and social structure across all of Britain, or even across a region.

The survey also highlighted another problem – the sex of some of the burials excavated by antiquarians might have been guessed at, based on the presence of a sword or mirror indeed, rather than assessed independently by an osteoarchaeologist. If that's the case, it would lead to a completely circular argument, of course: this burial contains a mirror – it must be female; oh look – mirrors occur in female graves. There are two burials that have been discovered relatively recently where the bones and artefacts 'don't match' – a possible male Romano-British burial with a mirror from St Albans, and a possible female burial (though the bones are really too fragmentary to be sure) with a sword from East Yorkshire.

Spreading the net more widely, the antiquarian's assumption about strictly divided-up grave goods between men and women perhaps says more about Victorian society than it does about the Iron Age (or other eras – remember Buckland and the Red Lady with her shell beads!). Women are in fact found buried with a great range of grave goods – from beads to items of potentially ritual significance like mirrors and spoons, to weapons. The archaeological evidence presents us with a much more fluid, diverse representation of female gender, at least. (And in fact it looks more diverse than some ideas about female gender today – especially if we look at the Catholic Church's edicts, or indeed, the highly gender-stereotyped division between pink-packaged toys for girls versus blue-boxed toys for boys in 21st-century Britain!)

The association of swords and male burials was more robust, but still not exclusive – and more diverse than previously assumed. The idea that the sword always signifies a warrior is challenged by the inclusion of such weapons in young children's graves. And while there is evidence for violent warfare during the Iron Age, it seems to have been sporadic – not endemic. Spears are in fact the most common weapon in burials – and they may relate to hunting rather than warfare. They may also have been part of the burial rite itself – some fifteen burials have been discovered where the body was pierced with spears, in the grave.

Thinking about identity more widely, we approach those Iron Age burials, indeed all archaeology, peering at it through our own cultural lens. And in our culture we have ideas about possessing personal wealth, and expressing our status in society through the things we buy and wear. We expect our ancestors to have done the same.

Even if mirrors and swords are marking out gender identities in some way, they're probably about other aspects of identity too. Or indeed, they might be 'about' something else entirely – the meaning of a particular grave good may not be about the identity of the deceased at all – or only very indirectly. It might have to do with mythology around death itself, or something that a mourner felt the need to bring to that ceremony, for instance.

Another pertinent point is that mirrors – particularly – are very rare. Examining the evidence from these burials, archaeologist Alexis Jordan notes that this rarity makes it 'likely that few people ever saw more than one mirror burial in their lifetime'. This in turn makes it very unlikely that Iron Age people across Britain would even have thought of a 'mirror burial' as a thing. It's a pattern *we* see – but those individual mirror burials may not be connected by much more than chance: the inclusion of the mirror in the grave meant something in the context of each of the individuals – but that 'something' may have been very personal, and different, in each case.

Some archaeologists have advocated a much more focused, fine-grained approach to burial archaeology: viewing the grave as a physical biography, taking in all sorts of objects, each of which has its own history or biography; objects that have each been made, mended, broken, changed purpose, handed on, gifted, transformed – that each bring their own story. And with prehistoric archaeology, we usually have no written reference for the meaning of those objects – though we may be able to make some inferences from later, or even contemporary, cultures, where we do have ideas written down. It is really important not to jump to conclusions, not to decide that one hypothesis must be true because we like it. We should think about all the possibilities, rather than dismissing any out of hand. This reminds me of medical diagnosis: you think about all the possible causes for patients' symptoms and the findings you make from physical examination. You throw the net wide, then use targeted investigations – specific blood tests, x-rays, other scans – to narrow the diagnosis down. Sometimes you may still be left with a few possibilities – not just one. Unless you can extract any more information, you have to be honest with yourself and keep all those possibilities open. In archaeology, it may be impossible to refine the 'diagnosis' down, and so you may often be left with a string of possible explanations – for the special treatment of a particular individual at death, for the inclusion of a particular mirror in a specific grave. The possibilities are so much wider than 'mirror = special woman'.

It may sound weird, and not at all neat, but what we need to do is embrace and preserve ambiguity – not to swap it for a simple answer, a quick fix, an all-too-satisfying but overly simplistic certainty. We oversimplify ourselves if we try too hard to oversimplify our ancestors.

The problem of working out what grave goods might actually have meant is coloured not only by our own cultural biases but by what we find easiest to detect. Even though the determination of biological sex in a skeleton isn't 100 per cent accurate, we're pretty good at it – and so we have a point of reference. And then we see everything else in relation to that: biological sex. If we start off thinking we'll find patterns among grave goods that relate to binary gender roles in society, we'll find them – and we may miss a lot of interesting connections with other aspects of identity, or culture more generally. 'We must unbind our thinking,' writes Alexis Jordan in her thoughtful, thought-provoking article on mirror and sword burials, 'and allow patterns that may or may not primarily be organised by sex and gender identities to reveal themselves'.

That Iron Age burial discovered on Hillside Farm, on Bryher, in the Isles of Scilly, is pertinent because it delightfully refused to fall into a simple category. It threw a real spanner in the works. Or rather, not a spanner but a mirror. And a sword. And a scabbard. The skeleton had disintegrated fairly comprehensively; it's no good how accurate your sexing methods are if there's simply not enough of a skeleton left to sex. (Such burials have been disappointing osteoarchaeologists for decades, though we now have a chance to sex the remains if we can secure the help of a friendly palaeogeneticist, and if there's enough DNA preserved to find the traces of a Y chromosome – or not.)

But even without knowing the sex of this ancient Scillonian, the grave threw up a challenge to the binary gender assumptions that had become engrained in Iron Age archaeology – the 'two-sex/two-gender' model – where mirror means woman; sword means man.

If we *expect* to find people that fall into one of two categories, we bind our findings to that dichotomy. We won't see any diversity, because we've reduced it to two classes. Other findings that could be interesting are side-lined or homogenised – squeezed into or out of our existing model for How The Past Was.

Can we avoid the binary trap and keep our eyes open for variability or ambiguity? And how can we make sense of Hillside Farm? We can start with a fine-grained, forensic approach to that physical biography in the grave.

We have: the fragmented bones of an un-sexable individual, laid to rest in a crouched position, lying on their right side, in a pit framed with boulders – the local way. More grave goods than in any other single burial from this time, in this place: a belt-ring, fittings from a shield, a brooch, a ring, pieces of textile and hide, a bronze scabbard – and an iron sword, close to the chest, and bronze mirror, close to the face. Phew.

Radiocarbon dating places the burial in the first or second century BCE. The brooch looks to be of a first-century style. So, this burial dates to the end of the British Iron Age, close to the arrival of the Romans and the changes they would bring. There was another cist nearby – these people might have been buried in a cemetery.

The sword and shield appear to have been deliberately broken. The scabbard was laid with its decorated surface lowermost. They have passed from the world of the living. And do the mirror and sword together symbolise a deviation from gender norms? Rising above those norms, or deviating from them? Unifying them? Again, our own prejudices about sex and gender come to the fore. Some have suggested the burial is that of a male warrior, and the mirror is also a weapon. But it could be the other way round of course – the weapons could be symbolic of connections and not of martial power at all. And it could be – if we 'unbind our thinking' – that the primary meaning of sword and mirror are: nothing much to do with the sex or gender of the individual in the grave. Think: they could symbolise elements of stories; they could represent alliances; they could be gifts from mourners; they could be about old battles, won or lost; they could be about putting a version of the past to bed; they could be about imagining a future.

Once thought to represent a strong and unified regional tradition, the Iron Age, stone-lined cist burials of the southwest are very diverse. (They may reflect traditions within smaller communities, even families.) So the Hillside Farm burial is not necessarily a deviation from a norm – rather, another facet of a very varied approach to mortuary ritual.

For Melanie Giles, the importance of this burial from the Isles of Scilly is that it *is unique* – it makes us focus on the individual story, whether we're looking at someone who does perhaps represent an Iron Age idea of a 'third gender', or indeed, someone who warranted a burial demonstrating 'a doubling of power, uniquely embodied in one person'.

What starts off looking like an 'exception to the rule' may be an important clue that there is something much more interesting going on.

Sex, gender and power

This whole chapter seems to be a cautionary tale about stereotypes – encouraging us instead to break away from them, to open our eyes to a more diverse perspective on the past, and to embrace and celebrate challenges to our theories and models.

The potential bias we bring is practically doubled-up in the Iron Age, when we have our own prejudices and cultural lens to squint through – *and* that classical perspective, in the words of the Greek and Roman writers. They tell us about their view of 'Celtic Society' – complete with stereotypical gender roles and a social hierarchy. There is a distinct possibility, of course, that they are trying to understand their northern neighbours by shoehorning the societies of northern Europe to fit into a classical, Mediterranean model.

The classical writers tell us that Iron Age society was arranged in a hierarchy that bears a striking resemblance to the ideal in Greek and Roman society: peasants at the bottom; artisans, bards and druids in the middle; then nobles; and a single chieftain at the lofty apex of a triangular or pyramidal structure. Women could only gain access to the higher echelons by marrying rich and powerful men. For a long time, archaeologists simply accepted that, and interpreted their finds accordingly. In the 1980s, the discovery of an Iron Age cemetery in Switzerland where 90 per cent of the richest burials were women really set the cat among the pigeons. But the archaeologists furrowed their brows and dug in their heels and pronounced that, in this case, wealth was not indicative of status. Or at least, the wealth buried with those women could not possibly represent their own status – instead, those richly ornamented female corpses were standing as status symbols for their husbands. Does the idea of a high-status Iron Age woman, powerful and wealthy in her own right, still cause anxiety? Luckily, a new generation of archaeologists is urging us to tear up those old preconceptions and look at what the archaeology is telling us on its own terms – to be open to the idea of a different sort of past.

The archaeology actually allows us to step away from those preconceptions for a moment – not expecting a certain power structure or approach to gender – and look at the evidence on its own terms.

It's interesting that there's very little evidence of gender differences represented within Neolithic funerary practices. Gender seems to be visible in some Bronze Age burials. That long view shows us that the way we construct gender – the personal experience of one's sex and social roles associated with it – is not inevitable or universal, even if it can feel that way to us. Different cultures have produced varied systems and ideas – across the world and through time.

Where we do have British Iron Age burials, most show no signs of a gendered approach to death and burial. Inhumations in the south and southwest of England show no particular gender divisions, and most of the Yorkshire ones don't either. It's only in the high-status burials in East Yorkshire – the ones that, let's face it, really catch our eye – that gender does stand out.

We can sort the grave goods from these burials into categories. And where we can determine biological sex from the human remains, the categories of grave goods often 'match up' with that. But it's not the strict, exclusive binary we might once have expected, through our modern lenses tinted even more by the Roman writers (even just a few decades ago).

When we try to sort the grave goods into just two groups, we find exceptions to the categories we impose – which hint at divergent identities. In fact, it could be that there's even a tendency to create more categories – third and fourth genders – when two main categories are more closely and clearly defined, than if gender is seen as something more fluid and labile. This long view is not only interesting in its own right – it perhaps makes us look at the way we see gender today in a different way. It seems that it's not just the way that gender might be represented in a human society that can change; the fundamental concept of gender can be different.

The female chariot burials tell us something very interesting about those individuals – and about the Iron Age society to which they belonged. Even while being cautious about forcing all Iron Age burials into one of two categories, the amassed evidence presents us with two major classes – which seem to be the physical representation of a (largely) two-gender system operating in society. This is certainly true for those high-status graves in East Yorkshire. Osteological males are more likely to be buried with weapons; osteological females with mirrors. There was a need to display – to confirm – gender, even in death. Most people fitted (or were seen as fitting) into one of two distinct categories. Most – but not all. And this is where we have to be really careful of being too narrow in our interpretations, of draping our own culture too heavily over the traces of the past. Perhaps the female charioteers from Yorkshire – and that mirror-and-sword burial from the Isles of Scilly – represent another possible, if rarer, way of being: a third gender. And then perhaps there was a fourth gender we haven't even spotted; a fifth; a sixth. It's interesting that the mirror burials, too, seem to represent something different. There are five early burials with iron mirrors, four of which contained female remains, but only one contained jewellery. It seems the mirror is compatible with a vehicle burial, but not with jewellery. It could represent a female aspect or role within a more masculine gender. It gets very complicated! But we need to think about all these possible constructions of – potentially multiple – genders.

In the 1980s, burials of apparently high-status European Iron Age women with typical male accoutrements were explained away as being transvestites – which may say much more about the narrowness of perspectives on gender in the 1980s, rather than in the Iron Age. Instead of shoehorning those women into essentially male identities, it seems that there may have been a range of female gender identities available. The most common was linked with exotic jewellery, but there were also identities linked with chariots and weapons, and with ritual objects like those mirrors. And they seem to have been quite separate identities – the women with swords or buried with chariots were not displaying jewellery. On the other hand, the burial identity of men, when it was obviously gendered, does not seem to have been so diverse. Would it have been difficult not to have been a macho man in Iron Age society?

There are some twenty-five known chariot burials in Britain now, eleven of which where the osteological sex of the skeleton has been determined. Of those, three are female – nearly a third. So are they really exceptions to the rule, whatever the rule was? Or just part of a much more diverse approach to gender and roles for women in society?

But then we also need to remember to open our minds to wider possibilities – to come up with a range of hypotheses to explain what we see; a spread of differential diagnoses – accepting that the story encapsulated in those graves is not *all* about gender, but about a much more complex biography. Melanie sees so many aspects represented in those graves – life history, age, events, skill – and gender is just part of that picture, not the overriding signal.

For those women buried with chariots, age in particular could have been the thing that marked them out for special status in life, and special treatment in death. Studies of the bones in the cemeteries reveal that the risk of disease, accident and injury was fairly even between the sexes. But mortality was higher for women in their twenties and thirties than for men of an equivalent age – probably because of deaths associated with pregnancy and childbirth; there are more old men (over forty-five years of age) than old women in the cemeteries. Elderly women could have had a special status of their own.

There are tantalising hints that some of the bodies may have spent time above ground before being interred. Perhaps this was ceremonial – they may have been kept as mummies for some time before burial. But there are other possibilities; the reasons could have been much more about expedience – waiting until frozen ground thawed enough to dig a grave, for instance, or for far-flung relatives to gather for the funeral.

Other clues emerge from scrutinising grave goods – uncovering the histories of the individual artefacts and then considering how those link up with the story of the woman interred in each female grave. At a fine scale, the artefacts might reveal 'micro-traditions' – family customs that hint at relationships between individuals, perhaps even lineages and dynasties. At Wetwang Slack, careful digging and dating allowed the sequence of burials in the cemetery to be disentangled. Clusters formed around primary interments – typically, an older woman buried with beads would be the 'founder figure' – her grave forming a focus for subsequent burials of more women, with or without beads. Those gendered clusters also make us think about whether women's status was in some ways independent from men's. We're not seeing wealthy men buried with wealthy women, at any rate.

Finally, one of the female chariot burials from Wetwang Slack has recently produced an unexpected surprise. The grave contained a sealed bronze canister. At least, the archaeologists initially thought it was completely sealed shut, and suggested that it might have held something of symbolic, even mystical, importance.

Now it turns out that the canister was locked, rather than sealed, shut. And it contained something organic – that's as far as the analysis has gone. What was it? A craft kit, with material for sewing? Perhaps food? Or some dry fungus to use as tinder? Or some kind of relic, even a human organ? The imagination runs wild. At some point, science will tether it down – and I hope it's more exciting than a sewing kit. Whatever it is, though, it was somehow important to this woman – perhaps she was known as a guardian or keeper of this enigmatic object, carrying it off with her into the afterlife.

Perhaps the Romans were right to be wary of the formidable females of Britain – wise women, prophetesses, priestesses, Ladies, Queens; we'll never capture exactly how they saw themselves and how their communities saw them, but they appear charismatic, formidable, powerful even in death.

Invasion neurosis

The spectacular burials from East Yorkshire allow us to paint intimate portraits of a few striking individuals. But they're also part of a wider story of connections with the near continent.

349

When the Reverend Stillingfleet excavated the original Arras burials, he was fascinated by the detail of the objects in the barrows – those intimate portraits – but knew their real importance would emerge when they could be placed in much wider context. He ended his report, to the Archaeological Institute, rather grandiloquently: 'It is by the collation of discoveries made in our islands with the result of the researches of our northern continental neighbours that a mass of evidence will in due time be collected, in regard to the customs of the various tribes, who have peopled Britain, in different eras.'

There are lots of connections in those Arras graves with traditions on the near continent – from the broad style of the graves, to the goods placed in them with the body. The foods are interesting – in northern France, there was a longstanding custom of placing meat in the grave, and it tended to be gendered: beef for women and pork for men. In Yorkshire, men and women could have either, it seems. In western Europe, the burial record for the earlier part of the Iron Age shows that women could hold high status, and probably power as well. Later on in the Iron Age, European society seems to become more patriarchal – but there are still some examples of high-status women.

The question of where that Arras culture comes from is still a live one. Like the debate over whether large-scale migration happened in the Neolithic and then again in the Bronze Age – archaeologists have amassed huge armouries of data from burials and settlements, and then argued themselves blue in the face about what it all meant. Isotope analysis promised a resolution – but only if we could catch those elusive first-generation immigrants. Ancient genomics finally holds out the possibility of some resolution. And we have seen that the dawn of the Neolithic was accompanied by a large influx of people, with another large-scale migration and fairly comprehensive population replacement in the Bronze Age. With the help of genomics to settle questions of whether large-scale migrations took place, the baton passes back to the archaeologists to work out the even more interesting questions of *why* and *how*. For the Neolithic and Bronze Age, ancient DNA does record a significant influx of people into Britain. When it comes to the Iron Age, the old traditional 'standard model' held that the Iron Age 'Celts' originated in central Europe and then spread out, eventually reaching British and Irish shores, bringing with them a cultural package including a range of Iron Age stuff – and Celtic languages.

Both history and archaeology have pointed to migrations potentially being important in the Iron Age. But is this simply a feature of human populations all the way through prehistory, into history? What level of migration could be considered business as usual? Are the Iron Age migrations into Britain, for example, as pronounced as the migrations we can detect, genetically, in the Neolithic and Bronze Age?

The idea that the Iron Age Celts moved into Britain first emerged from studies of languages. In the early eighteenth century, the Welsh antiquarian Edward Lluyd – who was Keeper of the Ashmolean Museum – undertook a pioneering survey of languages. Setting English aside, he noted the similarities between the other languages spoken across the British Isles – and that of Brittany. He called these languages 'Celtic' – which really just meant 'ancient' at that time. He sorted those Celtic languages into two main branches, which he suggested had arrived in two separate waves of 'invasion' from the continent. There was a consonant change between the two waves of Celtic invaders – q was replaced by p. Archaeologists then tried to match up changing patterns of material culture in the first millennium BCE with this two-wave model – first a load of 'Q-Kelts' or Goidels arrived, followed by a heap of 'P-Kelts' or Brythons. The language of the Goidels persisted in some areas, evolving into Gaelic languages: Irish, Scottish Gaelic and Manx. The language of the second wave, Brythonic or Brittonic, was the ancestor of Welsh, Cornish and Breton languages.

There seemed to be some archaeological support for this two-wave model – with the spread of two archaeologically distinct cultures from central Europe to Britain in the first millennium BCE: first the Hallstatt culture (named after an Iron Age site in Austria, where it was first defined), succeeded by La Tène (named after a site in Switzerland).

But by the early twentieth century, archaeologists were wondering if they'd been overly keen to shoehorn the archae-ological record into an existing model – allowing confirmation bias to shape their conclusions. They couldn't be sure when those 'Celtic' languages had actually arrived or developed in Britain and Ireland, after all. And with no evidence of Hallstatt culture in Ireland, the neat link between language and material culture was looking fragile.

By the 1960s, any models that lumped together ethnicity, material culture and language were viewed with suspicion – as old hat, dangerous-sounding culture-history. Archaeologists were pointing to evidence of continuity in culture, and ques-tioning that theoretical link between aspects of cultural change and ideas of population turnover. Cautioning against falling into the grip of an 'invasion neurosis', Grahame Clark, Professor of Archaeology at Cambridge University, suggested that the appearance of high-status, ornate, foreign-looking objects were more likely to be a signal not of an invading aristocracy, but of the increasing wealth of the native elite.

But really, plumping for either explanation – invasion or migration versus cultural continuity and diffusion of ideas – means we run into trouble very quickly. Our understanding of the past becomes constrained by well-worn ruts in our ways of thinking. By putting theory before evidence in this way, we really are putting the cart before the horse. The chariot before the ponies.

Once again, we should really try to approach the evidence as objectively as possible – exploring it for patterns with an open mind, rather than starting out by looking for support for one model or another. If we approach the archaeological record *expecting* to see evidence for a two-gender social system, or two waves of Celtic invaders, or indeed, cultural continuity – we're likely to discover what we set out to find. Instead, we should be ready for the archaeology to tell us something different. To surprise us.

There's plenty of careful analysis of Iron Age archaeology going on – looking for patterns at a local, regional, national and continental scale – that will help us better understand how culture evolved in the first millennium BCE. There's a theme of connectedness along the Atlantic-facing shores of western Europe, including the British Isles, for instance – with another link between Britain and the near continent across the North Sea. Ideas and people were clearly flowing along those maritime routes – both into and out of Britain. Careful dating of sites and objects will help to resolve the direction that ideas were travelling in.

The bones and teeth of the Iron Age dead also have the

potential to shed light on the origins and connections of the Arras culture. Isotope studies have shown that most of the individuals in the Wetwang and Garton Slacks cemeteries were local – with little evidence of long-distance mobility over their lives. That's a different pattern from that seen in Bronze Age people on the Yorkshire Wolds – who moved around a lot. The disparity probably reflects a shift from a pastoral, sheep- and goat-herding lifestyle into the Bronze Age to a more settled agricultural way of life in the Iron Age. As for long-distance migration – as we've noted before, you have to catch a first-generation immigrant to detect any isotopic signal of migration in their teeth. A few people buried in high-status graves had travelled some distance over their lifetimes – their status may have been tied up with that experience and worldliness. Isotopes are useful, but won't go far in answering our questions about the scale of migrations. In order to answer the enduring question of how much the spread of ideas was linked to the spread of people at any particular time – we need to unlock the information held in ancient genomes.

And for now, the question of the scale and tempo of Iron Age migration is one we cannot answer – we just don't have the large-scale ancient DNA data for the Iron Age that we have for the Neolithic and Bronze Age. Early suggestions are that there's no large-scale migration in the first millennium, though. Clearer answers will come soon, and Pontus' ambitious project at the Crick Institute will certainly shed light on the comings and goings of our ancestors during the Iron Age.

From that wide-angle perspective on the geopolitics of the Iron Age in western Europe, let's fall back to earth and home in again on those charioteers from the Yorkshire Wolds – the 'Pocklington King' as I like to think of him – and the women with their chariots and their precious mirrors at Arras and Wetwang.

Just like written eulogies or obituaries, funerals present an opportunity to provide a portrait of the deceased that is likely to be idealised: triumphs trumpeted; virtues extolled; short-comings glossed over, forgotten. There'll be bias written into the grave goods just as surely as there's spin in Tacitus. But still, those Iron Age Arras graves provide us with an astonishingly complete glimpse into ancient lives – we see an individual more clearly and closely than anywhere else, thanks to the complexity, the detail of that burial rite. In those graves we find not the broken and discarded artefacts that fill up village middens, but often either carefully looked-after or even brand new objects – each connected in some way with that individual. We can't see those connections in settlements, where objects are so often completely divorced from their owners or their users.

Those must have been extraordinary funerals. Perhaps the chariots were used as hearses to convey the bodies to the graves in each case. In each of the women's burials, the chariots were dismantled and laid, in pieces, in the base of the pit, before the body was lowered in – each with a mirror – symbolising power or prophesy, or perhaps both.

But having seen all the artefacts for myself, as well as the skeleton, and having had those conversations with Paula Ware and Melanie Giles, it's the funeral of the man from Pocklington that shimmers so vividly in my imagination. What an impressive scene it must have been. This leader, this defender, this chieftain perhaps – lying in the open grave, fully clothed, with his two brooches, placed in his chariot; his trusted ponies going with him on the journey. And then there's the accompanying feast, with suckling pigs being roasted – and people bringing some of the pieces of roast meat to place in the grave.

'We think that a lot of people would have gathered around the graveside, to view this body,' said Melanie, as we stood looking at the man's skeleton. 'This is a moment that sticks in their memory. They didn't write records, but presumably they sang songs and told stories.'

Long after they'd covered him up and mounded up the earth over his grave, he would have been remembered, his name and his story living on. But eventually it was forgotten, and so was he. For more than 2,000 years. Until his story was uncovered again, at the tip of an archaeologist's trowel.

'In one sense, we're the last witnesses to that drama, the spectacle of that funeral,' mused Melanie. 'It really is the most spectacular British Iron Age burial I've seen.'

And Melanie has seen *a lot* of Iron Age burials.

9.

AT SALISBURY MUSEUM, 26 JULY 2019

I'm back at Salisbury Museum. It is the day after the second-hottest day ever recorded in Britain, with temperatures reaching just over 38°C. I spent the day working at home, in my own library, with the windows open, blinds half-drawn and a fan pointing right at me.

Today the temperature has dropped considerably, but the air still feels thick with heat and moisture. I'm the only person alive in the library at Salisbury Museum, my back to the windows – which I've opened so a very faint breeze comes in – facing shelves full of cardboard boxes. The labels on the boxes include *LETTERS AND PERSONALIA, LOCAL MAPS, LOCAL HISTORY* and – intriguingly – *FIRMIN & BRADBEER HAUNCH OF VENISON*. I might have to sneak a look inside that one later.

But for now, I'll resist the urge – because I have my work cut out for me. Four hefty volumes, bound in blue with gold decoration and lettering, sit on the table to my left. These are Pitt Rivers' records of his *Excavations in Cranborne Chase*.

I open the first volume. Inside it are two loose plans – one of the Romano-British village at Woodcuts Common; the other, on a smaller scale, of Rushmore House and its grounds,

357

showing the position of that Romano-British village on the common, to the east of the kitchen garden of Rushmore.

In the preface, Pitt Rivers explains how he came to inherit Rushmore, and the name-change that came with the gift.

'I inherited the Rivers estates in the year 1880,' he writes, 'in accordance with the will of my great uncle, the second Lord Rivers, and by descent from my grandmother, who was his sister, and daughter of the first lord. The will was excessively binding, and provided amongst other things that I was to assume the name and arms of Pitt Rivers within a year of my inheriting the property . . .

. . . the only inconvenience I can be said to have suffered by it has been the severance of my name from the previous publications . . .'

And he goes on to describe how his inheritance enabled him to indulge his passion for archaeology, after he retired from active service:

Of [the antiquities on my own property] there were, especially near Rushmore, consisting of Romano-British Villages, Tumuli and other vestiges of the bronze and stone age, most of which were untouched and had been well preserved.

He goes on to write about what he hopes to achieve by undertaking these excavations – he wants to understand the *identity* of the people who lived on Cranborne Chase through the ages. Where did they come from? Was there an unbroken line of descent from early Britons through to later centuries? He seems quite sure that the people living in Wiltshire, 'remote from the great centres of Roman occupation', would have been – for the most part – indigenous Britons; descendants of the Iron Age people in the same locality. But what about later centuries, when the histories tell us that the Saxons invaded, for instance, and largely replaced British populations?

> It is to investigations of sites such as these that we must look for a solution of the problem which has so largely occupied the attention of historians, viz., to what extent were the Britons exterminated (as some authors have supposed) by the Saxons after their abandonment by the Romans, in what proportion does Celtic [Iron Age British] blood circulate in the veins of the existing population of England . . .

He comments that the people whose remains he discovered at 'Woodcuts Village', in its pits and ditches, were 'a remarkably small race of people'. And he remarks on the findings of earlier antiquarians who'd investigated long barrows, finding that 'a long-headed race of small stature, whose average height is estimated at 5 feet 6 inches, inhabited Britain in the Stone Age. These were succeeded by a tall, round-headed people of larger size, estimated at 5 feet 8 inches [not *that* much taller then!], and these again were replaced in after times by the Saxons, whose stature was also large. But of the peculiarities of Roman Britons little as yet is known . . .'

And he justifies his careful recording of the archaeology he has uncovered:

> It will, perhaps, be thought by some that I have recorded the excavations of this village and the finds that have been made

in it with unnecessary fulness, and I am aware that I have done it in greater detail than has been customary, but my experience as an excavator has led me to think that investigations of this nature are not generally sufficiently searching, and that much valuable evidence is lost by omitting to record them carefully.

Well, I'm certainly grateful that he recorded everything so meticulously. It means I can take a skull out of the archive and cross-reference it with the excavation records – matching it not only with descriptions and measurements, but even with photographs.

This first volume is filled with plans and sections of the excavations at Woodcuts, and then whole sections on artefacts – pages and pages of beautiful bow-shaped fibulae, bronze bosses, worked flints – and then, what I'm really interested in: the human remains. Pitt Rivers had the skull of each individual carefully drawn, from the front, from the side and from the top. With each set of drawings, there's a fold-out table of the measurements he made – using, as he's careful to point out, Professor Flower's and Professor Busk's craniometers.

When I come to make my own measurements on the skulls, I'm confident that I can cross-reference back to Pitt Rivers' analyses and compare my results with his. What I'm hoping is that I can capture a large set of measurements from each skull – most in the form of distances between certain anatomical landmarks – and use those to investigate shape differences across the sample. It will be interesting to see whether – and then how – the shape of the skull reflects genetic patterns of difference. And I want to know if Pitt Rivers really was on to something with his ideas of population replacement. The ancient genome data we already have from Britain suggests that his inferences might well have been correct – that he really was able to detect a change in the population through a change in skull shape and size. But with ancient DNA from the very skulls he analysed, and a modern craniometric assessment, we could look into those patterns in more detail.

But I won't be taking any of the skulls out of their boxes until Tom and Turi have done all the DNA sampling – just to avoid any unnecessary contamination.

I dig into the second volume. This one relates to excavations around Rushmore, across three distinct periods, which Pitt Rivers describes as 'the Bronze Age, the period of the Romanised Britons, and the Anglo-Saxon period'.

He starts this book describing his excavations of the barrows near Rushmore – among the earliest archaeological investigations he carried out after he inherited the estate. The sites have wonderful names – Tinkley Down, Scrubbity Coppice, Barrow Pleck ('pleck' being a local term for a woodland clearing). And the very first barrow he excavated, Barrow No. I, contained cremated remains, together with some 'minute fragments of bronze' that he surmised may have been all that was left of a weapon, buried with the cremated bone. Pitt Rivers describes the form of the barrow as being very simple – like an upturned bowl, with no ditch around it; perhaps an early type of barrow, though the form persisted among later, ditched types.

Barrow No. III was unusual – it contained two cremations in its centre, in basins cut into the underlying chalk. Then there were a further eight cremations placed in it as secondary interments, and one inhumation, the skeleton lying in a crouched position on its left side. Pitt Rivers wrote that this barrow 'Afford[ed] proof that both systems of burial were here practised at the same time' – although he had no way of directly dating the burials, of course.

Some of the barrows looked as though they had been started with a particular purpose – with a basin-shaped pit dug down into the chalk, presumably with the intention of collecting cremated bone from the funeral pyre and placing those remains in the pit, before covering the whole thing over with a mound of soil. But then it looked as though the pyre had been made *in situ*, and perhaps it was too difficult to collect up the bone or disturb the pyre – as the underlying pit was effectively left empty of cremated bone, and fragments were just scattered through the overlying soil.

Pitt Rivers was particularly interested in Barrow No. IX. It was large, with a ditch around it. Inside the mound, Pitt Rivers discovered the cremated remains of an individual lying within a wooden, boat-shaped coffin, made from a tree trunk. 'This is remarkable,' he wrote, 'as the coffin itself was adapted to contain a crouched skeleton, but the fact of its containing a burnt one would appear to be another instance of change of purpose.' The barrow also contained a flint knife and flint flakes.

Most of the barrows contained fragments of rough British pottery and some contained flint flakes. One – No. X – contained a large British urn, but no evidence of cremated human remains. Pitt Rivers noted that he'd found another urn like this on Winklebury Hill, empty of cremated bone but full of fragments of flint, and that his mentor, Canon Greenwell, had found similar examples in the Yorkshire Wolds. Perhaps, Greenwell had suggested, these 'empty' barrows served as cenotaphs or memorials, without needing to contain the physical remains of the person to whom they were dedicated.

Pitt Rivers noted that the absence of cremated bones in these barrows was likely to be real, not an artefact of preservation, as burnt bone usually survives well in such deposits.

This second volume of excavation reports also included records of Pitt Rivers' excavations on the edge of his estate, and just beyond – at Rotherley 'Romano-British Village' and Winklebury Camp.

Only two of the burials described in this volume contained bones that were complete enough to be assessed – the crouched skeleton in Barrow XX and the inhumation in Rotherley Village. Pitt Rivers estimated the stature of the Barrow XX individual to be somewhere around 5 feet 6.5 inches. The other individual was taller, at around 5 feet 9.5 inches. 'From this it will be seen,' notes Pitt Rivers, 'that the two skeletons considerably exceed those of the Romanised Britons found in the villages at Woodcuts and Rotherley.' The second skull was too fragmentary to yield accurate measurements of skull shape and size, but the Barrow XX skull had a cephalic index of 845mm – 'a typical Bronze Age skull'.

I move on to volumes three and four, but it's getting late in the day. I take photographs of the pages that I haven't had the time to read and transcribe today, and of some of the plans – and those beautiful plates of skulls.

At nearly six o'clock, I close up the four volumes and place them back on their shelves. I pack up my laptop and camera, and finally I allow myself to lift down that intriguing box labelled *HAUNCH OF VENISON* – and take a look inside.

It doesn't, somewhat disappointingly, contain a hunk of meat, or even a bone. It's full of documents – birth certificates, ration cards, and a large hardback ledger. I open it, and written in a flowing hand on the first page is:

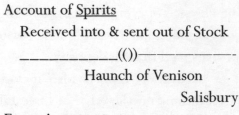

Account of <u>Spirits</u>

Received into & sent out of Stock

————————((·))————————-

Haunch of Venison

Salisbury

From August 1876

The Haunch was a pub, then. A quick internet search reveals that it is still in operation, and very proud of its reputation as 'Probably the oldest hostelry in Salisbury and certainly the most haunted.' It also has a 'smoke-preserved mummified hand' behind an iron grille, in an old bread oven next to the fireplace. I make a note to myself to pay it a visit sometime.

Everything is back in its place. I gather up my things, carefully lock the two doors to the library, and make my way downstairs, where I give the keys of the library back to Adrian Green. I'll be back in Salisbury in just six days' time. Adrian has kindly agreed to take me on an archaeological tour of Cranborne Chase – including a visit to the resting place of Pitt Rivers himself.

10.

ON CRANBORNE CHASE, 1 AUGUST 2019

I take the train to Salisbury again, and Adrian picks me up from the station. He drives out west from the city, along the Chalke Valley, until we reach Berwick St John. We turn left out of the village, and up onto the hill, where we park up in a lay-by.

Getting out of the car, we cross the road into a field at the northern end of the Rushmore Estate. We're high up in the landscape and the view to the south is quite idyllic.

We walk down through a field of wheat that's just been cut. Tractors are moving bales of straw. Boots kick, clattering, against the stubble. We are heading down towards one of Pitt Rivers' sites – the ancient settlement of Rotherley. Passing through an iron gate at the field boundary, we enter a grassy field. Close to the top of the sloping, undulating field is a curious stone obelisk, like a diminutive trig point – just before the field starts to slope down to Rotherley Bottom.

There's an inscription on the side of it. It's covered in yellow and grey lichen, but still legible. I run my fingers over the letters, and read it out loud: '*The Romano-British village was excavated and the pits and ditches partially filled up again by Lieutenant General Pitt Rivers FRS in the years 1886, 1887.*'

Moving anticlockwise round the obelisk, I read the next side:

'*Ninety two pits, fifteen human skeletons, two British coins, eleven Roman coins and numerous relics of the Roman Age were discovered. Of the skeletons, eleven were crouched, two were contracted and two extended* – there's a lot of detail!'

'It gets even better as you go round . . .' Adrian enthuses.

'*Stature – the average stature of eleven males was five foot, one to three inches . . . females four foot ten . . . Skulls – of fourteen skulls found, one was brachycephalic, three were* – what does it say? – *mesaticephalic, six were dolichocephalic, three were hyperdolichocephalic* – even longer – *one was uncertain*. What amazing detail. It's a report – it's a bone report in summary.'

It wasn't enough for Pitt Rivers to mark the spot – he wanted to provide any visitors with extra information, on this nineteenth-century version of an English Heritage information board.

'But it's also about what he's interested in,' says Adrian, 'and what he thinks the public will be most interested in – the human remains.'

Adrian had brought Pitt Rivers' plan of Rotherley with him. We spread it out, pinpointing our position on it. Within the settlement, Pitt Rivers had marked plenty of pits – but no obvious dwellings. But Adrian points out a set of four postholes arranged in a square, perhaps originally holding large timber posts for an above-ground granary – or holding up the roof of a roundhouse, even though its outer perimeter hadn't been identified. Another set of four postholes was labelled: '*Supposed granary. Grains of wheat found in all these holes.*'

'What he's recording in his plan are features dug into the chalk,' says Adrian. 'Anything above that, he missed out. But look here to the north – this is where he's finding burials . . . in these pits . . .'

The pits had been dug into the chalk – probably originally for storage, but later used for burials. It looks like an earlier settlement to the north of the site may have been abandoned – and then used as a cemetery. It's difficult to pick out the sequence of events, though – the plan is a dense palimpsest, containing everything Pitt Rivers had found, all the eras squashed together. This is, of course, how we find archaeology in the landscape – all those years, decades, centuries, millennia, stacked up and interleaved. The archaeologist's job is disentangling those layers – and that's become easier with the advent of absolute dating techniques such as radiocarbon dating. But even without such methods available to him, Pitt Rivers had some idea of different dates across the site. A handful of coins, for example, showed that the site extended into the Roman period.

'He's got pottery too,' Adrian explains. 'He recognises the difference between what he calls British pottery, of the Iron Age period, and then "Romano-British" pottery – Samian ware imported from the continent, and, later on, New Forest ware. But he wasn't looking at how the site evolves over time.'

This would be something we'd be able to decipher, with our new project. With radiocarbon dating, we'd know where each burial fitted into the sequence. And the ancient DNA should show us how much the population changed over time.

'They might all be related – an extended family over several generations,' muses Adrian.

When Pontus and his team get round to sampling and sequencing the Rotherley human remains, we'll be able to look at those sorts of questions: what happened here, when Britain became part of the Roman Empire? Did the same family carry on, farming this landscape as they'd done for generations? The archaeology didn't seem to show any evidence for discontinuity, for a break – but would the ancient DNA results speak of continuity as well?

'I think Pitt Rivers would be quite pleased to think that archaeologists in the twenty-first century were coming back to his excavations here,' says Adrian, 'reading the inscriptions on his monument, and thinking: we can apply some new techniques here, and perhaps finally answer some of his questions.

'It justifies everything he did – retaining all that material, and the detail he went into when he recorded the site. That's the beauty of it – that we can pick up where he left off, and reinterpret this place. I think he knew that no interpretation was ever fixed, and that things would move on, and different generations would have their own version of history.'

I remember something from those hefty excavation volumes back in the museum.

'In the prefaces of his excavation record, he says: I know it looks like I'm recording everything in such an extraordinary level of detail, and people might think that's over and above what's required, but I'm doing this for posterity. I'm recording as much as I possibly can – because it *might* be useful.'

We start walking down the eastern flank of the hill, still looking at Pitt Rivers' plan as we go. The archaeology was more jumbled here, with patches of scattered flints – perhaps floor surfaces inside buildings. Adrian tells me of something wonderful that had been found down in the dip, in the foundations of one of the buildings – he draws out a picture of it: a large tablet of Kimmeridge shale, about a foot long. It has a pattern incised into its surface. And I recognise the pattern.

'That's the pattern on the covers of his excavation volumes – embossed in gold!'

'Yes, he takes that incomplete pattern from the broken object and completes it – and uses it as a sort of monogram on all his publications.'

It was beautiful object. It seemed at odds with Pitt Rivers' assessment of the site, though. He was almost dismissive about the settlement, interpreting it as fairly crude and impoverished, with people living a very basic subsistence lifestyle.

'But they had a very nice table!' laughs Adrian. 'Well, a table or a tray of some sort. This is only half of it – I'd love to know where the other half is.'

There were other refined Roman objects from the site, too, including a small bronze box – the type that was used to keep a seal in.

'Are these the kind of things that you'd expect to find on a farm?' I ask.

'Well, it shows you the penetration of the Roman way of life, Roman culture. We're here, nearly on the edge of the Roman Empire, but they're still using, consuming, products like this that we would think of as being "Roman".'

'One of the things I really want to understand is the identity of these people – where their families came from. The Roman Empire is imposed on them – and they're buying into it. They're aspiring to certain aspects of Roman life. In some ways, it's to do with fashion, I suppose.'

'So you think they're most likely to be Romanised native Britons?'

'That's what I'd assume – but I may be completely wrong. I think they're likely to be people who have lived here for generations, but the ancient DNA will allow us to actually test that idea. We have this "school textbook" idea of the Roman period – lots of people coming over and settling here, another influx. But when you look at the archaeological evidence – when you look at a site like this – what you see is a mixing, a blending of cultures and ideas, in terms of objects and beliefs. I think people are probably retaining their old pre-Roman religious beliefs, but combining them with a smattering of high Roman culture – you see that all over the place.'

It makes sense if you think about *why* the Romans extended their empire to Britain – they were interested in the resources here, including the agricultural resources.

'If you wipe out the population here, and replace it with another population, you've lost all your farmers,' I reflect.

'Yes, of course you have, and these people knew how to farm this landscape. They knew it intimately. So – you're going to want to bring them into the fold. I think you start at the top, with the people in power. You bring them in, bind them to your way of life – and that eventually trickles down to the rest of society as well. The old affiliations of the Iron Age probably persist – the people who ruled the roost on a local level were likely the same people who were ruling before the Roman occupation happened.'

The way we carve up history into separate eras can obscure continuity. Look at a map of Britain today, even, and the place names hold ancient resonance.

'Obviously the Romans came in and labelled groups of people, and that's not necessarily how those people saw themselves – but they're probably reflecting local language and local labels. When you have a county like Dorset, with the county town of Dorchester, and you have an Iron Age tribe that the Romans tell us was called the Durotriges – it looks like we're still administering Britain according to an Iron Age pattern,' I suggest.

'Yes, I'd like to think that,' agrees Adrian. 'We can still see that continuity. I certainly don't think the Romans destroyed all the pre-existing culture – it's much more complicated than that. And some of what we have today does go right back to then.'

We look at the plans of Rotherley again. The detail on the plans is extraordinary. One burial is labelled 'Skeleton 15, crouched, with bronze ring on finger'.

'He'd have been pleased, I think, to see us up here, poring over his plans like this!' smiles Adrian.

As we walked down the flank of the hill, I notice a curious, keyhole-shaped feature on Pitt Rivers' plans.

'This feature – he calls it a "hypocaust": is it really? That's under-floor heating for a villa?' I query.

'Yes – that's not what it is. It's actually a small grain-drying oven. Something that was used for malting barley. So it's precisely the sort of thing you'd expect to find on a Roman farmstead. If you wanted to brew your own beer, you'd need that. I suppose it's a form of hypocaust – it has a furnace at one end, almost like a kiln. But Pitt Rivers misunderstood what they were used for. They're quite commonplace on Roman sites in Dorset.'

There's a spot where the ground has slumped and torn open of its own accord, creating a natural archaeological section. Pieces of flint stick out of the earth. We're in the area of the plan where the sunken huts are shown – that slightly messy, less definite part of the site. Adrian is surprised, though, that there were no obvious pieces of pottery.

'Either the settlement wasn't that dense. Or perhaps Pitt Rivers just removed it all.'

'Surely he wouldn't have been that assiduous?'

'Yes, I don't think he stripped the whole site.'

The ground is quite uneven – we are walking over banks and

ditches. Crickets are chirping in the grass. 'Are these the remnants of his digs – or were there lumps and bumps here already? Was that what drew him to excavate the site?'

'Yes – a few finds had turned up around rabbit burrows, and he then spotted that there were earthworks. He made models of the landscape before and afterwards, so we have a really good idea of what was visible before. But I think a lot of what we see here today is from his excavations – soil has been thrown up and not replaced. I think he did that on purpose – filling trenches up enough so they're not dangerous, but leaving indications here so that people can understand the site.'

'I like that layered archaeology; we've got the Romano-British village here and then we've also got the archaeology of Pitt Rivers' excavations here.'

'It would be interesting to re-excavate the site, to look at his techniques – and understand the settlement more.'

We walk back up the hill and into the wheat field where the huge tractors are still moving bales into great stacks. Then we cross the road to walk out onto Winklebury hillfort.

'This fort's on a peninsula, jutting out at the top of the Chalke Valley. It's heavily defended with banks and ditches on the landward side, but the defences around the side are quite light, as the slopes are naturally steep.'

'So it's similar to a coastal, promontory hillfort,' I observe.

'Yes, it is. But there are some questions about it. It doesn't look finished. Some of the gaps in the defences are quite large in places. It might have been experimental, left incomplete.'

What looked like a bank crowning the crest of the hill turns out to be just a patch of very tall thistles, reaching up to our hips. It's hard to avoid getting prickled.

'But it looks like there's something interesting here,' I say in defiance, fighting my way through the thistles. 'Whenever there's a change of vegetation like this, you do wonder if there's archaeology hidden under it . . .'

'Well, you're right, there is,' says Adrian. 'Roughly where we're standing, just to the south of the hillfort itself, there was a group of Bronze Age barrows. They were later reused for Saxon burials – that's fairly common.'

This echoed that reuse of Neolithic tombs in the Bronze Age.

'It seems to be about more recent incomers wanting to establish their right to the land,' muses Adrian.

Linking yourself to the landscape and the ancestors that lived there before; even if you were actually nothing to do with those ancestors, you could create that connection by associating yourselves with their burial mounds.

'It's interesting as "Winklebury" is an Anglo-Saxon name,' Adrian continues. "Winkle" may have been someone's name, while "bury" means a fort or enclosure. So somewhere around here, there should be an Anglo-Saxon settlement – and it may be under the modern village of Berwick St John. The burials up here were quite early, though – fifth or sixth century CE. And clearly, in the Saxon period, there are people who are coming in, but also local people adopting what we see as "Saxon" culture.'

'And that's combined with forging a new identity – when Britain stops being part of the Roman Empire.'

'Yes, they're having to create a whole new value system – one that's no longer pegged to the people you've been paying your taxes to, who were governing the land. It's quite fluid.'

'So much of British identity still seems to be about that – we're constantly wrestling with how close we feel to the rest of Europe.'

We suddenly come up to a huge bank and a V-shaped ditch

at least 4 metres deep, crossing the promontory from edge to edge. The bank on the far side is even higher.

'This is one of the first sites that Pitt Rivers excavated, not long after he took on the Cranborne Chase Estate,' explains Adrian. 'The irony of that is that this isn't actually on his estate – it's on the Grove family's land, next door.'

'What did Pitt Rivers find here?'

'Well, as a military man, he was interested in the defensive ditches. A lot of his energy went into trying to establish when they were constructed, so he put sections in across this huge ditch here – but also across the banks around the perimeter of the hill.'

We cross the ditch and walk to the end of the promontory. A skylark flies up, pouring out its bubbling song. The sides of the hill are incredibly steep.

'We're looking out over the top end of the Chalke Valley – that's the river Ebble below us that runs down to the Avon just south of Salisbury. So this hillfort dominates the headwaters of this river.'

Adrian fishes out Pitt Rivers' plans of this site.

'Here we go. Here's the hill. More or less exactly where we're standing, Pitt Rivers put one of his trenches in.'

I look just beyond Adrian, 'Is it just there? There's a dip . . .'

'There *is* a dip! Yes – I'd buy that. More evidence of Pitt Rivers' work.'

'Without his plan, you might think this was an entrance through the bank to the hillfort, but it is actually the remains of Pitt Rivers' trench.'

'That's the archaeology of archaeology, right there,' smiles Adrian. 'He excavated here in 1881, 1882. We don't have models – but he produced absolutely huge diagrams. We don't have room to display them in Salisbury Museum – they're bigger than the display cases. They show all the trenches and sections – but on a scale that they could have used for presentations. He did lectures and talks for local societies. He was a Fellow of the Royal Society, but also involved with the Society of Antiquaries and the Anthropological Society – all these groups in London associated with big ideas in archaeology and anthropology.'

He'd made a name for himself before he inherited Cranborne Chase – and so that name was not 'Pitt Rivers'.

'A lot of his published work was as "Lane Fox" – that's when he established his reputation.'

I remember something else from my digging around in the archives.

'Ah, yes, he grumbles about that a bit in one of the prefaces to the excavation volumes – he accepts that he must take the name of "Pitt Rivers" but laments the fact that he's losing the connection with his publication record under "Lane Fox".'

'In fact, if he hadn't inherited Cranborne Chase and done all this work here, he would still have been famous because of what he'd already done in archaeology,' replies Adrian.

'We'd still have heard of him – he'd still be famous – but as Lane Fox.'

We keep exploring, finding other gaps in the bank, which presumably did go back to the Iron Age. They could have been entrances. Or those discontinuities in the earthworks could have been filled in with fences, perhaps. Or the fort was left unfinished for some reason. This is one of those archaeological puzzles that we may never be able to solve.

As well as investigating the banks, Pitt Rivers had explored the inside of the hillfort. He uncovered what he described as a 'pit dwelling', although Adrian thinks it more likely to have been a small quarry.

'He loved a pit dwelling,' says Adrian, grinning. 'They were all the rage in the nineteenth century. He thought that's where "primitive people" lived. They lived in holes in the ground!'

We find the 'pit dwelling' marked on the plan – it looks like a mound as we approached it, but it turns out to be a mass of tall brambles growing out of a depression.

There was something a bit more civilised running through the centre of the hillfort, though: a surfaced road, which Pitt Rivers had dubbed 'Mid Street'. It reminded me of those chalk trackways criss-crossing the Yorkshire Dales. Also inside the hillfort, Pitt Rivers uncovered lots of pits, some of them containing charred grain.

'And the best thing,' says Adrian 'is he kept some of it! As environmental samples, just like a modern archaeologist – he was keeping environmental evidence to be analysed, so he could find out what crops were they growing.'

'And what were they growing?'

'Wheat – just as we do today.'

But, apart from the 'pit dwelling', there was no recorded evidence of structures on Pitt Rivers' plan of Winklebury Hillfort.

'He failed to uncover more subtle evidence, perhaps of wooden buildings. If you've got those pits, you assume there's occupation here.'

'It would be a bit odd to have those grain storage pits – that's your food and your wealth – with no one up here to protect it.'

The evidence now points to settlement in the hillfort – perhaps on a seasonal basis, tied in with harvesting of crops, rather than all year round. Adrian thinks the large entrances suggest livestock may have been brought up here too – that the hillfort could be seen as a 'big Iron Age cattle pen'. The hillfort was inevitably multifunctional – it could be used to protect assets like grain and cattle, but it was also a very imposing, showy feature in the landscape – perhaps acting as a status symbol as well.

It's lovely up on the hillfort in the sunshine. There are heathland butterflies, buttercups, harebells. Adrian and I are the only two humans there – looking for traces of the ancients, wondering what it had been like 2,000 years ago.

As we walk back up the promontory, we spot a cluster of Bronze Age barrows. Adrian wanders off to investigate.

'What have you found?'

'I don't know what I've found,' he laughs.

'Stones. That's a stone. I can recognise that as a stone.'

'But – it's not local, not from round here. It's not chalk and it's not flint.'

'It looks like a chunk of limestone. There's another one there . . . and there . . .'

'There's limestone not too far away from here.'

The stones were evenly spaced and covered in lichen. More Pitt Rivers monuments perhaps? Adrian was intrigued.

'Something for further research,' he mused.

Bodies, burning and burial

After a very respectable lunch at the King John pub in the village of Tollard Royal, right at the centre of the Rushmore Estate, Adrian continues the tour. We walk down the road from the pub and through a clanking gate into a churchyard.

'This is the church of St Peter ad Vincula – St Peter in chains. Quite an unusual dedication. This is the local parish church – look out for Pitt Rivers family graves. Anyone in the main line is called "Pitt Rivers"; other children who weren't going to inherit, they were called "Fox Pitt" or "Lane Fox Pitt".'

We walk up to the top of the sloping churchyard, where there is an ornate cross with a Celtic knot at the top, and a coat of arms at the base.

'This is his eldest son.'

I read the inscription. '*Alexander Edward Lane Fox Pitt Rivers.* Four surnames!'

'He was born in November 1855, died in August 1927 – and inherited the estate in 1900, when Pitt Rivers died.'

There are more family graves clustered around, some almost hidden under luxuriant nettles.

'I'm just seeing if I can find . . . Alice,' says Adrian.

'I'm here. Right here,' I reply.

Adrian laughs.

'Alice Pitt Rivers, I was thinking of! His wife.'

'But where's Pitt Rivers himself?'

'He's in the church.'

We enter the church itself.

'It probably won't take you long to spot his tomb,' says Adrian. 'It's not the knight.'

Towards the east end is a stone knight, with his feet resting on a dog. At the other end, to our left, there's a carved, marble-framed niche in the wall of the church – containing a black casket. And on the casket is a roundel depicting a Bronze Age urn, a mace-head and a skull; a sword buried underground; a pick and theodolite – archaeological finds and tools.

'This must be Pitt Rivers.'

'Yes, and this imagery is based on a medal designed by Sir John Evans – also a well-known archaeologist, and a friend of

Pitt Rivers – who would bury a bronze medal like this wherever he conducted excavations.'

The design was something like a logo, then. The medals: his calling cards. The theodolite and skull represented those twin passions: field survey and craniometry.

'"Pitt Rivers was here",' I remark.

'Exactly. And – in this case – *right* here. His cremated remains are in that casket.'

'He died in 1900. Cremation would have been extremely unusual at the time.'

'Yes – very rare. But he was very particular about it. There are stories that he used to argue with his wife, Alice, about it. Even in church. But she's buried outside – and he's in here, with this memorial.'

'The vast majority of people at the end of the nineteenth century are buried, not cremated – it was *not* in vogue.'

'Yes – which leads you to speculate: why. Was it to do with all the research that he'd done here, his interest in archaeology – all the cremated remains he uncovered on Cranborne Chase? That in some way he felt this was appropriate?'

'I suppose doing all of that research must have given him the ability to lift himself out of his contemporary culture, where we often perceive that what we do here, now, is *normal*, and everything else is abnormal – whether that's in other countries or in the past. And seeing how things changed over time – lots of different modes of funerary practice, burial, cremation – perhaps he felt liberated to choose something personal, that suited him.'

'And there's also the question of his religious beliefs – which I don't think we understand. I suspect he may not have been all that religious. The well-established Christian funerary practice was inhumation, so destroying the body through cremation may have been quite abhorrent to people.'

'And yet he's ended up in a church. Is it a protest? Is he here at the back, saying: "Here I am, I'm an atheist"?'

'Yes – we don't know.'

We pore over the inscription on the tomb, and it is quite determinedly not religious. It is instead a potted biography. Adrian reads it out, deciphering it as he goes:

'*Augustus Henry Lane Fox Pitt Rivers FRS* – Fellow of the Royal Society – *FSA* – that's Fellow of the Society of Antiquaries, *DCL . . . of Rushmore Grenadier Guards, was on the staff of DAQMG* – Deputy Assistant Quartermaster General – *at the Battle of Alma.* That's his only active service – in the Crimean War. Then he's the Assistant Quartermaster General at Cork. That's where he started to do some of his first archaeological work, in southern Ireland . . . then commander of a brigade depot at Guildford – and – *First Instructor of Musketry at Hythe and Malta.* Now that's really important, because he was responsible for researching and introducing the musket rifle into the army in the middle of the nineteenth century – that's probably his major military contribution. And the development of the rifle, how it evolved, is what led to his interest in collecting, looking at the evolution of culture . . . Then, *Devoted the last twenty years of his life to anthropological research.* The word archaeology is not mentioned – it's considered part of anthropology. He's *Inspector of Ancient Monuments.* That's a whole separate chapter in his career, which he took on in 1882, going around the country checking on sites that were on the first Schedule of Ancient Monuments. Then it backtracks: *Born 12 April 1827. Passed away 4 May 1900. Erected in loving memory by his eldest son Alexander Edward Lane Fox Pitt Rivers.*'

'Whose grave we saw outside.'

'And – *Also of his wife the Hon. Alice Margaret born 30 July 1828 and died 19 May 1910.* So she outlived him by ten years.'

'And didn't join him in here, in the casket?'

'No, she's out there, and he's in here. She was buried. He was cremated.'

'I'm so intrigued that he dared to do that. To be cremated.'

Pitt Rivers doesn't seem to have been *particularly* interested in death – in funerary or mortuary rituals. Graves were just another – if important – trace of past human activity in the landscape. With the added benefit that a skull, in an inhumation, of course, might permit the anthropologist to start tracing the comings and goings of ancient populations.

Of the 19,605 artefacts that Pitt Rivers donated to the University of Oxford (ending up in the eponymous museum there), only 254 related to death in some way. And although he wrote about the grave goods he discovered in his excavation records, he certainly didn't afford them the same attention he gave to the evolution of design or warfare. He would describe grave goods as 'religious emblems', but gave little away when it came to his own religious beliefs. But there are a couple of clues – one, a short paragraph from a draft of a lecture, written in 1875, that hints he was perhaps more of a deist than a theist. He doesn't seem keen on the idea of God as a supernatural being, and was more open to the idea that divinity – if it existed anywhere – existed everywhere:

What then if we do find that religion is subject to the same laws of evolution as all other human ideas. Are we to infer from this that we can see God in nothing, or may we not rather infer that we may see him in everything instead of peeping at him through the narrow chinks & crevices which have been prescribed for us during an ignorant age.

The paragraph certainly implies that Christianity – a Roman religion emerging from a Bronze Age tradition, after all – had enchained itself to a philosophical view of the world that was not only ancient – but ignorant.

When it came to human origins, Pitt Rivers took a determinedly scientific stance, accepting evolution, rather than divine creation, as the best explanation – and also seeing that as a positive philosophy. Here he is, addressing the Salisbury Archaeological Institute in 1887:

. . . I cannot myself see how human conduct is likely to be affected disadvantageously by recognizing the humble origin of mankind. If it teaches us to take less pride in our ancestry, and to place more reliance on ourselves, this cannot fail to serve as an additional incentive to industry and respectability. Nor are our relations with the Supreme Power presented to us in an unfavourable light by this discovery, for if man was created originally in the image of God, it is obvious that the very best of us have greatly degenerated. But if on the other hand we recognize that we sprung from inferior beings, then, there is no cause for anxiety on account of the occasional backsliding observable amongst men, and we are encouraged to hope that with the help of Providence, notwithstanding frequent relapses towards the primitive condition of our remote forefathers, we may continue to improve in the long run as we have done hitherto.

In this passage, we're presented with an optimistic view of humanity, where humans are freed to improve themselves — rather than required to atone for any original sin. Pitt Rivers clearly believed in human progress and advancement. Perhaps he's *too* progressivist, even — leaving you wondering how he might have castigated any 'backsliders'! Whether he would have described himself as a deist, agnostic or atheist, we will never know, but his general philosophy on life was far from nihilistic.

As far as going to church (which is never a very good measure of someone's religiosity anyway), Pitt Rivers would only turn up for weddings, funerals and religious festivals like Christmas and Easter. But his funeral did take place in a religious setting, at that church of St Peter ad Vincula in Royal Tollard — with his cremated remains ending up there, too.

Pitt Rivers was beset with illness for most of his life, stemming from his diabetes. Having retired early from active service, he then kept himself busy with his archaeological investigations. It seems he expected to die sooner than he actually did: in a letter dated 1897, about buying a new property, he mentions 'I am only going to be here for so short a time.' And yet he lived another thirteen years after that. In 1898, he wrote, 'I am very infirm now, having had diabetes continuously for 17 years. I can hardly do more than go from room to room but I still keep working a little slowly'.

He died on 4 May 1900, at his home on the Rushmore Estate. Rather oddly, his body was photographed, in his bed, two hours after death. Mortuary photographs like this were more common earlier in the nineteenth century. To modern eyes, they are frankly disturbing — especially the ones showing dead people posed alongside the living. The live faces often look slightly blurred, as long exposures were required — while the dead are sharply in focus. It seems to have been in fashion when photography was still quite rare and expensive – if you hadn't got round to capturing a likeness of a loved one in life, a death portrait was your last chance. Some attempted to portray the dead as still living – propping them up to participate in family portraits, or painting eyes onto the photograph. Others showed the dead arranged as though they were 'only sleeping'. Pitt Rivers' death portrait is neither. His body is formally laid out on his death bed, covered with a sheet, leaving his head bare. He is quite definitely dead in it. Not sleeping, not pretending to be alive. It's an unusually objective example of a death portrait.

It's also quite a late example – and what we don't know is whether Pitt Rivers himself had left instructions for this to happen, or if someone in his household took it into their own hands. It seems unlikely that it was a mourning relative, though, as the photograph wasn't kept in the family. Just eighteen years after it was snapped, it was snapped up by the Pitt Rivers Museum – from an antiquarian bookseller in Oxford.

Whoever took the photograph, though, was clearly ready to capture that moment. Perhaps it was one of his archaeological assistants – more used to recording excavations and photographing much more ancient human remains. Was this Pitt Rivers' obsession with recording, with capturing history, then, extending to his own death? Was it important to him to have this record created before his body was destroyed by cremation?

Much as we cannot pin Pitt Rivers down on his religious beliefs (though his grandson thought he probably was an atheist, and the glaring omission of anything even vaguely religious on his tomb inscription speaks volumes), neither can we be sure of what he thought happened after death. He certainly can't have believed in any bodily resurrection – he seems too scientific in his approach to the world for that – and archaeology, of course, reveals that the human body in death decays just as any animal remains do. Cremation tends not to be the first choice of someone who believes that there's any residue of a 'soul' in dead, physical remains, after all. And yet we know that Pitt Rivers attended a few séances. We're left wondering if he was open-minded about spiritualism (many reputable nineteenth-century scientists were), whether he was dragged along by his wife and, grumbling, complied – or whether his interest was more anthropological. He certainly can't have been someone who worried about being haunted by the ghosts of the Cranborne Chase dead, disgruntled at having been dug out of their tombs, their skulls gripped in his ingenious craniometer, to be sized up.

Pitt Rivers left no such physical remains to be pored over by future anthropologists. His body was cremated some distance away from Rushmore – in Woking, in Surrey, just five days after his death. This was only fifteen years after the first official cremation in Britain, and at that time Woking's was one of just four British crematoria.

The driver for cremation was more 'mortuary' than 'funerary'. If texts are lost in the future, and archaeologists in centuries to come try to interpret attitudes to death in the twentieth and twenty-first centuries from physical remains alone, they may well conclude that there was a major change of religion in Britain over this period. And yet the argument for cremation that emerged in the nineteenth century and prevailed in the twentieth was economic and sanitary, not religious. The burial grounds of Britain's major cities were full to bursting. In the overflow burial ground of St James' Piccadilly, in Euston, coffins were stacked, up to nine deep, in shafts that had been dug down to 7 metres beneath the surface of the ground. Struggling to understand how cholera epidemics emerged and spread, many connected the contagion with the noxious smells emanating from putrefying corpses in overfilled churchyards. Cremation seemed to present a cleaner – and cheaper – alternative, and had already taken off in Germany. But in Britain, Anglican bishops were uncomfortable about adopting such a 'heathen practice'.

In 1874, the eminent surgeon Sir Henry Thompson published a paper entitled *The Treatment of the Body after Death*, in which he argued that cremation 'was becoming a necessary sanitary precaution against the propagation of disease among a population daily growing larger in relation to the area it occupied'. Cremation also spared cost, spared space in churchyards, spared mourners the misery of standing around in cold, wet churchyards, and might even – if society could stomach it – provide a source of ashes for fertiliser. The idea quickly gained ground – quite literally – as Thompson acquired a site in Woking from the London Necropolis Company, for the purpose of building the UK's first crematorium. In March 1879, the facility was tested to see how well it would perform, cremating a dead horse. It was very effective, but the inhabitants of Woking were unimpressed and, led by the vicar, complained to the home secretary. What if cremation was used to dispose of a dead body – before an autopsy could be carried out? The home secretary, Sir Richard Cross, effectively shut down the Woking crematorium until further notice.

But some people were not to be deterred. In 1882, Captain John Hanham, of the small village of Manston in Dorset, faced a dilemma. His third wife knew that Hanham's second wife lay in a vault under the church, which regularly flooded whenever rain swelled the River Stour. She made Hanham promise that, were she to pre-decease him, he would have her body cremated – but of course, that was legally questionable. She died in 1876, and Hanham opted for a temporary fix, storing her corpse in a lead coffin in a mausoleum in the grounds of his home, Manston House. Meanwhile, he was negotiating with the authorities to be able to fulfil his dead wife's wishes. Then his mother died too, also wishing to be cremated. Finally, in October 1882, Hanham was granted permission to carry out the cremation of the two bodies – in his own, purpose-built crematorium at Manston House.

The following year, another cremation was attempted – this one on an open pyre, carried out by a very strange character, a certain Dr William Price, in Llantrisant, Glamorgan. Price was a well-known Welsh eccentric – and a proponent of the neo-Druidic movement, seeking to revive the forgotten religion of Iron Age Celtic druids (whatever that actually was). At the age of eighty-one, Dr Price married a 21-year-old farmer's daughter, Gwenllian Llewellyn. Two years later she miraculously gave birth to a son, whom they named Iesu Grist. Little Iesu lived only five months. Three days after the child died, on 13 January 1884, Price carried the small body up onto a hill to place it on a funeral pyre. This was an eccentricity too far for the locals, who marched up the hill to put a stop to the cremation, and Price was arrested. When he appeared at Cardiff Assizes, he argued that cremation was neither legal nor strictly illegal – and the judge agreed. In March, Price was allowed to carry out the cremation of his son. And when Price himself died in 1893, he was cremated atop a huge pyre of coal, on the same hillside.

The judgement at Cardiff Assizes in 1884, that cremation wasn't *actually* illegal, was the first step towards making the practice into a viable option under the law. But a parliamentary Bill to do just that was rejected in the same year. Nevertheless, the crematorium at Woking was stoked up again, and in March 1885, the first human body was cremated there – that of a well-known painter called Jeanette Pickersgill. By the end of the year, just three cremations had taken place – and more than 500,000 burials. By 1892, over 100 cremations were carried out within the year, and meanwhile, another crematorium was built in Manchester. Three years later, Glasgow got its first cremato-rium, and Liverpool followed suit the year after.

So this is the context of Pitt Rivers' cremation. In 1900, there were just four crematoria in the whole of Britain – with Woking having been the first, and also the only one in southern England. Pitt Rivers' was one of only 424 cremations carried out in the UK that year – of the 587,830 people who died in England and Wales in 1900, just 0.07 per cent were cremated. And it would be two more years before an Act of Parliament was finally passed, making cremation fully legal and regulated. Pitt Rivers' choice of mortuary treatment, then, was untraditional, unorthodox and avant-garde. No wonder his wife argued with him about it.

There was still huge popular opposition to cremation up to the First World War. The war and the dreaded flu outbreak that followed may have been instrumental in forcing a more pragmatic approach to the disposal of dead bodies. In 1944, William Temple became first the Archbishop of Canterbury to be cremated, signalling an acceptance of the method by the Church of England. In 1963, the Pope said that Catholics could be cremated if that was what they really wanted. The practice was also growing among the Jewish community. There was celebrity endorsement, too, with several members of the royal family choosing this rite, along with H. G. Wells.

There was no turning back now. By 1968, the number of

cremations in the UK exceeded the number of burials. By the year 2000, when 617,000 people died in the UK, 70 per cent were cremated rather than buried, and at the close of the second decade of the twenty-first century, the percentage had risen to 78 per cent.

That change in the rate of cremation in Britain – from 0.7 per cent to 70 per cent in a century – is quite extraordinary. It happened across a time period where there were certainly shifts in religious belief – the most profound being reducing religiosity, as Britain became increasingly secular – but the change in mortuary practice was happening within religious groups as well. Atheists and agnostics – or at least, people with a more down-to-earth, scientific and pragmatic approach to death, including Pitt Rivers himself – may have been at the forefront of the change in practice, driving it to begin with, but the shift doesn't map neatly onto a spread of secularism or a recession of faith.

It's a sobering thought – a useful lesson from more recent history – to bear in mind when we try to reconstruct ideas based on physical evidence of behaviour. We should be wary of interpreting a change in mortuary or funerary rites as a change in religion. Different aspects of culture are not wrapped up together in tightly constrained packages – they are more loosely associated with each other. Nevertheless, we can interpret the transition from majority burial to majority cremation over the twentieth century in Britain as reflecting changes in belief very generally – with increasing secularism. There's the health and hygiene argument too – articulated by Sir Henry Thompson – essentially an economic imperative. But the history of cremation shows that it really was a grassroots movement, rather than a top-down, government-led transition.

Focusing simply on that dichotomy – cremation versus

burial – obscures what is actually a very varied approach to rituals around death in 21st-century Britain. The placement of a body in the ground, or in a furnace, is one element of much more complex behaviour. If a body is to be buried, that could be in a churchyard (if you can find one that isn't full), in woodland, or even – as one public health expert has suggested might be a space-saving option – along motorway verges (which recalls the Roman tradition of roadside burials). What sort of coffin or casket do you opt for? Satin-lined solid oak, veneered plywood, wicker or cardboard? If a body is cremated, what happens to the 'ashes'? (I use inverted commas as the remains are not, strictly, ash. They are ground-up, burnt fragments of bone.) They might be kept in an urn on a mantelpiece. Or deposited in one of the stone-lined Neo-Neolithic funerary mounds that are springing up across the country. The ashes could be scattered from a hill or cliff – or, in a more explosive approach to scattering, even shot up in a firework, as one ex-vicar of Glastonbury chose for her final exit. Or of course, cremated remains can be buried, just as they were sometimes in antiquity. A few companies offer what seems to be a last-ditch attempt to make cremation a bit greener, by supplying biodegradable urns containing tree seeds, ready to be planted. Other remarkable possibilities include pressing cremated remains into vinyl records, incorporating them in a marine reef, and even compressing them into diamonds. The possibilities are almost endless.

Perhaps the most interesting trend in mortuary practice in the twentieth into the twenty-first century is that tightly controlled traditions gave way to a more individual, personal approach to mortuary rites – even if personal choice ends up being that someone doesn't really care what happens to their body after death.

ANCESTORS

I've spent much of my academic career looking at the remains of the dead, in various states. As a bone expert, working closely with archaeologists, I've examined the skeletal remains of individuals from Neolithic tombs, Bronze Age cists and Anglo-Saxon burial grounds. I've pored over the tiny fragments of burned bone from the Roman cremation cemetery at Caerleon in South Wales. I've helped the police with a number of cases where skeletal remains have turned up in unexpected places. And as an anatomist, teaching medical students and qualified doctors, I've dissected many, many cadavers to demonstrate the structure of the human body to my students. Even with amazing digital apps and atlases of human anatomy, some even using augmented reality, I still think that the learning that comes from the opportunity to examine the real thing is different – and deeper. The cadavers that enable that teaching to continue are those of people who generously bequeath their bodies to medical science. After the body is embalmed, dissected, learned from, dissected into even smaller pieces and learned from some more, the fate of those remains is invariably cremation. Families are invited to attend those cremations, of course, but rarely attend, as they've usually held a funeral, without a body, closer to the time of death. A great uncle of mine left his body to medical science, and the funeral happened with a bunch of flowers 'standing in' for a coffin. It seemed strange to me at the time, but perhaps our continued focus on the dead body is actually stranger. Cremation may move us away from such a strong fixation on the physical remains of the dead, but we still tend to organise memorial services around the act of cremation itself – even if the families of the deceased never pick up the ashes afterwards. (The storerooms of crematoria are full of urns of ashes never collected.) The memorials to those who have donated their bodies to medical science still stand out as the exception. But there does seem to be some demand for completely outsourcing the mortuary process – one company in America runs a service where you can book a slot for a corpse to be picked up, and the ashes get mailed back to you within a week.

The humanist philosopher Harold Blackham wrote about the British fixation on the dead body in a 1966 essay on re-evaluating ritual:

> In our own culture the ritual disposal of the corpse accentuates the end, the loss, and at the same time attempts to assuage the grief by the company and sympathy of the mourners and the words of comfort publicly declared and privately spoken.

Even at that time, more than fifty years ago, he felt the tradition was antiquated and superstitious.

'Surely it is time,' he wrote, 'to look critically at this ritual.'

> Why this concentration upon disposal of the remains? It is a wrong focus. It turns the knife in the wound. It is gratuitous, even superstitious. In so far as we no longer believe in the resurrection of the body and the immortality of the soul, the more reason for concentrating upon recalling and fixing the image of the living person whilst fresh in memory. In so far as we still hold fast to the beliefs of religious faith, there is no need to keep this focus upon the corpse. Even for the most private person, the unencumbered memorial meeting is the real tribute to the dead and the real admonition to the living, for it helps to redeem the loss in a living image and it asks for a life worth valuing.

In 2020, the need to memorialise lives lost and collectively make sense of grief suddenly came into very sharp focus with the unleashing of a global coronavirus pandemic. In the weeks leading up to lockdown in the UK, the government was holding meetings with religious leaders and humanist groups to consider the response to an inevitable sharp rise in mortality. Crematoria were urged to prepare to double their capacity – and, tragically, they needed to.

Cremations of those who had tested positive for the virus were carried out in strictly controlled conditions, with no bodies resting in coffins while eulogies were spoken and songs sung. The crematoria were working flat out, while the chapels stood empty, or almost empty. While I'm writing this – and Covid-19 is still ravaging populations across the world – it's not clear how the pandemic will transform our societies and our attitudes in the long run. But perhaps our approach to memorialisation of the dead will change in its wake. Perhaps we will extract ourselves from that focus on the disposal of a corpse – which does seem superstitious, if you think about it – and simply meet up to remember a life. Perhaps it's better to have a bunch of flowers to dwell on, after all, than a coffin.

Having focused so much on burial in the archaeological record – even enshrining that act as a marker of true 'modernity' in human cognition and behaviour – it seems we may have moved beyond it ourselves. Though then, of course, we must remember that burial was not the predominant mortuary ritual throughout most of human prehistory, and even history. The real marker of human culture is that it *varies*, after all. An archaeological approach to understanding ourselves in this respect – understanding how we make sense of death in our lives – reveals the complexity of this question. We see that humans have practised many different mortuary and funerary rituals through time. We see ancient hominins, perhaps, caching the dead in rocky fissures (unless it was hyenas doing it); we see that some Neanderthals, sometimes, buried their dead; we see cannibalism; we see cremation giving way to burial and burial giving way to cremation. We can contextualise our own response to death and the dead by making even wider comparisons – looking at other animals. Paul Pettitt is currently exploring 'primate thanatology' – looking for roots and resonance of human behaviour through ethnographic study that embraces other animals' behaviours. Among chimpanzees, mothers have been seen carrying dead infants around with them; individuals may visit, smell, touch, hit – and sometimes devour – a corpse. There are so many questions. Do other apes know that everyone dies? Do they pay more attention to the death of a close relative or close 'friend'? Is there a general tendency to clear bodies away from living spaces? That last tendency might turn out to be a general 'primate thing' (or perhaps even more widespread – among other animals too). It could explain something about humans: why mortuary rituals become more evident in the archaeological record as communities become more settled – perhaps starting with hiding bodies away in fissures and caves, progressing to covering up bodies, or 'disappearing' them by burning or excarnation. Burial may be not so much a marker of modernity, then, but simply a corollary of population growth and more permanent settlement in a landscape.

Back to the present – and our pressing problem of how to clear dead bodies from living spaces. While we consider the possibility of separating the business of disposal of the corpse from a meaningful memorial ritual, it looks like cremation itself may also have to be updated. We may have passed peak cremation, as a new economic imperative has emerged to influence the debate. Public health officials urge councils to consider greener alternatives to incinerating dead bodies. Gas-fired cremation may be quick, but it's hardly an eco-friendly option. Each cremated body results in 400 kilograms of CO_2 emissions – about the same as burning two tanks of diesel in an SUV. Toxic mercury vapour from tooth fillings also escapes into the atmosphere from the chimneys of crematoria.

Burial may be more ecologically friendly – but does require space, of course. Woodland burial sites have burgeoned across the UK, meeting the demand for those wanting to keep their carbon footprint low after death. Natural burials – with no added chemicals – present the lowest environmental impact. But if a body has been embalmed before burial, toxic fluids from that process will of course seep out into the soil. And the cost of a burial can be proscriptive, at around four times that of a cremation.

One method being pioneered in America recalls the suggestion, by Sir Henry Thompson, that the ashes of the dead could be used as fertiliser. It is human composting. While cremation leaves very little useful residue, placing a dead body in a steel composting vessel, with woodchips and straw, for just a month, can generate a reasonable volume of mulch. Another alternative is alkaline hydrolysis, carried out by placing the body in hot potassium hydroxide solution, in a machine called a Resomator. There's already such a facility in Leeds. Resomation – or 'aquamation' – originally designed for disposing of infected livestock during the foot-and-mouth epidemic – comes from the US too, where it's legal in nineteen states. Once again, the organic effluent can be used as fertiliser.

But old traditions – and ways of thinking – die hard. I'm a humanist, and I don't believe in any sort of life after death. I think death is the end of life – and that's it. I treat the skeletons and embalmed bodies that I look at with respect because they were *once* human beings, and not because I believe any residue of those personalities still infuses those bones and formalinised soft tissues. In many ways, though, that focus on a corpse, once thought to be so emblematic of true human nature, now seems the antithesis of it. Removing the body from the colony is the most basic act. An ant would do the same for a colony-member. As Harold Blackham urged, the most human response to death – the humanist response – is to accept that someone is gone, and remember their life. Not to fixate on their corpse.

If it feels wrong, consider this: that we may be closing the loop. Human funerary practices began with simple necrophoresis – removing the dead, slipping them into fissures or pushing them into the back of rock shelters; sometimes scooping out a hollow, laying plants over them to cover them up. Then there was burial, with beads and ochre. Then there was – all manner of things, from cannibalism to cremation, mummification to excarnation, burials with beakers and graves with chariots. And now, we're back looking at necrophoresis again: disappearing the physical remains of the dead, and instead, keeping their memory alive.

Sometimes, when I consider why religions have played such a huge part in human cultures, and why they still exist today, I think that a huge part of it is the consolation they offer in the face of that inevitable, unavoidable fact: everyone dies. We think that primates understand this; perhaps crows do too. By ten years old, children know that death is inevitable for all living things, and irreversible. And yet many religions sell a promise of something that no one has ever seen: a continued existence after death. There are cryptocurrencies that sell the promise of immense wealth at some undetermined time in the future. People have got rich in such schemes, it's true, but only by getting commission from other people they've roped in to sell the product. Most people get nothing at all, apart from a slightly lighter purse – and a bit of hope. That empty promise pales, though, beside the ultimate promise: life after death. Everyone knows it's impossible – and yet it's enticing enough for some to suspend disbelief, to reject what the 10-year-old knows.

But what that 10-year-old also conceives is that the dead continue to exist, in some immaterial way, after death. In the Ponzi scheme, that's heaven. There they are – looking down on us, judging us, approving or disapproving of us. In the real fabric of society and politics, the dead still leave us with a moral challenge: are we worthy inheritors? Or indeed, can we progress morally beyond their benchmarks? Can we be so bold as to topple a statue of someone long dead whose morals we disapprove of? Can we speak ill of the dead? The cognitive dissonance that accompanies the sight of a corpse seeps back in when we start to question their morals and motives. We always prefer to think of our ancestors as heroes, don't we? And yet we should dare to disagree. They cannot hold *more* moral authority because they are dead. We should let the worst of their ideas rot away as their bodies have.

This brings us back to the rotting of bodies. And the burgeoning trade in dissolving and composting bodies in vats.

I look at the world from a scientific perspective. I prefer natural explanations to supernatural ones. The natural explanations can be tested against reality. I see nothing in the supernatural ones (including religion) to recommend them. I can find no comfort in believing things that are unbelievable. And yet – there's something about death that seems impossible to compute: the non-existence of each of us. If you are there, reading these words, you must be alive. I, on the other hand, could be dead. My words will still be there (I hope, in some vain way). My body will not.

If Pitt Rivers were here now, I think he might go for Resomation. He might have chosen cremation to annoy his wife, to scandalise the worshippers at St Peter ad Vincula or to echo the ancestors in the Bronze Age barrows. But it probably seemed like the most rational, modern option available. He knew where his legacy lay – not in his bones, but in his books. And inscribed on that monument on Cranborne Chase.

But I don't think I'm quite ready to ask my family to compost me or dissolve me when I die. Even though there will be nothing left of 'me' to worry about it, of course. I would seriously consider leaving my body to medical science, though – I'd quite like to think of medical students learning from my innards after I've departed, just as I've learned and taught from the cadavers of so many generous people.

Alternatively, I'd like to have a 'natural' burial. It is perhaps the most eco-friendly option, after all. I would return to the earth; become part of the landscape. Plants would grow from me.

And if my relatives were to inter me in a small grave, laying me in it carefully, in a crouched position, along with a handmade pot and perhaps an amber bead, I would sure as hell confuse the archaeologists of the future.

POSTSCRIPT: THOSE WHO WENT BEFORE

I started my journey in the Crick Institute, as Pontus, Tom and Pooja were preparing to embark on the most ambitious ancient DNA project ever attempted in Britain. I thought I would end there – with the preliminary results of that study. But the pandemic that has extracted such a dreadful toll already in 2020 into 2021 – claiming more than 100,000 lives within 12 months in the UK alone – has meant that this science project, like so many others, is on hold. The Crick shut its doors to all but essential workers early on – transforming itself into a huge coronavirus testing facility.

On Monday 16 March, I was in London, meeting up with Pooja. Not talking about the Thousand Ancient Genomes project, and not in the Crick this time, but at the Wellcome Trust, where I was interviewing her for a history programme about the Restoration period in London.

We set up to film in the beautiful Reading Room of the Wellcome Collection on Euston Road, where we leafed through the Bills of Mortality from 1665 to 1666 – the year of the Great Plague. Together we pored over those Bills of Mortality, looking at the mounting deaths, week on week. The relevance was too terrible, too chilling. The Channel 4 commissioner had asked us to bring out contemporary rele-vance as much as possible in these history programmes. I don't think she ever contemplated quite how painfully relevant this particular programme could end up being.

As Pooja and I talked, two people came in quietly and started pulling down the blinds in the Reading Room. The Wellcome Trust was shutting down around us.

We did just one day of filming on that programme. That same evening, I drove home to North Somerset – and stayed there for the next three months, as the whole country went into lockdown.

The Pitt Rivers skulls are still in their boxes in the archive at Salisbury Museum. When we're able to start our research again, Tom Booth will go and take samples from the temporal bones – or the ossicles if they're present – and then I will go and make my measurements on those skulls. We'll be able to radiocarbon-date those bones too, and that will help us to understand the historical sequences at Pitt Rivers' sites – pinning down what happened, when. We'll be able to test his ideas about long-headed, dolichocranic people in the Neolithic being replaced by short-headed, brachycephalic people in the Bronze Age.

All of this effort to understand the past better is about under-standing ourselves, as well. Humans are, I think, uniquely aware of our own mortality, the brevity of our lives and the context of those lives. We are just the latest human beings to occupy this landscape – it doesn't belong to us in any way other than it forms part of our own story. And yet we can feel con-nected to a place by thinking about all those who have walked here before us.

Some people can get obsessed by ancestry, by trying to

establish genetic links with long-dead relatives. The lineages that always seem to cause the most excitement are those suggesting links to royalty. Sometimes those ancestral links are used to try to establish claims to territory. That can never really work as you have too many genetic ancestors to really make sense of any such inheritance, if you go back more than just a handful of generations. The geneticist and writer Adam Rutherford has written reams on how futile and spurious such lineage quests are. The doubling of ancestors at each generation means that, statistically speaking, you should have had over 2 trillion ancestors a thousand years ago – clearly several orders of magnitude more than the number of people who were alive on the planet at the time – and even today. What this means is that each thousand-year-old ancestor in your family tree appears many times, in different positions – the tree folds in on itself. And it also collapses into everyone else's family trees as well. Any two Europeans, for instance, are likely to find a common ancestor popping up in both their family trees going back just a few centuries ago. A thousand years ago, they are likely to have many common ancestors. And those Europeans, a millennium ago, are likely either to be the ancestors of most Europeans today – or none of them. That is the fate of lineages – they either die out or spread like wildfire, down through the generations. People love to find out they are related to Charlemagne, or have Viking ancestry. But if you're of broadly European descent – you will have. You don't need a test to prove it. As Adam Rutherford puts it, 'The truth is that we all are a bit of everything, and we come from all over. If you're white, you're a bit Viking. And a bit Celt. And a bit Anglo-Saxon. And a bit Charlemagne.' And the further back you go in your family tree, the more globally interconnected it becomes. From a purely genetic point of view, though, there is a complication. The DNA of each of your distant ancestors is not just diluted, generation by generation – it can completely disappear from your genome. This is just a quirk of how DNA is shuffled and sorted into eggs and sperm. So there are members of your family tree way back, from whom you have no DNA at all. It's been lost in time. Are they any less your ancestors?

Tracing ancestry using DNA turns out to be very useful for reconstructing ancient population history – looking at mobility and migration in the past, as we hope to do with the Thousand Ancient Genomes project. But it is much less informative and interesting from a personal, individual point of view – other than providing you with a picture of deep interconnectedness with everyone else. The genetic changes through which we glimpse those past migrations have very little, in fact, to do with identity.

As for using ancestors to back up modern political claims – to power or territory – that's clearly wrong-headed and futile too. I think we can feel a real sense of connection with individuals in the past – learning about their lives and understanding more about them – without needing a *genetic* connection to them. You can feel a sense of connection that is about common humanity – human experience.

If we try to connect with the past through individuals we believe to be *our own ancestors* in anything more than a very generic sense, it quickly gets overwhelming. There's a paradoxical situation: when we go back through centuries, millennia, we accumulate thousands and thousands of ancestors – too many to feel any real connection to, too dispersed across the world to feel that we have roots in just one place; and of course the paradox also that, among those ancestors who exist in our real family trees, many have left no genetic trace in us today. They are our ancestors on paper, but not in our genes.

The word 'ancestor', in fact, does not enshrine an idea of descent – although we use it that way legally, technically, biologically. The word itself is a descendant of a Latin word, via Old French, that is also extant in English, if less widely used: antecessor. It comes from *ante*, before, and *cedere*, to go – so it literally means 'one who went before'.

Don't try to *possess* these ancestors, then. Look at their lives, try to understand their societies and their cultures, find a new perspective on your own culture and sense of self through this exercise – but do not claim them for your own.

Instead, I feel connections through that human experience of being in a landscape – walking along the cliffs of Ronaldsay and imagining the early farmers there creating the chambered tomb; standing on the top of Winklebury Hill and imagining what it must have been like to have lived around there in the Iron Age; walking along the Gower coast and thinking about the people who lived and died there in the Ice Age.

I think we can explore those connections with landscape and discover a sense of belonging – a sense of place, of home – by examining the past in this way, by capturing moments in the life of one ancestor at a time. Especially those we see so clearly, in their time-capsule burials. We can imagine that other person's life and connect with them. Walking in the footsteps of someone long gone, seeing a version of a view they once saw, experiencing the landscape they inhabited – that's an incredible connection to the past.

And the past belongs to everyone.

ACKNOWLEDGEMENTS

So many people have helped me write this book. Many are mentioned in the text, their research and insights woven in. And I am hugely grateful to the wonderful, generous-hearted friends and colleagues who have read drafts so carefully and helped me find a path through great swathes of research, and have also corrected me where I've gone astray. It is customary, but also essential, to note that any flaws remaining are mine alone.

Enormous thanks to: Pontus Skoglund, Pooja Swali and Tom Booth at the Crick Institute; Adrian Green, Director of Salisbury Museum; Paul Pettitt, Durham University; Matt Pope, Institute of Archaeology, UCL; Graeme Barker and Emma Pomeroy, Cambridge University; Silvia Bello, Natural History Museum; Dan Lee, Orkney Research Centre for Archaeology (University of the Highlands and Islands Archaeology Institute); Julian Thomas, University of Manchester; Keith Ray (formerly county archaeologist for Herefordshire); Jim Leary, University of York; Andrew Fitzpatrick, University of Leicester; Melanie Giles, University of Manchester; Paula Ware, Director of MAP Archaeological Practice; Miles Russell, University of Bournemouth; Chris Stringer, Natural History Museum. Thank you all so much.

I must also give a shout out to all the researchers, producers and contributors who have worked on the BBC series *Digging for Britain* over the years.

I am also very grateful to my fantastic literary agent, Luigi Bonomi, for endless encouragement and support, and to Iain McGregor and Holly Harris at Simon & Schuster for being wonderful editors to work with; thank you to project editor Kaiya Shang and copy editor Victoria Godden, too.

Thanks for all the help via Twitter on Gaelic pronunciation in North Uist – @sweenyness, @Maggier3, @fion_argh, @arranlouise, @revelationVI, @maffie71!

And to my wonderful friend Janina Ramirez for decoding Old English and the hidden meaning in Cat's Brain.

Finally, I must thank my family – and especially Auntie Linda, for giving me the gift of time to write this year.

REFERENCES

A thousand ancient genomes, 22 May 2019

Asensi, V., Fierer, J. (2018) Of rats and men: Poussin's Plague at Ashdod. *Emerging Infectious Diseases* 24: 186–187.

Chouikha, I., Hinnebusch, B. J. (2012) *Yersinia*-flea interactions and the evolution of the arthropod-borne transmission route of plague. *Current Opinion in Microbiology* 15: 239–246.

Freeman, F. R. (2005) Bubonic plague in the Book of Samuel. *Journal of the Royal Society of Medicine* 98: 436.

Rasmussen, S., *et al.* (2015) Early divergent strains of *Yersinia pestis* in Europe 5,000 years ago. *Cell* 163: 571–582.

The Red Lady

Bennett, E. A., *et al.* (2019) The origin of the Gravettians: genomic evidence from a 36,000 year old Eastern European. *BioRxiv* doi.org/10.1101/685404

Chazan, M. (1995) Conceptions of time and the development of Paleolithic Chronology. *American Anthropologist* 97: 457–467.

Jacobi, R. M., Higham, T. F. G. (2008) The 'Red Lady' ages

gracefully: new ultrafiltration AMS determinations from Paviland. *Journal of Human Evolution* 55: 898–907.

Kacki, S., *et al.* (2020) Complex mortuary dynamics in the Upper Paleolithic of the decorated Grotte de Cussac, France. *PNAS* https://doi.org/10.1073/pnas.2005242117

Kobl-Ebert, M. (1997) Mary Buckland (nee Morland) 1797–1857. *Earth Sciences History* 16: 33–38.

Koslowski, J. K. (2015) The origin of the Gravettian. *Quaternary International* 359–360: 3–18.

O'Connor, A. and Graves, C. P. (2003) Canon Greenwell (1820–1918) and his contribution to archaeological research. *Bulletin of the History of Archaeology* 13 (2): 28–30.

Power, R. C., L'Engle Williams, F. (2018) Evidence of increasing intensity of food processing during the Upper Palaeolithic of Western Eurasia. *Journal of Paleolithic Archaeology* 1: 281–301.

Reynolds, N., *et al.* (2017) The Kostenki 18 child burial and the cultural and funerary landscape of Mid Upper Palaeolithic European Russia. *Antiquity* 91 (360): 1435–1450.

Sommer, M. (2004) 'An amusing account of a cave in Wales': William Buckland (1784–1856) and the Red Lady of Paviland. *British Journal for the History of Science* 37: 53–74.

Svoboda, J. (2007) The Gravettian on the Middle Danube. *PALEO* 19: 203–220

Weart, S. (2009) The discovery of rapid climate change. *Physics Today* 56: 10.1063/1.1611350

The Flower People

Boyd Dawkins, W. (1874) Cave Hunting: Researches on the evidence of caves respecting the early inhabitants of Europe. Macmillan & Co., London.

Compton, T., Stringer, C. (2015) The Morphological affinities of the Middle Pleistocene hominin teeth from Pontnewydd Cave, Wales. *Journal of Quaternary Science* 30: 713–730.

Culotta, E. (2019) New remains discovered at site of famous Neanderthal 'flower burial'. *Science* doi:10.1126/science.aaw7586.

Dibble, H. L,. *et al.* (2015) A critical look at evidence from La Chapelle-aux-Saints supporting an intentional Neanderthal burial. *Journal of Archaeological Science* 53: 649–657.

Fiacconi, M., Hunt, C. O. (2015) Pollen taphonomy at Shanidar Cave (Kurdish Iraq): An initial evaluation. *Review of Paleobotany and Palynology* 223: 87–93.

Green, H. S., *et al.* (1981) Pontnewydd Cave in Wales: a new Middle Pleistocene hominid site. *Nature* 294: 707–713.

Pettitt, P. B. (2002) The Neanderthal dead: exploring mortuary variability in Middle Palaeolithic Eurasia. *Before Farming* 2002/1: 1–26.

Pomeroy, E., *et al.* (2017) Newly-discovered Neanderthal remains from Shanidar Cave, Iraqi Kurdistan, and their attribution to Shanidar 5. *Journal of Human Evolution* 111: 102–118.

Pomeroy, E., *et al.* (2019) Issues of theory and method in the analysis of Paleolithic mortuary behaviour: a view from Shanidar Cave. *Wenner-Gren Foundation workshop; University of Cambridge, UK, January 2019.*

Pomeroy, E., *et al.* (2020) New Neanderthal remains associated with the 'flower burial' at Shanidar Cave. *Antiquity* 94: 11–26.

Rendu, W., *et al.* (2014) Evidence supporting an intentional Neanderthal burial at La Chapelle-aux-Saints. *PNAS* 111: 81–86.

Rendu, W., *et al.* (2016) Let the dead speak . . . comments on Dibble et al.'s reply to 'Evidence supporting an intentional burial at La Chapelle-aux-Saints'. *Journal of Archaeological Science* 69: 12–20.

Sommer, J. D. (1999) The Shanidar IV 'Flower Burial': a re-evaluation of Neanderthal Burial Ritual. *Cambridge Archaeological Journal* 9: 127–137.

The Cannibals of Cheddar and the Blue-Eyed Boy

Bello, S., *et al.* (2015) Upper Palaeolithic ritualistic cannibalism at Gough's Cave (Somerset, UK): The human remains from head to toe. *Journal of Human Evolution* 82: 170–189.

Currant, A. P., Jacobi, R. M., Stringer, C. B. (1989) Excavations at Gough's Cave, Somerset 1986–7. *Antiquity* 63: 131–136.

Irwin, D. J. (1986) Gough's Old Cave – its history. *Proceedings of the University of Bristol Sepaeological Society* 17: 250–266.

Jacobi, R. M., Higham, T. F. G. (2009) The early Lateglacial re-colonization of Britain: new radiocarbon evidence from Gough's Cave, southwest England. *Quaternary Science Reviews* 28: 1895–1913.

Olalde, I., *et al.* (2018) The Beaker phenomenon and the genomic transformation of northwest Europe. *Nature* 555: 190–196.

Parry, R. F. (1928) Recent Excavations at the Cheddar Caves. *Nature* 3080: 735–736.

Pearson, M. P., *et al.* (2016) Beaker people in Britain: migration, mobility and diet. *Antiquity* 90: 620–637.

Richards, M. P., *et al.* (2000) Hough's Cave and Sun Hole Cave human stable isotope values indicate a high animal protein diet in the British Upper Palaeolithic. *Journal of Archaeological Science* 27: 1–3.

Seligman, C. G., Parsons, F. G. (1914) The Cheddar Man: A skeleton of late Palaeolithic date. *The Journal of the Royal Anthropological Institute of Great Britain and Ireland.* 44: 241–263.

Tratman, E. K. (1975) Problems of 'The Cheddar Man', Gough's Cave, Somerset. *Proceedings of the University of Bristol Spelaeological Society* 14: 7–23.

The Founding Farmers

Brace, S., *et al.* (2018) Population replacement in early Neolithic Britain. *BioRxiv* doi.org/10.1101/267443

Brace, S., *et al.* (2019) Ancient genomes indicate population replacement in early Neolithic Britain. *Nature Ecology & Evolution* 3: 765–771.

Cassidy, L. M., *et al.* (2020) A dynastic elite in monumental Neolithic society. *Nature* 582: 384–388.

Historic England (2018) *Causewayed Enclosures: Introductions to Heritage Assets.*

Hofmanova, Z., *et al.* (2016) Early farmers from across Europe directly descended from Neolithic Aegeans. *PNAS* 113: 6868–6891.

Laporte, L., Tinevez, J-Y. (2004) Neolithic houses and chambered tombs of western France. *Cambridge Archaeological Journal* 14: 217–34.

Meyer, C., *et al.* (2015) The massacre mass grave of Schöneck-Kilianstädten reveals new insights into collective violence in Early Neolithic Central Europe. *PNAS* 112: 11217–11222.

Osborne, J. F. (2011) Secondary mortuary practice and the bench tomb: structure and practice in Iron Age Judah. *Journal of Near Eastern Studies* 70: 35–53.

Sanchez-Quinto, F., *et al.* (2019) Megalithic tombs in western and northern Neolithic Europe were linked to a kindred society. *PNAS* 116: 9469–9474.

Scheib, C. L., *et al.* (2019) East Anglian early Neolithic monument burial linked to contemporary Megaliths. *Annals of Human Biology* 46: 145–149.

Schulting, R. (2009) Skeletal evidence and contexts of violence in the European Mesolithic and Neolithic. In Gowland, R., Knusel, C. (eds) *The Social Archaeology of Funerary Remains.*

Sheridan, A. (2020) Incest uncovered at the elite prehistoric Newgrange monument in Ireland. *Nature* 582: 347–349.

Skoglund, P. (2012) Neolithic farmers and hunter-gatherers in Europe. *Science* 336: 466–469.

At Salisbury Museum, 8 July 2019

A biography of Augustus Henry Lane Fox Pitt Rivers http://web.prm.ox.ac.uk/rpr/index.php/pitt-rivers-life/10 -biography-of-general-pitt-rivers/

Lane Fox, A. H. (1874) *The Evolution of Culture.*

Rolian, C., Lieberman, D. E., Hallgrimsson, B. (2010) The coevolution of human hands and feet. *Evolution* 1558–1568.

Pitt Rivers, A. H. L. F. (1887) Excavations in Cranborne Chase near Rushmore on the borders of Dorset and Wiltshire Vol I.

The Amesbury Archer

Callaway, E. (2018) Divided by DNA: The uneasy relationship between archaeology and ancient genomics. *Nature* 555: 573–576.

Carlin, N. (2018) Haunted by the ghost of the Beaker folk? *Biochemist* 42 (1): 30–33.

Case, D. T., Burnett, S. E., Nielsen, T. (2006) *Os acromiale:* Population differences and the etiological significance. *Homo* 57: 1–18.

Deter, C. A., *et al.* (2019) Aspects of human osteology and skeletal biology. In Parker Pearson, M. *et al.* (eds) The Beaker People. Prehistoric Society Research Paper 7: 253–291.

Fitzpatrick, A. P. (2002) 'The Amesbury Archer': a well-furnished early Bronze Age burial in southern England. *Antiquity* 293: 629–630.

Fitzpatrick, A. P. (2011) The Amesbury Archer and the Boscombe Bowmen: Bell Beaker burials at Boscombe Down, Amesbury, Wiltshire. *Wessex Archaeology Report 27.*

Fitzpatrick, A. P. (2013) The arrival of the Bell Beaker set in Britain and Ireland. In Koch, J. T., Cunliffe, B. (eds) *Celtic from the West 2:* 41–70.

Olalde, I., *et al.* (2018) The Beaker phenomenon and the genomic transformation of northwest Europe. *Nature* 555: 190–196.

Parker Pearson, M., *et al.* (2009) Who was buried at Stonehenge? *Antiquity* 83: 23–39.

Parker Pearson, M., *et al.* (2016) Beaker people in Britain: migration, mobility and diet. *Antiquity* 90: 620–637.

Parker Pearson, M., *et al.* (2017) The origins of Stonehenge: on the track of the bluestones. *Archaeology International* 20: 52–57.

Piguet, M., Besse, M. (2009) Chronology and Bell Beaker common ware. *Radiocarbon* 51: 817–830.

Pitts, M. (2015) What has the mesolithic got to do with Stonehenge? Not a lot. *Mike Pitts – Digging Deeper* blog.

Pitts, M. (2018) A close look at Blick Mead and Star Carr. *Mike Pitts – Digging Deeper* blog.

Rogers, B., *et al.* (2016) Aurochs hunters: the animal bones from Blick Mead. *Durham Research Online.*

Rogers, B., *et al.* (2019) Isotopic analysis of the Blick Mead dog: a proxy for the dietary reconstruction and mobility of Mesolithic British hunter-gatherers. *Journal of Archaeological Science* 24: 712–720.

Stevens, C. J., Fuller, D. Q. (2012) Did Neolithic farming fail? The case for a Bronze Age agricultural revolution in the British Isles. *Antiquity* 86: 707–722.

Yammine, K. (2014) The prevalence of os acromiale: a systematic review and meta-analysis. *Clinical Anatomy* 27: 610–621.

The Charioteers

Allison, K. J. (ed.) (1969) A history of the county of York East Riding: Volume 1. *Victoria County History, London.*

Allison, K. J., *et al.* (2002) A history of the county of York East Riding: volume 7. *Victoria County History, London.*

Dent, J. S. (2020) Excavations in Garton Slack and Wetwang Slack 1963–1989. In Halkon, P. (ed.) *The Arras Culture of Eastern Yorkshire.* Oxbow Books, Oxford, 33–46.

Duric, M., Rakocevic, Z., Donic, D. (2005) The reliability of sex determination of skeletons from forensic context in the Balkans. *Forensic Science International* 147: 159–164.

Giles, M., Green, V., Peixoto, P. (2020) Wide connections: women, mobility and power. In Halkon, P. (ed.) *The Arras Culture of Eastern Yorkshire*. Oxbow Books, Oxford, 47–66.

Halkon, P., *et al.* (2019) Arras 200: revisiting Britain's most famous Iron Age cemetery. *Antiquity* 93: 1–7.

Halkon, P. (2020) Setting the scene – landscape and settlement in Iron Age eastern Yorkshire. In Halkon, P. (ed.) *The Arras Culture of Eastern Yorkshire*. Oxbow Books, Oxford, 1–16.

Jordan, A. M. (2016) Her mirror, his sword: unbinding binary gender and sex assumptions in Iron Age British mortuary traditions. *Journal of Archaeological Method and Theory* 23: 870-899.

Pope, R., Ralston, I. (2012) Approaching sex and status in Iron Age Britain with reference to the nearer continent. In *Atlantic Europe in the First Millennium BC: Crossing the Divide.*

Robb, J., Harris, O. J. T. (2018) Becoming gendered in European prehistory: was Neolithic gender fundamentally different? *American Antiquity* 83: 128–147.

Selliah, P., *et al.* (2020) Sex estimation of skeletons in middle and late adulthood: reliability of pelvic morphological traits and long bone metrics on an Italian skeletal collection. *International Journal of Legal Medicine*. Published online 16 April 2020.

Stephens, M., Ware, P. (2020) The Iron Age cemeteries at Pocklington and other excavations by MAP. In Halkon, P. (ed.) *The Arras Culture of Eastern Yorkshire*. Oxbow Books, Oxford, 17–32.

Stillingfleet, E. W. (1847) Account of the opening of some barrows on the Wolds of Yorkshire. *Proceedings of the Royal Archaeological Institute of Great Britain*. York, 26–32.

Postscript: those who went before

Anderson, J., Biro, D., Pettitt, P. (2018) Evolutionary thanatology. *Philosophical Transactions B* 373: 20170262.

Ashton, J. (2019) Necropolis in crisis: housing the living is one thing, there is also a problem in housing the dead. *Journal of the Royal Society of Medicine* 112: 313–315.

History of Modern Cremation in the UK 1874–1974, *The Cremation Society*: cremation.org.uk

Pettit, P., Anderson, J. R. (2020) Primate thanatology and hominoid mortuary archaeology. *Primates* 61: 9–19.

INDEX